The Official
Diary of the Season
2003-2004

Derby County

Reporter: Steve Nicholson

DERBY COUNTY

Evening Telegraph

First published in 2004 by:
First Edition Limited, 32 Stamford Street, Altrincham,
Cheshire, WA14 1EY in conjunction with the Derby
Evening Telegragh, Derby Express Newspapers,
Northcliffe House, Meadow Road, Derby, DE1 2DW.

Statistics provided by: The Press Association.

Text provided by: Derby Evening Telegraph.

Photographs provided by: Derby Evening Telegraph and
where indicated Raymond's Press Agency.

ISBN: 1-84547-087-7

Contents

Junior celebrates with the fans after his penalty secured Derby's biggest win for six years.

Manager's Foreword

On behalf of the players and everyone at Derby County I'd like to thank you for your continued support and urge you to join us for what I hope will be an exciting - and successful - Coca-Cola Championship season.

This book tells the story of the 2003-04 campaign. It was a season of highs and lows... but it was certainly never dull!

It marked a period of transition for the club. This was my first season as manager and October saw the appointment of a new board of directors.

Along the way we enjoyed mixed footballing fortunes - from a disappointing opening day defeat to that terrific 4-2 victory over our closest rivals. Facts and figures from every 2003-04 match are featured within these pages, alongside pictures of some of the most memorable moments.

This publication is also your guide to the 2004-05 Coca-Cola Championship season - and here at the club we can't wait for the campaign to kick-off. I am delighted with the players we have signed this summer, their quality will really add to a squad that I believe is now strong enough to compete with the best in this league.

So get behind us home and away during the season - we plan to give you something to cheer about.

George Burley
Manager
Derby County

DERBY [0] 0 Stoke [2] 3

Defeats on the opening day are always deflating. To be beaten so easily, especially at home, must have left supporters fearing for the future. Stoke stuck to a simple game-plan and their organisation proved too much for the Rams.

Burley wanted to stick with a back three and wing-backs following the encouraging pre-season display against Real Mallorca. But an uncertain defence leaked two goals inside 20 minutes to end the game as a contest.

Whatever the shape or system, Derby should still have been capable of imposing their game on a hurriedly-assembled Stoke team, which had six players making their League debuts. But they never really started.

Mc Leod was involved early. He moved into the area and appeared to go down over the challenge of the sprawling veteran goalkeeper Ed De Goey. Then referee Howard Webb awarded a free-kick, much to Derby's annoyance, and then rather harshly booked McLeod for diving.

Five players made their League debuts for Derby, including skipper Ian Taylor, Caldwell, Costa and Tome. The youngster from Peru, did not look out of place in the game. In fact he was arguably Derby's best player.

Stoke's two early goals were always likely to be decisive and so it proved. Gifton Noel Williams beat Steve Elliott to the ball to score from close range after 15 minutes before poor Derby defending was punished five minutes later.

Wayne Thomas launched a long ball forward, Caldwell hesitated and then was out-muscled by Carl Asaba, who rolled the ball into the path of Chris Greenacre to fire low past Andy Oakes from 12 yards.

Stoke completed a miserable day for the Rams with a good third goal on the stroke of full-time.

Two of the substitutes combined, with Chris Iwelumo crossing and Lewis Neal thumping a volley past a stranded Oakes.

Result.......Result.......Result.

DERBY ....(0) 0   STOKE ....(2) 3
Noel-Williams 15
Greenacre 20
Neal 90

Att 21,517
Referee: Howard Webb

Stats......Stats.......Stats......Stats

DERBY				STOKE		
1st	2nd	Total		Total	2nd	1st
3	3	6	Corners	5	2	3
10	1	11	Fouls	19	9	10
2	0	2	Yellow cards	2	0	2
0	0	0	Red cards	0	0	0
0	1	1	Caught Offside	3	1	2
0	5	5	Shots on target	7	5	2
2	6	8	Shots off target	4	4	0
0	0	0	Hit woodwork	0	0	0
47	62	54%	Possession	46%	38	53

OVERALL it's very, very disappointing although we knew the game would provide a big physical challenge for our young players and it proved to be the case.
George Burley

I'D watched Derby on a couple of occasions pre-season and we'd for-mulated a game plan which we stuck to and I'm pleased it's come off.
Tony Pulis

Other Div 1 Results

Bradford 2 Norwich 2, Burnley 2 Crystal Palace 3, Ipswich 1 Reading 1, Millwall 2 Wigan 0, Nottm Forest 2 Sunderland 0, Preston 1 West Ham 2, Rotherham 0 Cardiff 0, Sheff Utd 0 Gillingham 0, Walsall 4 West Brom 1, Watford P Coventry P, Wimbledon 3 Crewe 1

DERBY [0] 0 Stoke [2] 3

| Goalkeeper Stats: Andy Oakes Saves: Catch 2, Crosses: Catch 2, Punch 1 | | | | | | | | | |

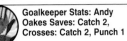

Derby Player Stats		Shots on target	Shots off target	Caught offside	Fouls conceded	Free-kicks won	Corners taken	Clearances	Defensive blocks
		L/R/H/Oth	L/R/H/Oth						
31 G Labarthe Tome	1st	-/-/-/-	-/-/-/-	-	-	-	-	-	-
▲ 32	2nd	-/3/-/-	-/2/-/-	-	-	2	-	-	-
11 Lee Morris	1st	-/-/-/-	-/-/-/-	-	2	-	1	-	-
▼ 63	2nd	-/-/-/-	-/-/-/-	-	-	-	1	-	-
7 Ian Taylor	1st	-/-/-/-	-/-/-/-	-	2	-	-	-	-
■ 38	2nd	-/-/-/-	-/-/1/-	-	1	-	-	-	-
20 Lewis Hunt	1st	-/-/-/-	-/-/-/-	-	-	-	-	-	-
▼ 32	2nd	-/-/-/-	-/-/-/-	-	-	-	-	-	-
5 Steve Elliott	1st	-/-/-/-	-/-/1/-	-	-	1	-	1	-
	2nd	-/-/-/-	-/-/-/-	-	-	-	-	-	1
14 Richard Jackson	1st	-/-/-/-	-/-/-/-	-	-	1	-	-	-
	2nd	-/-/-/-	-/-/-/-	-	-	1	-	-	-
18 Izale McLeod	1st	-/-/-/-	-/-/-/-	-	1	1	-	-	-
▼ 51 ■ 2	2nd	-/-/-/-	-/-/-/-	-	-	1	-	-	-
17 Paul Boertien	1st	-/-/-/-	-/-/-/-	-	-	-	-	-	-
▲ 51	2nd	-/-/-/-	-/-/-/-	-	-	1	-	-	-
15 Adam Bolder	1st	-/-/-/-	-/-/-/-	-	-	-	-	-	-
▲ 63	2nd	-/1/-/-	-/1/-/-	-	-	-	-	-	-
32 Gary Caldwell	1st	-/-/-/-	-/-/-/-	-	1	2	-	1	-
	2nd	-/1/-/-	-/-/-/-	-	-	1	-	1	1
8 Candido Costa	1st	-/-/-/-	-/-/-/-	-	2	3	2	-	-
	2nd	-/-/-/-	-/2/-/-	1	-	2	2	-	-
6 Pablo Mills	1st	-/-/-/-	-/-/-/-	-	-	1	-	-	-
	2nd	-/-/-/-	-/-/-/-	-	-	-	-	-	-
29 Tom Huddlestone	1st	-/-/-/-	-/-/1/-	-	2	1	-	2	-
	2nd	-/-/-/-	-/-/-/-	-	-	1	-	-	-

Subs not used: Grant, Valakari. - Formation: 5-3-2

| Goalkeeper Stats: Ed de Goey ▼ 54 Crosses: Punch 1 Neil Cutler ▲ 54 Saves: Tip Over 1, Catch 1 | | | | | | | | | |

Player Stats		Shots on target	Shots off target	Caught offside	Fouls conceded	Free-kicks won	Corners taken	Clearances	Defensive blocks
2	Wayne Thomas ■ 19	-/-/-/-	-/-/-/-	-	2	-	-	-	1
17	Darel Russell	-/-/-/-	1/-/-/-	-	2	2	-	-	-
21	Petur Marteinsson	-/-/-/-	-/-/-/-	-	-	1	-	-	-
18	Lewis Neal ▲ 80	2/-/-/-	-/-/-/-	-	-	-	-	-	-
9	Gifton Noel-Williams ▼ 81	-/2/-/-	-/-/1/-	1	2	1	-	-	-
3	Clive Clarke	-/-/-/-	-/-/-/-	-	1	2	4	1	-
8	Chris Greenacre ▼ 80	-/1/-/-	-/-/-/-	-	4	-	-	-	-
20	Keith Andrews	-/-/-/-	-/-/-/-	-	2	-	-	-	2
4	John Eustace	-/1/-/-	-/1/-/-	-	2	3	1	-	-
7	Carl Asaba	-/1/-/-	-/-/1/-	2	3	1	-	1	-
15	Chris Iwelumo ▲ 81	-/-/-/-	-/-/-/-	-	-	-	-	-	-
16	Marcus Hall ■ 21	-/-/-/-	-/-/-/-	-	1	-	-	1	-

Subs not used: Goodfellow, Commons. - Formation: 4-3-3

Derby Played: 1 Won 0 Drawn 0 Lost 1 For 0 Against 3 Pos 24

Huddersfield [0] 2 DERBY [1] 1

Derby County followed up their opening day disappointment by being dumped out of the Carling Cup by Third Division Huddersfield Town at the Alfred McAlpine Stadium.

Second-half goals from Jonathan Stead and John Thorrington gave Huddersfield a 2-1 first round victory. And this after the Rams had led at the interval through an Ian Taylor header.

But once Stead headed the equaliser, there was only going to be one winner and the decisive strike came from Thorrington with 20 minutes remaining.

Yet the opening 45 minutes gave the travelling Rams supporters hope. Valakari was constantly involved, tidying up and knitting together passages of play with his simple distribution. Recalled Grant was still the busiest of the two goalkeepers. He saved a curling shot from Jon Newby and then made an excellent double stop, first from Stead and then Newby.

Derby took the lead on 41 minutes from their first shot on target.

Tome's neat turn and dash towards the Huddersfield penalty area was halted by Rob Edwards' foul. As the home side organised a defensive wall, Tom Huddlestone took a quick free-kick which Ian Gray kept out with a sharp save. Boertien retrieved the ball and crossed for Taylor to head wide of Gray.

Candido Costa, more involved than against Stoke, flashed a shot high and wide in the opening minutes and Steve Elliott was only inches away with a header.

The turning point came with Huddersfield's equaliser after 58 minutes and once again poor Rams defending was punished. Thorrington delivered a deep cross and the unchallenged Stead rose high to plant a header across the diving Grant and into the bottom corner.

And the winning goal came after 70 minutes. Lee Fowler hit a free-kick high into the area, Efe Sodje had time to steer his header across goal and Thorrington stole in to finish from close range.

Result.......Result.......Result.

HUDDERSFIELD (0) 2   DERBY ....(1) 1
Stead 59   Taylor 41
Thorrington 70

Att 6,672
Referee: Eddie Ilderton

Stats......Stats.......Stats......Stats

HUDDERSFIELD				DERBY		
1st	2nd	Total		Total	2nd	1st
1	5	6	Corners	2	0	2
7	9	16	Fouls	12	8	4
1	3	4	Yellow cards	0	0	0
0	0	0	Red cards	0	0	0
6	0	6	Caught Offside	6	3	3
2	6	8	Shots on target	2	0	2
4	4	8	Shots off target	2	0	2
0	0	0	Hit woodwork	0	0	0
42	51	46%	Possession	54%	49	58

> **"** I was delighted with the attitude of the players and said to them at half-time that if we got a goal we'd go on and win, and we did.
> **Peter Jackson** **"**

> **"** THE league is our priority so this defeat may turn out to be a blessing in disguise. We're trying to get a squad together to keep Derby in Division One.
> **George Burley** **"**

Other Lge Cup Rnd 1 Results

Barnsley 1 Blackpool 2, Bradford 0 Darlington 0, Bristol R 0 Brighton 1, Cambridge U 1 Gillingham 2, Cardiff 4 Leyton Orient 1, Cheltenham 1 QPR 2, Chesterfield 0 Burnley 0, Colchester 2 Plymouth 1, Crewe 2 Wrexham 0, Doncaster 3 Grimsby 2, Luton 4 Yeovil 1, Macclesfield 1 Sheff Utd 2, Millwall 0 Oxford U 1, Northampton 1 Norwich 0, Port Vale 0 Nottm F 0, Preston 0 Notts C 0, Rotherham 2 York 1, Scunthorpe 2 Oldham 1, Southend 2 Swindon 3, Tranmere 1 Bury 0, Walsall 2 Carlisle 1, Watford 0 Bournemouth 0, West Brom 4 Brentford 0, Wigan 2 Hull 0, Wycombe 2 Wimbledon 0

Goalkeeper Stats: Lee Grant Saves: Catch 5, Crosses: Catch 2, Punch 2

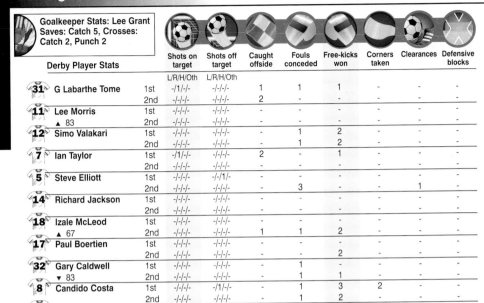

Derby Player Stats		Shots on target	Shots off target	Caught offside	Fouls conceded	Free-kicks won	Corners taken	Clearances	Defensive blocks
		L/R/H/Oth	L/R/H/Oth						
31 G Labarthe Tome	1st	-/1/-/-	-/-/-/-	1	1	1	-	-	-
	2nd	-/-/-/-	-/-/-/-	2	-	-	-	-	-
11 Lee Morris ▲ 83	1st	-/-/-/-	-/-/-/-	-	-	-	-	-	-
	2nd	-/-/-/-	-/-/-/-	-	-	-	-	-	-
12 Simo Valakari	1st	-/-/-/-	-/-/-/-	-	1	2	-	-	-
	2nd	-/-/-/-	-/-/-/-	-	1	2	-	-	-
7 Ian Taylor	1st	-/1/-/-	-/-/-/-	2	-	1	-	-	-
	2nd	-/-/-/-	-/-/-/-	-	-	-	-	-	-
5 Steve Elliott	1st	-/-/-/-	-/-/1/-	-	-	-	-	-	-
	2nd	-/-/-/-	-/-/-/-	-	3	-	-	1	-
14 Richard Jackson	1st	-/-/-/-	-/-/-/-	-	-	-	-	-	-
	2nd	-/-/-/-	-/-/-/-	-	-	-	-	-	-
18 Izale McLeod ▲ 67	1st	-/-/-/-	-/-/-/-	-	-	-	-	-	-
	2nd	-/-/-/-	-/-/-/-	1	1	2	-	-	-
17 Paul Boertien	1st	-/-/-/-	-/-/-/-	-	-	-	-	-	-
	2nd	-/-/-/-	-/-/-/-	-	-	2	-	-	-
32 Gary Caldwell ▼ 83	1st	-/-/-/-	-/-/-/-	-	1	-	-	-	-
	2nd	-/-/-/-	-/-/-/-	-	1	1	-	-	-
8 Candido Costa	1st	-/-/-/-	-/1/-/-	-	1	3	2	-	-
	2nd	-/-/-/-	-/-/-/-	-	1	2	-	-	-
29 Tom Huddlestone	1st	-/-/-/-	-/-/-/-	-	-	-	-	-	-
	2nd	-/-/-/-	-/-/-/-	-	1	-	-	-	-
6 Pablo Mills ▼ 67	1st	-/-/-/-	-/-/-/-	-	-	-	-	-	-
	2nd	-/-/-/-	-/-/-/-	-	-	-	-	-	-

Subs not used: Oakes, Bolder, Hunt. - Formation: 3-5-2

Goalkeeper Stats: Ian Gray Crosses: Catch 2

	Player Stats	Shots on target	Shots off target	Caught offside	Fouls conceded	Free-kicks won	Corners taken	Clearances	Defensive blocks
16	Efetobore Sodje	-/-/-/-	-/-/1/-	-	1	2	-	1	-
9	Jonathan Stead	-/1/2/-	-/2/1/-	1	3	5	-	1	-
4	Lee Fowler ▪ 75	-/-/-/-	-/1/-/-	-	4	-	2	-	-
11	Danny Schofield	-/1/-/-	1/-/-/-	2	-	-	-	-	-
6	Ian Hughes	-/-/-/-	-/-/-/-	-	2	-	-	3	-
10	Jon Newby	-/2/1/-	-/-/-/-	2	-	1	-	-	-
3	Rob Edwards ▪ 52	-/-/-/-	-/-/-/-	-	2	-	-	-	-
14	John Thorrington ▪ 70	-/1/-/-	1/-/-/-	-	1	-	3	-	-
5	Steve Yates ▪ 82	-/-/-/-	-/-/-/-	-	1	2	-	-	1
8	Anthony Carss	-/-/-/-	-/-/-/-	1	2	2	1	-	-

Subs not used: Booty, Thompson, Senior, Worthington, Booth. - Formation: 4-4-2

Derby County claimed their first point of the new season and in doing so provided a few pointers to encourage concerned supporters.

Manager George Burley received the commitment and desire from his players that he had demanded. In turn, the players looked more at ease with a 4-4-2 shape in which debutant Michael Johnson marshalled the defence.

Johnson collected a yellow card after only three minutes for a rash challenge but gradually settled and was impressive in the second half. Lee Bradbury held the ball up in attack, using it simply and sensibly.

Derby's best chance fell to Bradbury 10 minutes after the break. Tom Huddlestone's thumping strike was blocked and the ball fell to the forward in a position close to the penalty spot. However, he could only drive a low shot straight at grateful goalkeeper Jason Brown.

Lee Morris also wasted a good opportunity, flashing a shot high and wide when he should at least have hit the target.

Ian Taylor started to look his old self against Gillingham and made some useful breaks from midfield, particularly in the second period.

But Gillingham had the better of things in the first half without forcing a save out of Rams goalkeeper Lee Grant. Despite a handful of promising openings, a couple of which fell to ex-Rams striker Tommy Johnson, Gillingham failed to hit the target. Many of their shots were high or wide. Shooting low can often bring more reward as it almost did for Southall who fizzed an effort a foot wide of the post.

Grant's only saves of note came in the final 10 minutes of the game as the Gills made a late push for three points. He saved low down from David Perpetuini, did very well to parry a firm drive from Nosworthy and then kept out an effort from Johnson.

Result.......Result.......Result.

GILLINGHAM ......(0) 0   DERBY ....(0) 0
Att 7,850
Referee: C Penton

Stats......Stats.......Stats......Stats

	GILLINGHAM				DERBY		
1st	2nd	Total			Total	2nd	1st
1	5	6	Corners		5	2	3
10	7	17	Fouls		13	6	7
1	0	1	Yellow cards		3	0	3
0	0	0	Red cards		0	0	0
3	2	5	Caught Offside		1	1	0
0	4	4	Shots on target		5	3	2
7	2	9	Shots off target		5	3	2
0	0	0	Hit woodwork		0	0	0
43	50	46%	Possession		54%	50	57

> **WE** haven't been beaten yet this season after three games but I suppose people will say that we have thrown away two points.
> **Andy Hessenthaler**

> **THIS** was a good honest performance. Coming to Gillingham is never easy, but I thought we competed very well and had one or two good half chances.
> **George Burley**

Other Div 1 Results

Cardiff 0 Bradford 2, Coventry 0 Walsall 0, Crewe 1 Ipswich 0, Crystal Palace 1 Watford 0, Norwich 2 Rotherham 0, Reading 3 Nottm Forest 0, Stoke 2 Wimbledon 1, Sunderland 0 Millwall 1, West Brom 4 Burnley 1, West Ham 0 Sheff Utd 0, Wigan 1 Preston 1

Gillingham [0] 0 DERBY [0] 0

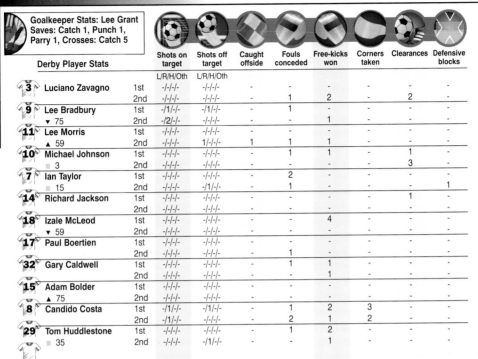

Goalkeeper Stats: Lee Grant Saves: Catch 1, Punch 1, Parry 1, Crosses: Catch 5

Derby Player Stats		Shots on target L/R/H/Oth	Shots off target L/R/H/Oth	Caught offside	Fouls conceded	Free-kicks won	Corners taken	Clearances	Defensive blocks
3 Luciano Zavagno	1st	-/-/-/-	-/-/-/-	-	-	-	-	-	-
	2nd	-/-/-/-	-/-/-/-	-	1	2	-	2	-
9 Lee Bradbury ▼ 75	1st	-/1/-/-	-/1/-/-	-	1	-	-	-	-
	2nd	-/2/-/-	-/-/-/-	-	-	1	-	-	-
11 Lee Morris ▲ 59	1st	-/-/-/-	-/-/-/-	-	-	-	-	-	-
	2nd	-/-/-/-	1/-/-/-	1	1	1	-	-	-
10 Michael Johnson ▪ 3	1st	-/-/-/-	-/-/-/-	-	1	1	-	1	-
	2nd	-/-/-/-	-/-/-/-	-	-	-	-	3	-
7 Ian Taylor ▪ 15	1st	-/-/-/-	-/-/-/-	-	2	-	-	-	-
	2nd	-/-/-/-	-/1/-/-	-	1	-	-	-	1
14 Richard Jackson	1st	-/-/-/-	-/-/-/-	-	-	-	-	1	-
	2nd	-/-/-/-	-/-/-/-	-	-	-	-	-	-
18 Izale McLeod ▼ 59	1st	-/-/-/-	-/-/-/-	-	-	4	-	-	-
	2nd	-/-/-/-	-/-/-/-	-	-	-	-	-	-
17 Paul Boertien	1st	-/-/-/-	-/-/-/-	-	-	-	-	-	-
	2nd	-/-/-/-	-/-/-/-	-	1	-	-	-	-
32 Gary Caldwell	1st	-/-/-/-	-/-/-/-	-	1	1	-	-	-
	2nd	-/-/-/-	-/-/-/-	-	-	1	-	-	-
15 Adam Bolder ▲ 75	1st	-/-/-/-	-/-/-/-	-	-	-	-	-	-
	2nd	-/-/-/-	-/-/-/-	-	-	-	-	-	-
8 Candido Costa	1st	-/1/-/-	-/1/-/-	-	1	2	3	-	-
	2nd	-/1/-/-	-/1/-/-	-	2	1	2	-	-
29 Tom Huddlestone ▪ 35	1st	-/-/-/-	-/-/-/-	-	1	2	-	-	-
	2nd	-/-/-/-	-/1/-/-	-	-	1	-	-	-

Subs not used: Oakes, Valakari, Elliott. - Formation: 4-4-2

Goalkeeper Stats: Jason Brown Saves: Fumble 1, Catch 2, Crosses: Catch 1

	Player Stats	Shots on target	Shots off target	Caught offside	Fouls conceded	Free-kicks won	Corners taken	Clearances	Defensive blocks
6	Ian Cox	-/-/-/-	-/-/1/-	-	-	1	-	1	-
2	Nyron Nosworthy	-/1/-/-	-/1/-/-	1	1	-	-	-	1
18	Chris Hope	-/-/-/-	-/-/-/-	-	3	-	-	4	1
22	Danny Spiller	-/1/-/-	-/-/-/-	1	2	1	2	-	-
11	Tommy Johnson	1/-/-/-	2/1/-/-	-	1	-	-	-	-
10	Paul Shaw ▼ 48	-/-/-/-	1/-/-/-	1	2	-	-	-	-
16	Richard Rose ▲ 48	-/-/-/-	-/-/-/-	-	-	2	-	1	-
29	Mamady Sidibe	-/-/-/-	-/-/-/-	2	4	-	-	-	-
7	Nicky Southall	-/-/-/-	1/1/-/-	-	-	5	4	2	-
3	John Hills	-/-/-/-	-/-/-/-	-	1	1	-	1	-
26	David Perpetuini ▪ 24	1/-/-/-	1/-/-/-	-	3	3	-	1	-

Subs not used: Bartram, L Johnson, Crofts, Beckwith. - Formation: 4-4-2

Derby Played: 2 Won 0 Drawn 1 Lost 1 For 0 Against 3 Pos 21

DERBY [1] 2 Reading [3] 3

Derby County's season promised to be tough enough without gifting goals to the opposition. Reading punished the defensive mistakes in this game to leave Pride Park Stadium with a 3-2 victory they just about deserved.

And yet there were encouraging points as Derby almost snatched a draw against a team many, including Burley, believed would push strongly for promotion. Lee Morris was lively. His pace will always trouble defenders and three times he went close in the first period, the nearest being when his stooping header struck a post with the score at 1-1.

Junior came off the substitutes' bench around the hour mark and injected more enthusiasm and belief but Derby's defending was alarming in the first half as Reading helped themselves to their three goals.

Reading striker Nicky Forster caused havoc with his movement and trickery and he had a role in the opening goal. The impressive Kevin Watson released Forster who crossed for Shaun Goater to bundle the ball home from close range.

Derby, to their credit, pulled themselves level three minutes later when a breakdown in communication between Ricky Newman and Hahnemann resulted in Newman panicking and knocking Costa over in the area.

There were few arguments about the penalty decision and Taylor confidently struck the spot-kick wide of the diving Hahnemann.

Michael Johnson, on his home debut, cleared off the line from Forster before Lee Grant's blunder handed Reading a 30th-minute lead. When Gary Caldwell and Johnson failed to deal with a lofted ball, Derby fell further behind. Reading picked up the pieces, worked the ball to Murray whose shot took a slight deflection to flash high beyond Grant.

While the Rams looked tighter in the second half, the visitors had no need to chase a fourth goal. This allowed Derby to regain a foothold but Reading held on.

Result.......Result.......Result.

DERBY ....(1) 2   READING ......(3) 3
Taylor 7(p)   Goater 3
Svensson 81   Murray 30, 36

Att 18,970
Referee: Colin Webster

Stats......Stats.......Stats......Stats

DERBY				READING		
1st	2nd	Total		Total	2nd	1st
0	2	2	Corners	8	3	5
8	7	15	Fouls	9	3	6
1	2	3	Yellow cards	1	0	1
0	0	0	Red cards	0	0	0
0	0	0	Caught Offside	6	1	5
4	5	9	Shots on target	8	1	7
1	4	5	Shots off target	0	0	0
0	0	0	Hit woodwork	0	0	0
46	46	46%	Possession	54%	54	54

" IF I compare this to the Stoke match I can see a great improvement. If we keep playing like this we will string some good results together.
George Burley "

" I didn't think we played that well. We went 3-1 up and thought we could go through the motions and you can't do that at Derby.
Alan Pardew "

Other Div 1 Results

Bradford 0 Gillingham 1, Burnley 0 Wigan 2, Ipswich 1 Coventry 1, Millwall 1 Crewe 1, Nottm Forest 1 Cardiff 2, Preston 0 Sunderland 1, Rotherham 1 West Ham 0, Sheff Utd 1 Norwich 0, Walsall 1 Stoke 1, Watford 0 West Brom 1, Wimbledon 1 Crystal Palace 3

Goalkeeper Stats: Lee Grant
Crosses: Catch 2

Derby Player Stats

Player		Shots on target L/R/H/Oth	Shots off target L/R/H/Oth	Caught offside	Fouls conceded	Free-kicks won	Corners taken	Clearances	Defensive blocks
10 Michael Johnson	1st	-/-/-/-	-/-/-/-	-	-	-	-	-	-
65	2nd	-/-/-/-	-/-/-/-	-	2	1	-	-	-
11 Lee Morris	1st	-/-/2/-	1/-/-/-	-	4	-	-	-	-
28	2nd	1/-/-/-	-/-/-/-	-	-	-	-	-	-
12 Simo Valakari	1st	-/-/-/-	-/-/-/-	-	1	-	-	-	-
▼ 59	2nd	-/-/-/-	-/-/-/-	-	-	-	-	-	-
7 Ian Taylor	1st	-/-/-/-	-/-/-/-	-	-	-	-	-	-
	2nd	-/-/-/-	-/-/1/-	-	-	-	-	-	-
33 Junior	1st	-/-/-/-	-/-/-/-	-	-	-	-	-	-
▲ 59	2nd	-/-/-/-	2/-/1/-	-	1	-	-	-	-
14 Richard Jackson	1st	-/-/-/-	-/-/-/-	-	-	1	-	-	-
	2nd	-/-/-/-	-/-/-/-	-	-	-	-	-	-
34 Mathias Svensson	1st	-/-/-/-	-/-/-/-	-	2	-	-	1	-
83	2nd	-/1/1/-	-/-/-/-	-	1	-	-	1	-
17 Paul Boertien	1st	-/-/-/-	-/-/-/-	-	-	-	-	1	-
	2nd	-/-/-/-	-/-/-/-	-	1	-	-	-	-
32 Gary Caldwell	1st	-/-/-/-	-/-/-/-	-	-	2	-	1	-
▼ 45	2nd	-/-/-/-	-/-/-/-	-	-	-	-	-	-
8 Candido Costa	1st	-/-/-/-	-/-/-/-	-	1	3	-	-	-
	2nd	-/1/-/-	-/-/-/-	-	-	1	2	-	-
29 Tom Huddlestone	1st	-/1/-/-	-/-/-/-	-	-	-	-	3	-
	2nd	1/-/-/-	-/-/-/-	-	2	-	-	-	-
6 Pablo Mills	1st	-/-/-/-	-/-/-/-	-	-	-	-	-	-
▲ 45	2nd	-/-/-/-	-/-/-/-	-	-	1	-	-	-

Subs not used: Oakes, Bolder, McLeod. - Formation: 4-4-2

Goalkeeper Stats: Marcus Hahnemann Saves: Catch 4, Crosses: Catch 3

Player Stats

	Player	Shots on target	Shots off target	Caught offside	Fouls conceded	Free-kicks won	Corners taken	Clearances	Defensive blocks
11	Andy Hughes	-/-/-/-	-/-/-/-	1	1	-	-	-	-
8	Adrian Williams	-/-/-/-	-/-/-/-	-	-	-	-	3	1
9	Shaun Goater ▼ 79	1/-/-/-	-/-/-/-	1	1	1	-	-	-
2	Graeme Murty	-/-/-/-	-/-/-/-	-	-	-	-	1	-
15	James Harper ▲ 45	-/-/-/-	-/-/-/-	-	-	-	-	-	-
10	Nicky Forster	-/4/-/-	-/-/-/-	4	4	1	-	-	-
25	Ricky Newman ■ 7	-/-/-/-	-/-/-/-	-	3	2	-	-	-
14	Steven Sidwell	-/-/-/-	-/-/-/-	-	-	1	-	-	-
4	Kevin Watson ▼ 45	-/-/-/-	-/-/-/-	-	-	1	-	-	-
6	John Mackie ▲ 45	-/-/-/-	-/-/-/-	-	-	2	-	-	-
16	Martin Butler ▲ 79	-/-/-/-	-/-/-/-	-	-	1	-	-	-
7	Scott Murray	1/2/-/-	-/-/-/-	-	-	3	8	-	-
5	Steve Brown ▼ 45	-/-/-/-	-/-/-/-	-	-	3	-	2	-

Subs not used: Ashdown, Tyson. - Formation: 4-4-2

Derby Played: 3 Won 0 Drawn 1 Lost 2 For 2 Against 6 Pos 22

Cardiff [2] 4 DERBY [0] 1

Portuguese winger Candido Costa was sent off as struggling Derby County slumped to their second defeat in three days.

The officials did not have the best of days but once again Derby shot themselves in the foot. Another goalkeeping error from Lee Grant turned the game in Cardiff's favour on the half-hour mark. To make matters worse, Costa's hot-headed moment two minutes before the break brought a red card and reduced the Rams to 10 men.

On-loan striker Mathias Svensson provided a glimmer of hope with his second goal in as many games three minutes after the break but Cardiff eventually ran out comfortable winners.

There were signs in the previous two games that Derby were improving and they started steadily against a fiercely-competitive Cardiff. Brazilian striker Junior looked enthusiastic on his first start up front alongside the willing Svensson and Lee Morris began brightly before quickly fading.

But Grant's mistake proved a key moment. Fresh from gifting Reading a goal, he totally misjudged a hopeful high cross from Alan Lee and watched in horror as the ball bounced in off the back post.

Cardiff doubled their lead six minutes before the break. Ian Taylor went to ground in the area in an attempt to halt John Robinson's surge. There was contact and the Cardiff player went down. Barry pointed to the spot and Graham Kavanagh fired the spot-kick past Grant.

It looked a hopeless situation for Derby on their first visit to Ninian Park in 18 years but they started the second half in spirited fashion and Svensson reduced the deficit by shooting low past Neil Alexander after a good move involving Junior and Taylor.

Robert Earnshaw restored the home side's two-goal cushion on 55 minute, firing high into an empty net after a good passing movement. The fourth goal arrived on 70 minutes. Defender James Collins met Langley's corner with a firm header.

Result.......Result.......Result.

CARDIFF..............(2) 4	DERBY ....(0) 1
Lee 30	Svensson 48
Kavanagh 40(p)	
Earnshaw 55	
Collins 70	

Att 15,091
Referee: N Barry

Stats......Stats.......Stats......Stats

CARDIFF				DERBY		
1st	2nd	Total		Total	2nd	1st
1	3	4	Corners	1	0	1
7	10	17	Fouls	17	7	10
1	1	2	Yellow cards	2	0	2
0	0	0	Red cards	1	0	1
3	1	4	Caught Offside	0	0	0
2	7	9	Shots on target	5	3	2
2	2	4	Shots off target	0	0	0
0	1	1	Hit woodwork	0	0	0
47	58	52%	Possession	48%	42	53

 WE started very strongly and it was a quality performance. Once we got that first goal the result really was never in doubt.
Lennie Lawrence

CARDIFF were outstanding against Forest and we knew it would be a tough game here but you cannot legislate for referees making wrong decisions.
George Burley

Other Div 1 Results

Crewe 1 Walsall 0, Gillingham 0 Burnley 3, Reading 0 Rotherham 0, Sunderland 2 Watford 0, West Brom 1 Preston 0

Cardiff [2] 4 DERBY [0] 1

Goalkeeper Stats: Lee Grant Saves: Catch 3, Round Post 1

Derby Player Stats		Shots on target L/R/H/Oth	Shots off target L/R/H/Oth	Caught offside	Fouls conceded	Free-kicks won	Corners taken	Clearances	Defensive blocks
17 Paul Boertien	1st	-/-/-/-	-/-/-/-	-	1	1	-	1	-
	2nd	-/-/-/-	-/-/-/-	-	2	1	-	1	-
13 Lee Grant	1st	-/-/-/-	-/-/-/-	-	-	-	-	-	-
	2nd	-/-/-/-	-/-/-/-	-	-	1	-	-	-
11 Lee Morris ▼ 52	1st	-/-/-/-	-/-/-/-	-	-	-	-	-	-
	2nd	-/-/-/-	-/-/-/-	-	-	-	-	-	-
10 Michael Johnson ■ 20	1st	-/-/-/-	-/-/-/-	-	1	-	-	1	-
	2nd	-/-/-/-	-/-/-/-	-	-	-	-	1	-
7 Ian Taylor	1st	-/-/-/-	-/-/-/-	-	1	1	-	2	-
	2nd	-/-/-/-	-/-/-/-	-	-	-	-	2	-
15 Adam Bolder ▲ 75	1st	-/-/-/-	-/-/-/-	-	-	-	-	-	-
	2nd	-/-/-/-	-/-/-/-	-	-	1	-	-	-
12 Simo Valakari ▲ 52	1st	-/-/-/-	-/-/-/-	-	-	-	-	-	-
	2nd	-/-/-/-	-/-/-/-	-	-	1	-	-	-
8 Candido Costa ■ 43	1st	-/-/-/-	-/-/-/-	-	1	-	1	-	-
	2nd	-/-/-/-	-/-/-/-	-	-	-	-	-	-
33 Junior ▼ 75	1st	1/-/-/-	-/-/-/-	-	2	2	-	-	-
	2nd	1/-/-/-	-/-/-/-	-	-	-	-	-	1
14 Richard Jackson	1st	-/-/-/-	-/-/-/-	-	-	1	-	1	-
	2nd	-/-/-/-	-/-/-/-	-	-	-	-	-	-
34 Mathias Svensson	1st	-/-/-/-	-/-/-/-	-	2	-	-	-	-
	2nd	1/1/-/-	-/-/-/-	-	2	3	-	-	-
6 Pablo Mills	1st	-/-/-/-	-/-/-/-	-	1	1	-	-	-
	2nd	-/-/-/-	-/-/-/-	-	1	1	-	-	-
29 Tom Huddlestone ■ 2	1st	-/1/-/-	-/-/-/-	-	1	1	-	1	-
	2nd	-/-/-/-	-/-/-/-	-	2	1	-	-	-

Subs not used: Oakes, Caldwell, McLeod. - Formation: 4-4-2

Goalkeeper Stats: Neil Alexander Saves: Catch 3, Crosses: Catch 2

	Player Stats	Shots on target	Shots off target	Caught offside	Fouls conceded	Free-kicks won	Corners taken	Clearances	Defensive blocks
3	Chris Barker	-/-/-/-	-/-/-/-	-	-	-	-	1	-
11	Peter Thorne ▲ 77 ■ 82	-/-/-/-	-/-/-/-	-	2	-	-	-	-
4	Gareth Whalley ▲ 78	-/-/-/-	-/-/-/-	-	2	-	-	-	-
8	Graham Kavanagh	-/2/-/-	-/-/-/-	-	1	-	3	-	-
24	Alan Lee ▼ 77 ■ 45	-/1/-/-	-/-/1/-	1	4	3	-	-	-
17	James Collins	-/-/1/-	-/-/-/-	-	3	3	-	6	-
2	Rhys Weston	-/-/-/-	-/1/-/-	-	-	-	-	1	-
12	Willie Boland	-/1/-/-	-/-/-/-	-	1	2	-	-	1
10	Robert Earnshaw	-/2/-/-	-/1/-/-	3	-	1	-	-	-
25	Richard Langley	1/-/-/-	-/-/-/-	-	2	5	1	-	-
7	John Robinson ▼ 78	-/-/-/-	-/-/-/-	-	1	1	-	1	-
21	Tony Vidmar	-/-/-/-	-/-/1/-	-	1	2	-	-	-

Subs not used: Prior, Bonner, Margetson. - Formation: 4-4-2

Derby Played: 4 Won 0 Drawn 1 Lost 3 For 3 Against 10 Pos 23

DERBY [0] 0 West Brom [0] 1

Derby County may have been improving with each game but their results were not. Four defeats and a draw in five Division One outings meant the Rams were rock bottom with a miserable one point from 15.

More worrying still was that Derby produced their best football of the season and yet still finished empty-handed. They squandered chances early with Mathias Svensson and Ian Taylor both going close and should really have been ahead at the interval.

After 76 minutes of a second half that had been much more even than the first, Rob Hulse struck the winning volley after Derby's indecision had seen them struggle to clear a free-kick.

There was a key incident after only 11 minutes of the game. Morris and Svensson combined with a neat one-two and Morris was away at pace. The trailing Larus Sigurdsson hacked him down from behind as he appeared to enter the area. Referee Michael Ryan gave a free-kick right on the edge of the box rather than a penalty and then only produced a yellow card for Sigurdsson.

Simo Valakari did well on his recall and young Tom Huddlestone enjoyed a good first half before he became careless with his passing.

Svensson provided a focal point to the attack. His style ruffled defenders and led to openings for team-mates. There were signs against West Brom of an understanding between him and his strike partner Morris, who was more of a threat when the shackles of standing on the left were removed.

The end product, whether it be pass, cross or finish, had to be improved because another visiting goalkeeper was allowed to leave Pride Park without being overly worked.

The victory was West Brom's fourth since losing heavily on the opening day and took them to top slot. George Burley's team clearly deserved something from the game but once again came away with nothing.

Result......Result......Result.

DERBY ....(0) 0   WEST BROM (0) 1
Hulse 76

Att 21,499
Referee: M Ryan

Stats......Stats......Stats......Stats

DERBY				WEST BROM		
1st	2nd	Total		Total	2nd	1st
1	1	2	Corners	3	2	1
5	8	13	Fouls	19	6	13
1	2	3	Yellow cards	2	0	2
0	0	0	Red cards	0	0	0
0	0	0	Caught Offside	3	1	2
9	3	12	Shots on target	6	4	2
2	3	5	Shots off target	2	1	1
0	0	0	Hit woodwork	0	0	0
55	60	58%	Possession	42%	40	45

> **DECISIONS** are not going for us. Was it in the box or outside? Was it a penalty or not? Was it a yellow card or a red?
> **George Burley**

> **IN** the second half we did better, did more when we were in possession and in the end we were thankful for Rob Hulse's goal.
> **Gary Megson**

Other Div 1 Results

Bradford 0 Sunderland 4, Burnley 1 Crewe 0, Ipswich 1 West Ham 2, Millwall 1 Crystal Palace 1, Nottm Forest 2 Norwich 0, Preston 1 Stoke 0, Rotherham 0 Wigan 3, Sheff Utd 2 Coventry 1, Walsall 1 Cardiff 1, Watford 2 Gillingham 2, Wimbledon 0 Reading 3

DERBY [0] 0 West Brom [0] 1

Goalkeeper Stats: Andy Oakes Crosses: Catch 1, Punch 1

Derby Player Stats

		Shots on target L/R/H/Oth	Shots off target L/R/H/Oth	Caught offside	Fouls conceded	Free-kicks won	Corners taken	Clearances	Defensive blocks
11 Lee Morris	1st	1/1/-/-	-/-/-/-	-	1	3	-	-	-
	2nd	1/-/-/-	-/-/-/-	-	1	3	-	-	-
10 Michael Johnson ▼ 68	1st	-/-/-/-	-/-/-/-	-	-	1	-	-	-
	2nd	-/-/-/-	-/-/-/-	-	-	-	-	-	-
17 Paul Boertien ■ 63	1st	-/1/-/-	-/-/-/-	-	-	-	-	-	-
	2nd	-/-/-/-	-/1/-/-	-	1	-	-	-	-
12 Simo Valakari	1st	-/-/-/-	-/1/-/-	-	-	1	-	-	-
	2nd	1/-/-/-	1/-/-/-	-	1	-	-	-	-
7 Ian Taylor ■ 76	1st	-/-/1/-	-/-/-/-	-	1	1	-	-	-
	2nd	-/-/-/-	-/-/-/-	-	1	-	-	1	-
8 Candido Costa	1st	-/1/-/-	-/-/-/-	-	2	1	1	-	-
	2nd	-/-/-/-	-/-/-/-	-	-	1	1	-	-
33 Junior ▲ 68	1st	-/-/-/-	-/-/-/-	-	-	-	-	-	-
	2nd	1/-/-/-	1/-/-/-	-	1	1	-	-	-
14 Richard Jackson	1st	-/-/-/-	-/-/-/-	-	-	-	-	-	-
	2nd	-/-/-/-	-/-/-/-	-	-	-	-	-	-
34 Mathias Svensson ■ 14	1st	2/-/-/-	1/-/-/-	-	1	2	-	-	-
	2nd	-/-/-/-	-/-/-/-	-	1	-	-	1	-
6 Pablo Mills	1st	-/-/-/-	-/-/-/-	-	-	2	-	1	-
	2nd	-/-/-/-	-/-/-/-	-	2	1	-	-	-
29 Tom Huddlestone	1st	-/2/-/-	-/-/-/-	-	-	2	-	-	-
	2nd	-/-/-/-	-/-/-/-	-	-	-	-	2	-

Subs not used: Grant, Bolder, McLeod, Caldwell. - Formation: 4-4-2

Goalkeeper Stats: Russell Hoult Saves: Catch 3, Crosses: Catch 3

Player Stats

		Shots on target	Shots off target	Caught offside	Fouls conceded	Free-kicks won	Corners taken	Clearances	Defensive blocks
3	Neil Clement	1/-/-/-	-/-/-/-	-	2	1	-	-	-
20	Artim Sakiri ▲ 74	1/-/-/-	-/-/-/-	-	-	-	-	1	-
12	Scott Dobie ▲ 25	-/1/-/-	-/-/-/-	1	-	2	-	-	-
24	Thomas Gaardsoe	-/-/1/-	-/-/-/-	-	-	1	-	3	-
25	Joost Volmer	-/-/-/-	-/-/1/-	-	1	2	-	2	-
15	Rob Hulse	-/1/-/-	-/1/-/-	1	3	2	-	1	-
4	James O'Connor ▼ 74 ■ 45	-/-/-/-	-/-/-/-	-	1	2	-	-	-
2	Bernt Haas	-/-/-/-	-/-/-/-	-	1	2	-	-	-
17	Larus Sigurdsson ■ 11	-/-/-/-	-/-/-/-	-	5	-	-	-	-
19	Lee Hughes ▼ 25	-/-/-/-	-/-/-/-	1	1	-	-	-	-
14	Sean Gregan	-/1/-/-	-/-/-/-	-	4	1	-	5	-
18	Jason Koumas ▼ 74	-/-/-/-	-/-/-/-	-	1	-	3	-	-
10	Andy Johnson ▲ 74	-/-/-/-	-/-/-/-	-	-	-	-	-	-

Subs not used: Murphy, Gilchrist. - Formation: 5-3-2

...August Team Stats.....Team Stats......Team Stats......Team S

League table at the end of August

		HOME				AWAY						
	P	W	D	L	F	A	W	D	L	F	A	Pts	Df
West Brom	5	2	0	0	5	1	2	0	1	3	4	12	3
Reading	5	1	1	0	3	0	2	1	0	7	3	11	7
Sheff Utd	5	2	1	0	3	1	1	1	0	2	1	11	3
Wigan	5	1	1	0	2	1	2	0	1	5	2	10	4
Crystal Palace	5	1	0	1	2	2	2	1	0	7	4	10	3
West Ham	5	1	1	0	1	0	2	0	1	4	3	10	2
Sunderland	5	1	0	1	2	1	2	0	1	6	2	9	5
Millwall	5	1	2	0	4	2	1	1	0	1	0	9	3
Nottm Forest	5	2	0	1	5	2	1	0	1	3	4	9	2
Stoke	5	1	1	0	2	1	1	1	1	4	2	8	3
Cardiff	5	1	0	1	4	3	1	2	0	3	2	8	2
Norwich	5	2	0	0	5	2	0	1	2	2	5	7	0
Crewe	5	2	0	0	2	0	0	1	2	2	5	7	-1
Walsall	5	1	2	0	6	3	0	1	1	0	1	6	2
Burnley	5	1	0	2	3	5	1	0	1	4	4	6	-2
Gillingham	5	0	1	1	0	3	1	2	0	3	2	6	-2
Rotherham	5	1	1	1	1	3	0	1	1	0	2	5	-4
Preston	5	1	0	2	2	4	0	1	1	1	2	4	-3
Bradford	5	0	1	2	2	7	1	0	1	2	1	4	-4
Wimbledon	5	1	0	2	4	7	0	0	2	3	5	3	-5
Coventry	4	0	1	1	1	3	0	1	1	2	3	2	-3
Ipswich	5	0	2	1	3	4	0	0	2	0	2	2	-3
Watford	4	0	1	1	2	3	0	0	2	0	3	1	-4
Derby	5	0	0	3	2	7	0	1	1	1	4	1	-8

August matches table

	P	W	D	L	F	A	Pts
West Brom	5	4	0	1	8	5	12
Reading	5	3	2	0	10	3	11
Sheff Utd	5	3	2	0	5	2	11
Crystal Palace	5	3	1	1	9	6	10
Wigan	5	3	1	1	7	3	10
West Ham	5	3	1	1	5	3	10
Sunderland	5	3	0	2	8	3	9
Nottm Forest	5	3	0	2	8	6	9
Millwall	5	2	3	0	5	2	9
Cardiff	5	2	2	1	7	5	8
Stoke	5	2	2	1	6	3	8
Norwich	5	2	1	2	7	7	7
Crewe	5	2	1	2	4	5	7
Burnley	5	2	0	3	7	9	6
Walsall	5	1	3	1	6	4	6
Gillingham	5	1	3	1	3	5	6
Rotherham	5	1	2	2	1	5	5
Bradford	5	1	1	3	4	8	4
Preston	5	1	1	3	3	6	4
Wimbledon	5	1	0	4	7	12	3
Coventry	4	0	2	2	3	6	2
Ipswich	5	0	2	3	3	6	2
Derby	5	0	1	4	3	11	1
Watford	4	0	1	3	2	6	1

August team stats details

Club Name	Ply	Shots On	Shots Off	Corners	Hit W'work	Caught Offside	Offside Trap	Fouls	Yellow Cards	Red Cards	Pens Awarded	Pens Con
Bradford	5	25	24	23	3	13	9	72	11	0	1 (-)	-
Burnley	5	21	30	28	2	17	18	62	12	0	1 (-)	-
Cardiff	5	40	26	39	2	14	8	52	7	1	1 (1)	1
Coventry	4	45	36	31	1	3	18	43	9	1	1 (-)	1
Crewe	5	31	27	34	3	25	18	35	4	0	- (-)	1
Crystal Palace	5	31	19	26	1	14	24	62	10	4	4 (3)	2
Derby	5	36	23	16	0	2	21	69	13	1	1 (1)	1
Gillingham	5	20	39	24	0	20	13	80	7	0	- (-)	-
Ipswich	5	36	28	29	1	25	17	47	11	0	1 (1)	-
Millwall	5	28	18	31	0	22	13	92	10	0	1 (-)	-
Norwich	5	25	23	26	0	16	15	76	10	0	2 (2)	3
Nottm Forest	5	26	30	45	0	15	5	61	8	0	1 (1)	1
Preston	5	37	41	34	0	16	10	70	13	1	- (-)	1
Reading	5	37	21	38	0	20	15	64	6	1	1 (-)	2
Rotherham	5	21	30	28	0	14	13	70	12	1	- (-)	-
Sheff Utd	5	28	24	27	2	14	10	48	4	1	1 (1)	2
Stoke	5	42	36	37	1	16	14	67	11	0	1 (1)	-
Sunderland	5	45	21	27	2	7	20	73	12	0	1 (1)	-
Walsall	5	23	19	26	1	16	20	51	8	2	1 (-)	1
Watford	4	15	27	28	0	18	24	62	6	1	- (-)	1
West Brom	5	24	28	26	2	19	7	70	8	0	1 (1)	-
West Ham	5	34	20	23	2	20	13	64	12	0	- (-)	-
Wigan	5	36	29	27	1	12	24	77	13	0	- (-)	1
Wimbledon	5	24	19	18	2	9	18	41	9	1	- (-)	2

AUGUST STATS

Monthly Top scorers

Shaun Goater (Reading)	4
Nathan Ellington (Wigan)	3
Paul Merson (Walsall)	3
Lee Hughes (West Brom)	3
Robert Blake (Burnley)	3
Jermain Defoe (West Ham)	3
Scott Murray (Reading)	3
Marlon Harewood (West Ham)	2
Robert Earnshaw (Cardiff)	2
David Johnson (Nottm Forest)	2

Penalties scored

2 Mark Rivers (Norwich), Dougie Freedman (Crystal Palace)

Assists

Nicky Forster (Reading)	4
Kevin Watson (Reading)	3
Paul McVeigh (Norwich)	2
Carl Asaba (Stoke)	2
Matthew Etherington (West Ham)	2
Graham Alexander (Preston)	2
Andy Reid (Nottm Forest)	2

Quickest goals

1:11 mins - Robert Earnshaw (Nottm Forest vs Cardiff)
1:33 mins - Eddie Lewis (Preston vs West Ham)
2:41 mins - Shaun Goater (Derby vs Reading)
3:33 mins - Sean Thornton (Preston vs Sunderland)
5:00 mins - Jermain Defoe (Preston vs West Ham)

Top Keeper

	Mins	Gls
Patrick Kenny (Sheff Utd)	336	1
Tony Warner (Millwall)	474	2
Ed de Goey (Stoke)	348	2
Mart Poom (Sunderland)	479	3
John Filan (Wigan)	476	3
M Hahnemann (Reading)	476	3
David James (West Ham)	475	3
Neil Cutler (Stoke)	134	1

Shots on target

Jermain Defoe (West Ham)	15
Patrick Suffo (Coventry)	12
Eddie Lewis (Preston)	11
Gifton Noel-Williams (Stoke)	11
Robert Earnshaw (Cardiff)	10
Alan Lee (Cardiff)	10
Kevin Kyle (Sunderland)	9
Dean Ashton (Crewe)	9
Paul Merson (Walsall)	9
Nicky Forster (Reading)	9

Shots off target

Dean Ashton (Crewe)	11
Patrick Suffo (Coventry)	10
Robert Earnshaw (Cardiff)	9
Ricardo Fuller (Preston)	9
Steve Jones (Crewe)	8
Nicky Southall (Gillingham)	8
David Johnson (Nottm Forest)	8
Tommy Johnson (Gillingham)	8
Jermain Defoe (West Ham)	8
Robert Blake (Burnley)	8

Caught offside

Jermain Defoe (West Ham)	14
Dean Ashton (Crewe)	13
Robert Earnshaw (Cardiff)	10
Danny Webber (Watford)	10
Nicky Forster (Reading)	10
David Johnson (Nottm Forest)	10
Darren Byfield (Sunderland)	9
Steve Jones (Crewe)	8
Darren Bent (Ipswich)	8

Free-kicks won

Heidar Helguson (Watford)	21
Alan Lee (Cardiff)	18
Dennis Wise (Millwall)	17
Kevin Kilbane (Sunderland)	16
Peter Ndlovu (Sheff Utd)	15
Steven Sidwell (Reading)	15
Gifton Noel-Williams (Stoke)	15
David Perpetuini (Gillingham)	15
Candido Costa (Derby)	14

Brazilian Junior (v Cardiff)

Fouls conceded

Kevin Kyle (Sunderland)	17
Alan Lee (Cardiff)	16
Noel Whelan (Millwall)	15
Tim Cahill (Millwall)	14
Stuart Nethercott (Millwall)	14
Mamady Sidibe (Gillingham)	13
Gifton Noel-Williams (Stoke)	13
Ian Cox (Gillingham)	12
Mikele Leigertwood (Wimbledon)	12

Fouls without a card

Gifton Noel-Williams (Stoke)	13
Mikele Leigertwood (Wimbledon)	12
Bruce Dyer (Watford)	12
Nicky Forster (Reading)	11
Andy Gray (Sheff Utd)	10
Robert Lee (West Ham)	9
Neil Shipperley (Crystal Palace)	9
Iwan Roberts (Norwich)	9
Heidar Helguson (Watford)	8

© Raymond's Press Agency

Candido Costa attempts to beat the Gillingham defence
during the frustrating 0-0 draw

Ian Taylor is beaten to the ball by Reading's 'keeper Marcus Hahnemann during the first half.

Junior leaps to avoid a hard tackle from West Brom's Bernt Haas in the disappointing 1-0 loss.

Steve Elliot and Stoke's Chris Greenacre both challenge for the same ball during Derby's opening day defeat.

The script was already written and Junior did not disappoint in the lead role. Once Derby County manager George Burley had handed centre stage to the Brazilian striker, the storyline began to unfold.

Junior had left Walsall in acrimonious circumstances at the end of last season and was making his first return to the Bescot Stadium with his new club. And it was he who snatched the only goal of the game with 10 minutes remaining. His first goal for the Rams brought a much-needed first victory of the season and hoisted the team off the bottom of Division One.

Derby, as in their previous game against West Bromwich Albion, should have been two up by half-time. Junior inexplicably headed a cross from Morris against the foot of the post after only six minutes when it looked easier to score.

Despite being constantly bumped and buffeted by his former team-mates, Junior handled the situation well. He saw a curling free-kick tipped over by James Walker before Morris twice found himself clear on goal.

On the first occasion, Paul Ritchie extinguished the danger with an excellent covering tackle. Then Walker was out quickly to smother a shot from Morris.

Taylor fired straight at Walker but his presence in the area lead to the decisive goal. Paul Boertien delivered from the left, Taylor's effort was blocked and the ball fell to Junior with his back to goal. He swivelled to send a low shot past the stranded Walker and just inside the post.

Walsall, poor in the first-half, did improve but fortunately, Paul Merson never took full control despite looking more than capable of doing so. When he did knit play together, Walsall looked more of a threat and Derby had to show plenty of character as the game wore on.

Despite some nervous moments late on, Derby emerged to taste victory for the first time in five months since beating Coventry City in April.

Result......Result......Result.

WALSALL ....(0) 0   DERBY ....(0) 1
Junior 80

Att 8,726
Referee: M Clattenburg

Stats......Stats.......Stats......Stats

WALSALL				DERBY		
1st	2nd	Total		Total	2nd	1st
1	6	7	Corners	7	1	6
8	7	15	Fouls	13	4	9
0	0	0	Yellow cards	2	1	1
0	0	0	Red cards	0	0	0
1	2	3	Caught Offside	3	2	1
3	3	6	Shots on target	5	2	3
3	2	5	Shots off target	5	3	2
0	0	0	Hit woodwork	0	0	0
38	50	44%	Possession	56%	50	62

I was upset about the way Junior left the club and although some managers might not say anything about that, that's not the way I am.
Colin Lee

JUNIOR is a natural goalscorer, he knows where the goal is and won the game for us. It's amazing how many players go back to haunt their old clubs.
George Burley

Other Div 1 Results

Bradford 2 Preston 1, Cardiff 5 Gillingham 0, Coventry 4 Stoke 2, Norwich 2 Burnley 0, Nottm Forest 3 Sheff Utd 1, Rotherham 0 Crewe 2, Sunderland 2 Crystal Palace 1, Watford 3 Millwall 1, West Brom 4 Ipswich 1, West Ham 1 Reading 0, Wimbledon 2 Wigan 4

Walsall [0] 0 DERBY [0] 1

Goalkeeper Stats: Andy Oakes
Saves: Catch 1, Punch 1, Parry 2,
Crosses: Fumble 1, Catch 3, Parry 1

Derby Player Stats

Player		Shots on target L/R/H/Oth	Shots off target L/R/H/Oth	Caught offside	Fouls conceded	Free-kicks won	Corners taken		Defensive blocks
3 Luciano Zavagno ▼ 51	1st	-/-/-/-	-/-/-/-	-	-	-	-		
	2nd	-/-/-/-	-/-/-/-	-	-	-	-	-	-
10 Michael Johnson	1st	-/-/-/-	-/-/-/-	-	1	1	-	1	1
	2nd	-/-/-/-	-/-/-/-	-	-	1	-	1	-
11 Lee Morris	1st	-/-/-/-	-/-/-/-	-	-	-	4	-	-
	2nd	-/-/-/-	-/1/-/-	1	-	-	1	-	-
17 Paul Boertien ▲ 51	1st	-/-/-/-	-/-/-/-	-	-	-	-	-	
	2nd	-/-/-/-	-/-/-/-	-	-	1	-	-	-
7 Ian Taylor	1st	-/-/-/-	-/-/-/-	-	-	2	-	1	-
	2nd	-/1/-/-	-/1/-/-	-	1	-	-	-	-
32 Gary Caldwell ▲ 87	1st	-/-/-/-	-/-/-/-	-	-	-	-	-	
	2nd	-/-/-/-	-/-/-/-	-	-	-	-	-	-
12 Simo Valakari ▪ 37	1st	-/-/-/-	-/-/-/-	-	3	1	2	-	1
	2nd	-/-/-/-	-/-/-/-	-	-	-	-	-	-
33 Junior ▼ 87	1st	1/-/2/-	1/-/-/-	1	3	3	-	-	-
	2nd	1/-/-/-	1/-/-/-	-	1	1	-	-	-
14 Richard Jackson	1st	-/-/-/-	-/-/-/-	-	-	1	-	-	1
	2nd	-/-/-/-	-/-/-/-	-	-	1	-	1	1
34 Mathias Svensson ▪ 70	1st	-/-/-/-	-/-/-/-	-	1	-	-	-	-
	2nd	-/-/-/-	-/-/-/-	1	2	3	-	1	-
6 Pablo Mills	1st	-/-/-/-	-/-/-/-	-	-	-	-	-	-
	2nd	-/-/-/-	-/-/-/-	-	-	-	-	-	-
29 Tom Huddlestone	1st	-/-/-/-	-/1/-/-	-	1	-	-	1	-
	2nd	-/-/-/-	-/-/-/-	-	-	-	-	1	-

Subs not used: Grant, Bolder, Holmes. - Formation: 4-4-2

Goalkeeper Stats: James Walker Saves: Tip Over 1, Catch 2, Punch 1, Crosses: Catch 2

Player Stats

	Player Stats	Shots on target	Shots off target	Caught offside	Fouls conceded	Free-kicks won	Corners taken	Clearances	Defensive blocks
6	Ian Roper	-/-/-/-	-/1/-/-	-	1	1	-	1	-
28	Deon Burton	-/-/-/-	-/2/-/-	3	4	1	-	-	-
11	Darren Wrack	1/-/-/-	-/-/-/-	-	3	2	-	-	-
50	Stefan Oakes ▲ 53	-/-/-/-	-/-/-/-	-	1	-	-	-	-
9	Jorge Leitao	-/1/1/-	-/1/-/-	-	-	2	-	-	-
10	Paul Merson	-/1/-/-	-/1/-/-	-	-	-	7	-	-
14	Jamie Lawrence ▼ 53	-/-/-/-	-/-/-/-	-	2	-	-	1	-
2	Darren Bazeley ▼ 71	-/1/-/-	-/-/-/-	-	-	-	-	-	-
12	Pedro Matias ▲ 71	-/-/-/-	-/-/-/-	-	-	-	-	-	1
7	Simon Osborn ▼ 90	-/1/-/-	-/-/-/-	-	-	5	-	1	-
26	Paul Ritchie	-/-/-/-	-/-/-/-	-	2	1	-	1	-
15	Neil Emblen ▲ 90	-/-/-/-	-/-/-/-	-	-	-	-	-	-
4	Danny Hay	-/-/-/-	-/-/-/-	-	2	-	-	2	-

Subs not used: Kerr, Corica. - Formation: 3-5-2

Derby Played: 6 Won 1 Drawn 1 Lost 4 For 4 Against 11 Pos 22

DERBY [1] 3 Watford [1] 2

Brazilian striker Junior was Derby County's match-winner for the second time in a matter of days but it was young winger Lee Holmes who stole the show.

His testing crosses from the left created two goals, including Junior's decisive header a couple of minutes from time that sealed a 3-2 victory at Pride Park Stadium. The win also brought to an end a worrying run of three consecutive home defeats.

Ian Taylor had put the Rams ahead with an excellent 25-yard volley, only for Watford to plunder an equaliser when Derby were down to 10 men and deciding whether or not to send on a substitute for the injured Michael Johnson.

On-loan Mathias Svensson put the Rams ahead again with his third goal in five games before Ashley Young pulled Watford level in the closing stages. Then Junior had the final say.

When Johnson had to go off injured, Watford took advantage. Tom Huddlestone, covering in defence, gave away an unnecessary free-kick. Lee Cook curled the ball in and Gayle got in front of everybody to glance home a header.

In answer, Svensson was off target with a volley and a header and Junior poked the ball agonisingly wide from 10 yards. Then Holmes was introduced and helped put Derby ahead with his first meaningful touch.

His cross from the left was somehow missed by Junior but the ball fell kindly for Svensson to smash home a volley.

Watford fought back again to equalise after 81 minutes, when Young scored from close range but Holmes was not finished. This time his cross stretched Chamberlain, who touched the ball beyond the back post, where Junior rose to score with a header from an acute angle.

Six points from two games meant that Derby were heading in the right direction at last, but much hard work remained.

Result.......Result.......Result.

DERBY ....(1) 3   WATFORD......(1) 2
Taylor 18   Gayle 38
Svensson 73   Young 81
Junior 88

Att 18,459
Referee: M Dean

Stats......Stats.......Stats.....Stats

DERBY   WATFORD

1st	2nd	Total		Total	2nd	1st
1	3	4	Corners	4	1	3
7	6	13	Fouls	12	5	7
0	0	0	Yellow cards	3	2	1
0	0	0	Red cards	1	0	1
2	2	4	Caught Offside	9	2	7
4	5	9	Shots on target	3	2	1
1	7	8	Shots off target	2	0	2
0	0	0	Hit woodwork	0	0	0
48	56	52%	Possession	48%	44	52

> **IAN** Taylor scored a spectacular goal to give us the lead but Michael Johnson going off definitely had an influence on them getting their first equaliser.
>
> **George Burley**

> **WE** worked really hard and got ourselves back into the game but then their second and third goals were bad goals for us to concede.
>
> **Ray Lewington**

Other Div 1 Results

No other games

DERBY [1] 3 Watford [1] 2

Goalkeeper Stats: Andy Oakes Saves: Catch 1, Crosses: Catch 4, Punch 5

Derby Player Stats		Shots on target	Shots off target	Caught offside	Fouls conceded	Free-kicks won	Corners taken	Clearances	Defensive blocks
		L/R/H/Oth	L/R/H/Oth						
3 Luciano Zavagno	1st	-/-/-/-	-/-/-/-	-	1	2	-	-	-
▼ 45	2nd	-/-/-/-	-/-/-/-	-	-	-	-	-	-
11 Lee Morris	1st	-/-/-/-	-/-/-/-	-	1	1	1	-	-
	2nd	1/-/-/-	1/-/-/-	-	-	2	1	-	-
10 Michael Johnson	1st	-/-/-/-	-/-/-/-	-	1	1	-	-	-
▼ 40	2nd	-/-/-/-	-/-/-/-	-	-	-	-	-	-
12 Simo Valakari	1st	-/-/-/-	-/-/-/-	-	-	-	-	-	-
▼ 67	2nd	-/-/-/-	-/-/-/-	-	-	-	2	-	-
7 Ian Taylor	1st	-/1/-/-	-/-/-/-	-	-	1	-	-	-
	2nd	-/-/-/-	-/-/-/-	-	-	1	-	-	-
33 Junior	1st	1/-/1/-	1/-/-/-	1	1	1	-	1	-
	2nd	1/-/1/-	1/-/1/-	2	-	-	-	-	-
14 Richard Jackson	1st	-/-/-/-	-/-/-/-	-	-	-	-	-	-
	2nd	-/-/-/-	-/-/-/-	-	-	-	-	1	-
34 Mathias Svensson	1st	-/-/-/-	-/-/-/-	1	2	-	-	-	-
	2nd	1/-/-/-	-/1/2/-	-	-	-	-	-	-
17 Paul Boertien	1st	-/-/-/-	-/-/-/-	-	-	-	-	-	-
▲ 45	2nd	-/-/-/-	-/-/-/-	-	3	-	-	-	-
32 Gary Caldwell	1st	-/-/-/-	-/-/-/-	-	-	-	-	-	-
▲ 40	2nd	-/-/-/-	-/-/-/-	-	1	1	-	1	-
30 Lee Holmes	1st	-/-/-/-	-/-/-/-	-	-	-	-	-	-
▲ 67	2nd	-/1/-/-	-/-/-/-	-	-	1	-	-	-
1 Andy Oakes	1st	-/-/-/-	-/-/-/-	-	-	1	-	-	-
	2nd	-/-/-/-	-/-/-/-	-	-	-	-	-	-
29 Tom Huddlestone	1st	1/-/-/-	-/-/-/-	-	1	-	-	-	-
	2nd	-/-/-/-	-/1/1/-	-	2	-	-	-	-

Subs not used: Grant, Bolder. - Formation: 4-4-2

Goalkeeper Stats: Alec Chamberlain Saves: Catch 2, Crosses: Catch 3

	Player Stats	Shots on target	Shots off target	Caught offside	Fouls conceded	Free-kicks won	Corners taken	Clearances	Defensive blocks
17	Jamie Hand ▼ 77	-/-/-/-	-/-/-/-	-	1	-	-	1	-
2	Neal Ardley ▲ 52	-/-/-/-	-/-/-/-	-	1	2	1	-	-
9	Danny Webber ▼ 52	-/1/-/-	-/-/-/-	4	-	-	-	-	-
5	Neil Cox ■ 82	-/-/-/-	-/1/-/-	-	1	1	-	3	-
22	Lee Cook ▼ 77	-/-/-/-	-/-/-/-	-	1	1	2	-	-
6	Sean Dyche	-/-/-/-	-/-/-/-	-	1	2	-	2	-
25	Paul Devlin ■ 2 ■ 45	-/-/-/-	-/-/-/-	-	4	1	1	-	-
7	Bruce Dyer	-/-/-/-	-/-/-/-	5	1	3	-	-	-
12	Gavin Mahon	-/-/-/-	-/1/-/-	-	-	1	-	1	-
27	Ashley Young ▲ 77	-/-/1/-	-/-/-/-	-	-	1	-	-	-
21	Scott Fitzgerald ▲ 77	-/1/-/-	-/-/-/-	-	-	-	-	-	-
3	Paul Robinson ■ 90	-/-/-/-	-/-/-/-	-	1	1	-	1	-
15	Marcus Gayle	-/-/-/-	-/-/-/-	-	1	-	-	3	-

Subs not used: Pidgeley, Doyley. - Formation: 4-4-2

Derby Played: 7 Won 2 Drawn 1 Lost 4 For 7 Against 13 Pos 18

DERBY [0] 1 Sunderland [0] 1

Derby had seemingly snatched victory in this game through skipper Ian Taylor's goal seconds before full time. But then former Rams goalkeeper Mart Poom, making his first return to the club he served for almost six years, provided a sensational conclusion to what had been an absorbing contest.

He earned a thoroughly-deserved point for his Sunderland team with a towering, unstoppable header in third minute of added time which brought a whole new meaning to "keeper saves the day".

Poom's late heroics denied Derby a third consecutive League victory, something they had not achieved for five years.

After a rough opening, Derby dug in, rode their luck but also had their moments without ever fully stretching Poom. Gary Caldwell was close with a header and Taylor even closer with a low left foot shot. Tom Huddlestone had a rasping drive deflected behind for a corner and Junior stung the hands of Poom from 25 yards.

Matt Svensson and Junior showed that they can unsettle defences, while there were glimpses of promise from 16-year-old Lee Holmes on his first start.

Sunderland should really have been ahead at half-time and it would have been an injustic had they left empty-handed. John Oster and the impressive Thomas Butler provided good width and a consistent supply of crosses.

Fortunately for the Rams, striker Kevin Kyle and Marcus Stewart were equally consistent in their failure to find a finish. Stewart had four decent chances, two of which he headed weakly at Andy Oakes and Kyle was off target on three occasions.

But it was Derby who snatched the lead when Taylor forced the ball home from Valakari's corner. But Poom, a quiet, unassuming character, had the final word.

With time running out, Oaks turned Julio Arca's shot round the post after the Rams had conceded a free-kick in their own half to hand Sunderland possession, a costly lapse.

He could do nothing, however, as Poom arrowed a header past him from the resulting corner taken by substitute Sean Thornton.

Result.......Result.......Result.

DERBY ....(0) 1   **SUNDERLAND** (0) 1
Taylor 90   Poom 90

Att 22,535
Referee: P Walton

Stats......Stats.......Stats......Stats

DERBY					SUNDERLAND	
1st	2nd	Total		Total	2nd	1st
2	3	5	Corners	11	4	7
7	10	17	Fouls	7	3	4
1	0	1	Yellow cards	1	1	0
0	0	0	Red cards	0	0	0
3	1	4	Caught Offside	10	3	7
4	4	8	Shots on target	9	8	1
3	2	5	Shots off target	6	3	3
0	0	0	Hit woodwork	0	0	0
24	37	30%	Possession	70%	63	76

> **IT'S** been a fantastic week for us. We've taken seven points from three games whereas at the start of the season we didn't look capable of getting one.
>
> **George Burley**

> **YOU** couldn't have written the script for that game and I don't think I'll be able to cope with stuff like that every week.
>
> **Mick McCarthy**

Other Div 1 Results

Burnley 4 Bradford 0, Crewe 3 Nottm Forest 1, Crystal Palace 2 West Brom 2, Gillingham 2 West Ham 0, Ipswich 4 Wimbledon 1, Millwall 2 Walsall 1, Preston 4 Rotherham 1, Reading 1 Coventry 2, Sheff Utd 5 Cardiff 3, Stoke 1 Norwich 1, Wigan 1 Watford 0

DERBY [0] 1 Sunderland [0] 1

Goalkeeper Stats: Andy Oakes Saves: Catch 2, Parry 1, Crosses: Catch 6, Punch 3

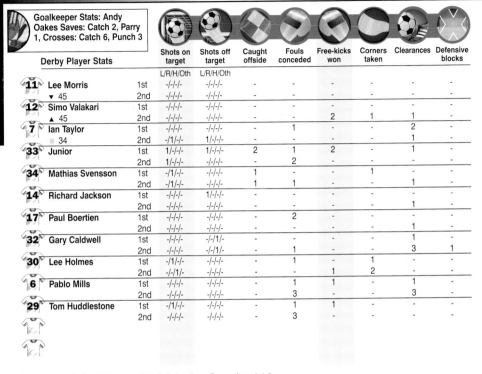

Derby Player Stats		Shots on target	Shots off target	Caught offside	Fouls conceded	Free-kicks won	Corners taken	Clearances	Defensive blocks
		L/R/H/Oth	L/R/H/Oth						
11 Lee Morris	1st	-/-/-/-	-/-/-/-	-	-	-	-	-	-
▼ 45	2nd	-/-/-/-	-/-/-/-	-	-	-	-	-	-
12 Simo Valakari	1st	-/-/-/-	-/-/-/-	-	-	-	-	-	-
▲ 45	2nd	-/-/-/-	-/-/-/-	-	-	2	1	1	-
7 Ian Taylor	1st	-/-/-/-	-/-/-/-	-	1	-	-	2	-
■ 34	2nd	-/1/-/-	1/-/-/-	-	-	-	-	1	-
33 Junior	1st	1/-/-/-	1/-/-/-	2	1	2	-	1	-
	2nd	1/-/-/-	-/-/-/-	-	2	-	-	-	-
34 Mathias Svensson	1st	-/1/-/-	-/-/-/-	1	-	-	1	-	-
	2nd	-/1/-/-	-/-/-/-	1	1	-	-	1	-
14 Richard Jackson	1st	-/-/-/-	1/-/-/-	-	-	-	-	-	-
	2nd	-/-/-/-	-/-/-/-	-	-	-	-	1	-
17 Paul Boertien	1st	-/-/-/-	-/-/-/-	-	2	-	-	-	-
	2nd	-/-/-/-	-/-/-/-	-	-	-	-	1	-
32 Gary Caldwell	1st	-/-/-/-	-/-/1/-	-	-	-	-	1	-
	2nd	-/-/-/-	-/-/1/-	-	1	-	-	3	1
30 Lee Holmes	1st	-/1/-/-	-/-/-/-	-	1	-	1	-	-
	2nd	-/-/1/-	-/-/-/-	-	-	1	2	-	-
6 Pablo Mills	1st	-/-/-/-	-/-/-/-	-	1	1	-	1	-
	2nd	-/-/-/-	-/-/-/-	-	3	-	-	3	-
29 Tom Huddlestone	1st	-/1/-/-	-/-/-/-	-	1	1	-	-	-
	2nd	-/-/-/-	-/-/-/-	-	3	-	-	-	-

Subs not used: Grant, Zavagno, Elliott, Labarthe. - Formation: 4-4-2

Goalkeeper Stats: Mart Poom Saves: Catch 1, Crosses: Catch 3

	Player Stats	Shots on target	Shots off target	Caught offside	Fouls conceded	Free-kicks won	Corners taken	Clearances	Defensive blocks
9	Kevin Kyle	-/-/-/-	1/1/1/-	8	2	4	-	-	-
15	Sean Thornton ▲ 82	-/-/-/-	-/-/-/-	-	-	-	3	-	-
10	Marcus Stewart	2/-/2/-	-/-/1/-	2	-	3	-	-	-
22	Joachim Bjorklund	-/-/-/-	-/-/-/-	-	1	2	-	2	1
25	Colin Healy	-/1/-/-	-/-/-/-	-	-	-	-	-	-
21	Paul Thirlwell	-/1/-/-	-/-/-/-	-	1	4	-	-	-
20	Thomas Butler ▼ 82	-/-/-/-	-/1/-/-	-	-	1	3	-	-
33	Julio Arca ■ 87	1/-/-/-	-/-/-/-	-	3	2	-	1	1
12	John Oster	1/-/-/-	-/1/-/-	-	-	-	5	-	-
16	Darren Williams	-/-/-/-	-/-/-/-	-	-	1	-	-	1
3	George McCartney	-/-/-/-	-/-/-/-	-	-	-	-	4	2

Subs not used: Ingham, Clark, Proctor, James. - Formation: 4-4-2

Derby Played: 8 Won 2 Drawn 2 Lost 4 For 8 Against 14 Pos 20

Nottm Forest [1] 1 DERBY [1] 1

George Burley was clearly the more pleased of the two managers and had every reason to be following this East Midlands showdown. There seemed to be more shape and purpose to the Rams' play and more of a goal threat thanks to the growing partnership of Matt Svensson and Junior.

But even a creditable point from Forest did not prevent the Rams from slipping a place to 21st in the Division One long table.

A typical derby match first half proved scrappy with endeavour outweighing quality. It was, however, lifted by two goals in three minutes. Rams struck first after 25 minutes when Svensson neatly headed behind the bemused Forest defence for Junior to rifle a low shot past Darren Ward.

It was the Brazilian's third goal for the club, an excellent finish from just inside the area that sent almost 4,000 travelling fans delirious.

But then Gareth Williams' pass allowed Andy Reid to capitalise on a flat-footed backline. He moved in from the left and though Andy Oakes got a strong hand on the shot, he could not prevent the ball from entering the net high off a post.

Either team could have won it in the second half, with the woodwork twice denying the Rams. Svensson turned Luciano Zavagno's inviting low cross onto the bar and Candido Costa's follow-up header was brilliantly tipped over by Ward.

Then Michael Johnson, returning after a neck injury was only a coat of paint away from giving the Rams their first win in Forest's backyard for 32 years. With two minutes remaining, he smashed the ball against the underside of the bar from eight yards. But Forest will feel disappointed about squandering three gilt-edged chances.

Having given their new blue away kit its first airing in a competitive match, the Rams were feeling anything but blue at the end having picked up another good point.

Result.......Result.......Result.

NOTTM FOREST (1) 1   DERBY ....(1) 1
Reid 28   Junior 25

Att 29,059
Referee: S Mathieson

Stats......Stats.......Stats......Stats

NOTTM FOREST				DERBY		
1st	2nd	Total		Total	2nd	1st
1	4	5	Corners	3	2	1
9	8	17	Fouls	22	11	11
1	1	2	Yellow cards	1	1	0
0	1	1	Red cards	0	0	0
3	3	6	Caught Offside	0	0	0
1	2	3	Shots on target	4	1	3
1	3	4	Shots off target	6	3	3
0	0	0	Hit woodwork	2	2	0
39	45	42%	Possession	58%	55	61

 I expected a very tough game and that's what we got. We had chances to win but Derby could say the same thing - they certainly worked hard.
Paul Hart

 OUR first game showed me we weren't strong enough to compete in this division but we've honed the squad, worked hard and a draw was a fair result.
George Burley

Other Div 1 Results

Bradford 1 Sheff Utd 2, Cardiff 3 Crewe 0, Coventry 1 Wigan 1, Norwich 2 Crystal Palace 1, Rotherham 1 Gillingham 1, Sunderland 2 Reading 0, Walsall 2 Preston 1, Watford 1 Ipswich 2, West Brom 1 Stoke 0, Wimbledon 2 Burnley 2

27th September

Nottm Forest [1] 1 DERBY [1] 1

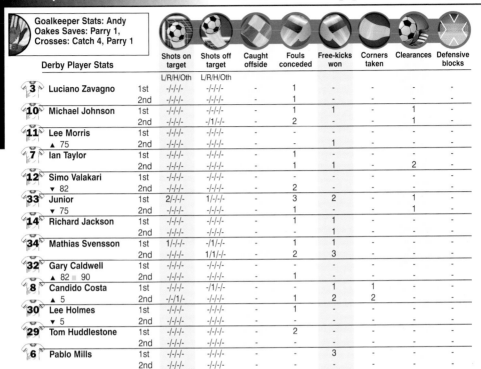

Goalkeeper Stats: Andy Oakes Saves: Parry 1, Crosses: Catch 4, Parry 1

Derby Player Stats

		Shots on target L/R/H/Oth	Shots off target L/R/H/Oth	Caught offside	Fouls conceded	Free-kicks won	Corners taken	Clearances	Defensive blocks
3 Luciano Zavagno	1st	-/-/-/-	-/-/-/-	-	1	-	-	-	-
	2nd	-/-/-/-	-/-/-/-	-	1	-	-	-	-
10 Michael Johnson	1st	-/-/-/-	-/-/-/-	-	1	1	-	1	-
	2nd	-/-/-/-	-/1/-/-	-	2	-	-	1	-
11 Lee Morris ▲ 75	1st	-/-/-/-	-/-/-/-	-	-	-	-	-	-
	2nd	-/-/-/-	-/-/-/-	-	-	1	-	-	-
7 Ian Taylor	1st	-/-/-/-	-/-/-/-	-	1	-	-	-	-
	2nd	-/-/-/-	-/-/-/-	-	1	1	-	2	-
12 Simo Valakari ▼ 82	1st	-/-/-/-	-/-/-/-	-	-	-	-	-	-
	2nd	-/-/-/-	-/-/-/-	-	2	-	-	-	-
33 Junior ▼ 75	1st	2/-/-/-	1/-/-/-	-	3	2	-	1	-
	2nd	-/-/-/-	-/-/-/-	-	1	-	-	1	-
14 Richard Jackson	1st	-/-/-/-	-/-/-/-	-	1	1	-	-	-
	2nd	-/-/-/-	-/-/-/-	-	-	1	-	-	-
34 Mathias Svensson	1st	1/-/-/-	-/1/-/-	-	1	1	-	-	-
	2nd	-/-/-/-	1/1/-/-	-	2	3	-	-	-
32 Gary Caldwell ▲ 82 ■ 90	1st	-/-/-/-	-/-/-/-	-	-	-	-	-	-
	2nd	-/-/-/-	-/-/-/-	-	1	-	-	-	-
8 Candido Costa ▲ 5	1st	-/-/-/-	-/1/-/-	-	-	1	1	-	-
	2nd	-/-/1/-	-/-/-/-	-	1	2	2	-	-
30 Lee Holmes ▼ 5	1st	-/-/-/-	-/-/-/-	-	1	-	-	-	-
	2nd	-/-/-/-	-/-/-/-	-	-	-	-	-	-
29 Tom Huddlestone	1st	-/-/-/-	-/-/-/-	-	2	-	-	-	-
	2nd	-/-/-/-	-/-/-/-	-	-	-	-	-	-
6 Pablo Mills	1st	-/-/-/-	-/-/-/-	-	-	3	-	-	-
	2nd	-/-/-/-	-/-/-/-	-	-	-	-	-	-

Subs not used: Grant, Boertien. - Formation: 4-4-2

Goalkeeper Stats: Darren Ward Saves: Catch 1, Crosses: Catch 2

Player Stats

	Shots on target	Shots off target	Caught offside	Fouls conceded	Free-kicks won	Corners taken	Clearances	Defensive blocks
14 Eoin Jess ▼ 88 ▲ 69	-/-/-/-	-/-/-/-	-	-	-	-	-	-
7 Andy Reid	2/-/-/-	-/-/-/-	2	1	4	2	-	-
11 Marlon Harewood	-/-/-/-	-/-/-/-	4	4	1	-	-	-
23 Wes Morgan	-/-/-/-	-/-/-/-	-	2	4	-	2	-
24 Gregor Robertson ▲ 88 ■ 90	-/-/-/-	-/-/-/-	-	1	-	-	-	-
22 Stephen McPhail	-/-/-/-	1/-/-/-	-	1	1	3	-	-
10 Gareth Taylor ▼ 69 ■ 2	-/-/-/-	-/-/-/-	-	3	1	-	1	-
6 John Thompson ■ 87	-/-/-/-	-/-/-/-	-	2	1	-	2	-
2 Matthieu Louis-Jean	-/-/-/-	-/1/-/-	-	-	1	-	-	-
8 Gareth Williams	-/-/-/-	-/-/-/-	-	1	1	-	-	-
21 Danny Sonner	-/-/-/-	1/-/1/-	-	-	2	-	-	-
5 Michael Dawson	-/-/1/-	-/-/-/-	-	2	6	-	4	-

Subs not used: Stewart, Roche, Cash. - Formation: 4-4-2

Derby Played: 9 Won 2 Drawn 3 Lost 4 For 9 Against 15 Pos 21

Bradford [0] 1 DERBY [1] 2

Lee Morris struck twice as Derby County beat Bradford City to extend their unbeaten run to five matches. His first goals of the season gave the Rams a 2-1 victory at Valley Parade.

Morris feels his best position is up front and Burley agrees but there had been no reason to split the blossoming partnership of Junior and the on-loan Mathias Svensson.

However, with Junior facing a number of weeks out with a worrying knee injury, Morris was handed his chance and took it. He finished expertly on the stroke of half time and again with 11 minutes remaining - both goals coming as Bradford held the upper hand only to squander some clear-cut chances.

Morris' eagerness to impress was evident and he had a good chance as early as the seventh minute. Released by Svensson's neat pass, he tried to lift the ball over the advancing Mark Paston, who blocked the effort.

After constant Bradford pressure, it seemed that the Rams would do well to reach the break on level terms, but they did better than that by stealing the lead deep into the two minutes of added time.

Huddlestone fed the ball into Morris who, with his back to goal, moved away from Gareth Edds and turned Jason Gavin before firing the ball right-footed past Paston. If conceding right on half time was a blow to Bradford, they did not show it. Instead, they reappeared showing plenty of fighting spirit.

Oakes produced an excellent save to keep out a Windass header from point-blank range but could do nothing about the equalising goal after 59 minutes.

But just as Bradford again took control of the game, Morris flattened them with the winner after 81 minutes. He latched onto a Svensson header, left Gavin for pace and finished with a low shot across the diving Paston and in off the foot of the post.

Result.......Result.......Result.

BRADFORD ....(0) 1   DERBY ....(1) 2
Gray 59   Morris 45, 79

Att 10,143
Referee: P Dowd

Stats......Stats.......Stats......Stats

	BRADFORD				DERBY	
1st	2nd	Total		Total	2nd	1st
2	3	5	Corners	4	3	1
6	6	12	Fouls	21	9	12
1	1	2	Yellow cards	2	0	2
0	0	0	Red cards	0	0	0
5	2	7	Caught Offside	2	1	1
2	4	6	Shots on target	7	2	5
6	3	9	Shots off target	3	2	1
0	0	0	Hit woodwork	0	0	0
39	50	45%	Possession	55%	50	61

THAT'S the best we've played this season. We've played worse than that and won. We created enough chances to win the game but didn't take them.

Nicky Law

THE way we played in the first 20 minutes is the standard I'm looking for all the time. We got a bit sloppy but showed real character.

George Burley

Other Div 1 Results

Cardiff 0 Wigan 0, Norwich 2 Reading 1, Rotherham 3 Stoke 0, Sunderland 3 Ipswich 2, Watford 1 Burnley 1, West Brom 2 Millwall 1, Wimbledon 1 Sheff Utd 2

Goalkeeper Stats: Andy Oakes
Saves: Parry 1, Crosses: Catch 3, Feet 1, Punch 1

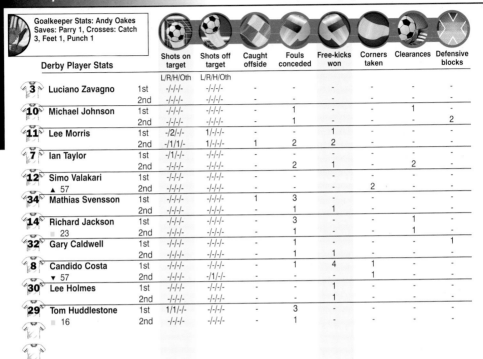

Derby Player Stats

		Shots on target L/R/H/Oth	Shots off target L/R/H/Oth	Caught offside	Fouls conceded	Free-kicks won	Corners taken	Clearances	Defensive blocks
3 Luciano Zavagno	1st	-/-/-/-	-/-/-/-	-	-	-	-	-	-
	2nd	-/-/-/-	-/-/-/-	-	-	-	-	-	-
10 Michael Johnson	1st	-/-/-/-	-/-/-/-	-	1	-	-	1	-
	2nd	-/-/-/-	-/-/-/-	-	1	-	-	-	2
11 Lee Morris	1st	-/2/-/-	1/-/-/-	-	-	1	-	-	-
	2nd	-/1/1/-	1/-/-/-	1	2	2	-	-	-
7 Ian Taylor	1st	-/1/-/-	-/-/-/-	-	-	-	-	-	-
	2nd	-/-/-/-	-/-/-/-	-	2	1	-	2	-
12 Simo Valakari ▲ 57	1st	-/-/-/-	-/-/-/-	-	-	-	-	-	-
	2nd	-/-/-/-	-/-/-/-	-	-	-	2	-	-
34 Mathias Svensson	1st	-/-/-/-	-/-/-/-	1	3	-	-	-	-
	2nd	-/-/-/-	-/-/-/-	-	1	1	-	-	-
14 Richard Jackson ■ 23	1st	-/-/-/-	-/-/-/-	-	3	-	-	1	-
	2nd	-/-/-/-	-/-/-/-	-	1	-	-	1	-
32 Gary Caldwell	1st	-/-/-/-	-/-/-/-	-	1	-	-	-	1
	2nd	-/-/-/-	-/-/-/-	-	1	1	-	-	-
8 Candido Costa ▼ 57	1st	-/-/-/-	-/-/-/-	-	1	4	1	-	-
	2nd	-/-/-/-	-/1/-/-	-	-	-	1	-	-
30 Lee Holmes	1st	-/-/-/-	-/-/-/-	-	-	1	-	-	-
	2nd	-/-/-/-	-/-/-/-	-	-	1	-	-	-
29 Tom Huddlestone ■ 16	1st	1/1/-/-	-/-/-/-	-	3	-	-	-	-
	2nd	-/-/-/-	-/-/-/-	-	1	-	-	-	-

Subs not used: Grant, Boertien, Mills, Tudgay. - Formation: 4-4-2

Goalkeeper Stats: Mark Paston Saves: Block 1, Catch 3, Crosses: Catch 1

Player Stats	Shots on target	Shots off target	Caught offside	Fouls conceded	Free-kicks won	Corners taken	Clearances	Defensive blocks
3 Paul Heckingbottom	-/-/-/-	-/-/-/-	-	1	3	-	-	-
5 David Wetherall	-/-/-/-	-/1/1/-	-	2	1	-	2	-
17 Jason Gavin ■ 78	-/-/1/-	-/-/-/-	-	2	2	-	-	1
8 Michael Branch	1/1/-/-	-/2/-/-	5	-	1	-	-	-
10 Dean Windass ■ 12	-/-/2/-	-/-/-/-	1	1	4	-	-	-
9 Nicky Summerbee	-/-/-/-	-/-/-/-	-	1	-	5	-	-
18 Ben Muirhead ▼ 81	-/-/-/-	-/2/-/-	-	2	4	-	-	-
20 Robert Wolleaston ▲ 81	-/-/-/-	-/-/-/-	-	-	-	-	-	-
19 Gareth Edds	-/-/-/-	-/-/-/-	-	2	-	-	-	-
11 Andy Gray	-/-/1/-	-/1/-/-	1	1	3	-	1	-
7 Paul Evans	-/-/-/-	-/2/-/-	-	-	3	-	-	1

Subs not used: Beresford, Cornwall, Francis, Emanuel. - Formation: 4-4-2

Derby Played: 10 Won 3 Drawn 3 Lost 4 For 11 Against 16 Pos 16

...September Team Stats.....Team Stats......Team Stats......Team S

League table at the end of September

		HOME					AWAY					Pts	Df
	P	W	D	L	F	A	W	D	L	F	A		
Sheff Utd	10	4	1	0	13	4	3	1	1	7	6	23	10
West Brom	10	5	0	0	12	3	2	1	2	5	7	22	7
Wigan	10	3	1	0	4	1	3	2	1	10	5	21	8
Norwich	10	5	0	0	11	4	1	2	2	5	7	20	5
Sunderland	10	4	0	1	9	4	2	1	2	8	6	19	7
West Ham	9	2	2	0	3	1	3	0	2	7	5	17	4
Nottm Forest	9	3	1	1	9	4	2	0	2	7	7	16	5
Millwall	11	3	2	0	8	3	1	2	3	7	10	16	2
Cardiff	10	3	1	1	12	3	1	2	2	7	9	15	7
Reading	10	2	1	1	6	3	2	1	3	8	8	14	3
Burnley	11	2	0	3	7	8	2	2	2	9	10	14	-2
Crewe	9	3	0	1	5	4	1	1	3	4	8	13	-3
Gillingham	11	2	1	2	7	8	1	3	2	5	10	13	-6
Walsall	10	3	2	1	10	6	0	1	3	2	5	12	1
Stoke	11	2	2	1	7	5	1	1	4	6	10	12	-2
Derby	10	1	1	3	6	10	2	2	1	5	6	12	-5
Crystal Palace	9	1	1	2	4	5	2	1	2	9	8	11	0
Ipswich	10	2	2	1	9	6	1	0	4	5	10	11	-2
Preston	9	3	0	2	10	7	0	1	3	3	6	10	0
Bradford	10	1	1	4	6	12	2	0	2	3	5	10	-8
Coventry	8	1	2	1	6	6	1	1	2	6	8	9	-2
Rotherham	10	2	2	2	5	6	0	1	3	1	11	9	-11
Watford	9	1	2	2	7	7	0	0	4	2	7	5	-5
Wimbledon	10	1	1	4	9	15	0	0	4	4	11	4	-13

September matches table

	P	W	D	L	F	A	Pts
Norwich	5	4	1	0	9	4	13
Sheff Utd	5	4	0	1	15	8	13
Derby	5	3	2	0	8	5	11
Wigan	5	3	2	0	7	3	11
West Brom	5	3	1	1	9	5	10
Sunderland	5	3	1	1	9	7	10
Ipswich	5	3	0	2	11	10	9
Burnley	6	2	2	2	9	9	8
Cardiff	5	2	1	2	12	7	7
Millwall	6	2	1	3	10	11	7
Coventry	4	2	1	1	9	8	7
Gillingham	6	2	1	3	9	13	7
Nottm Forest	4	2	1	1	8	5	7
West Ham	4	2	1	1	5	3	7
Preston	4	2	0	2	10	7	6
Walsall	5	2	0	3	6	7	6
Crewe	4	2	0	2	5	7	6
Bradford	5	2	0	3	5	9	6
Watford	5	1	1	3	7	8	4
Stoke	6	1	1	4	7	12	4
Rotherham	5	1	1	3	5	12	4
Reading	5	1	0	4	4	8	3
Wimbledon	5	0	1	4	6	14	1
Crystal Palace	4	0	1	3	4	7	1

September team stats details

Club Name	Ply	Shots On	Shots Off	Corners	Hit W'work	Caught Offside	Offside Trap	Fouls	Yellow Cards	Red Cards	Pens Awarded	Pens Con
Bradford	5	27	37	26	0	22	6	52	8	1	- (-)	-
Burnley	6	54	31	41	4	21	37	67	12	1	1 (-)	1
Cardiff	5	54	24	29	0	19	15	57	6	0	1 (1)	2
Coventry	4	40	32	24	1	9	18	51	3	2	1 (1)	1
Crewe	4	29	19	24	2	12	17	35	3	0	1 (1)	1
Crystal Palace	4	15	19	20	0	8	12	46	12	0	- (-)	2
Derby	5	33	27	23	2	13	35	86	6	0	- (-)	-
Gillingham	6	27	23	34	0	28	24	87	13	0	1 (1)	3
Ipswich	5	36	19	45	2	22	22	56	10	0	2 (2)	-
Millwall	6	37	25	31	3	32	13	110	14	1	2 (2)	1
Norwich	5	40	31	30	0	20	8	79	6	0	1 (1)	-
Nottm Forest	4	18	18	20	1	21	5	53	9	1	1 (1)	-
Preston	4	32	20	30	1	10	4	65	9	1	1 (1)	-
Reading	5	27	19	33	0	16	28	73	7	0	- (-)	-
Rotherham	5	40	24	31	0	7	11	78	13	1	2 (2)	1
Sheff Utd	5	37	19	21	0	8	17	75	7	1	3 (3)	2
Stoke	6	34	29	27	1	23	15	80	15	3	- (-)	1
Sunderland	5	38	25	37	0	22	17	51	12	1	1 (1)	-
Walsall	5	35	26	32	2	15	25	66	8	0	1 (1)	3
Watford	5	24	16	34	0	31	12	60	11	2	1 (1)	-
West Brom	5	36	23	34	2	25	22	60	10	1	- (-)	-
West Ham	4	29	14	25	3	18	14	50	9	1	- (-)	-
Wigan	5	23	29	27	2	16	18	66	11	1	- (-)	-
Wimbledon	5	22	28	16	0	9	32	59	11	0	- (-)	2

SEPTEMBER STATS

Monthly Top scorers

Robert Earnshaw (Cardiff)	6
Ricardo Fuller (Preston)	5
Peter Thorne (Cardiff)	4
Luke Chadwick (Burnley)	4
Peter Ndlovu (Sheff Utd)	4
Andrew Morrell (Coventry)	4
Rob Hulse (West Brom)	3
Patrick Agyemang (Gillingham)	3
David Connolly (West Ham)	3
Richard Naylor (Ipswich)	3

Penalties scored

3 Peter Ndlovu (Sheff Utd), **2** Neil Harris (Millwall), Darren Byfield (Sunderland)

Assists

Lee Cook (Watford)	3
Dennis Wise (Millwall)	3
Peter Thorne (Cardiff)	3
Paul Ifill (Millwall)	3
Michael Doyle (Coventry)	3
Gareth Farrelly (Burnley)	3
Clive Clarke (Stoke)	2

Quickest goals

1:21 mins - Shaun Derry (Norwich vs Crystal Palace)
4:05 mins - Patrick Suffo (Coventry vs Stoke)
4:19 mins - Jason Koumas (West Brom vs Millwall)
6:50 mins - Marlon Harewood (Burnley vs Nottm Forest)
7:34 mins - Bruce Dyer (Watford vs Millwall)

Top Keeper

	Mins	Gls
John Filan (Wigan)	477	3
David James (West Ham)	380	3
Robert Green (Norwich)	474	4
Darren Ward (Nottm Forest)	574	5
Alan Combe (Bradford)	98	1
Andy Oakes (Derby)	483	5
Russell Hoult (West Brom)	483	5
Mart Poom (Sunderland)	482	7

Shots on target

Robert Blake (Burnley)	17
Peter Thorne (Cardiff)	14
Junior (Derby)	12
Darren Byfield (Sunderland)	12
Kevin Kyle (Sunderland)	11
Peter Crouch (Norwich)	11
Richard Langley (Cardiff)	11
Marlon King (Nottm Forest)	11
Graham Kavanagh (Cardiff)	11
Jermain Defoe (West Ham)	11

Shots off target

Delroy Facey (Burnley)	10
Kevin Kyle (Sunderland)	10
Michael Doyle (Coventry)	8
Paul Evans (Nottm Forest)	8
Dean Ashton (Crewe)	8
Junior (Derby)	7
Nathan Ellington (Wigan)	7
Gifton Noel-Williams (Stoke)	6
Geoff Horsfield (Wigan)	6
Mathias Svensson (Derby)	6

Caught offside

Marlon Harewood (West Ham)	17
Kevin Kyle (Sunderland)	15
Geoff Horsfield (Wigan)	14
Danny Webber (Watford)	14
Michael Branch (Bradford)	13
Gifton Noel-Williams (Stoke)	12
Nicky Forster (Reading)	12
Delroy Facey (Burnley)	11
Darren Huckerby (Norwich)	10

Free-kicks won

Tim Cahill (Millwall)	17
Darren Huckerby (Norwich)	17
Marlon King (Nottm Forest)	14
Nigel Reo-Coker (West Ham)	14
Tomas Repka (West Ham)	13
Rob Hulse (West Brom)	13
Geoff Horsfield (Wigan)	13
Danny Spiller (Gillingham)	13
Kevin Kyle (Sunderland)	13

Forest v Derby

Fouls conceded

Ashley Ward (Sheff Utd)	22
Bob Peeters (Millwall)	20
Kevin Kyle (Sunderland)	14
Peter Crouch (Norwich)	14
Nicky Forster (Reading)	14
Tom Huddlestone (Derby)	14
Andy Todd (Burnley)	13
John Eustace (Stoke)	13
Keith Andrews (Wolverhampton)	13

Fouls without a card

Junior (Derby)	12
Ian Cox (Gillingham)	12
Dele Adebola (Coventry)	11
Darren Huckerby (Norwich)	10
Damien Francis (Norwich)	10
Delroy Facey (Burnley)	10
James Harper (Reading)	9
Ricardo Fuller (Preston)	9
Neil Shipperley (Crystal Palace)	8

Former Ram's goalkeeper Mart Poom, who later scored an amazing injury time equaliser, challenges Junior for the ball.

Ian Taylor jumps for the ball during the Midlands Derby. The match ended in a draw, with both goals being scored in a frantic 3 minute spell.

Andy Reid and Michael Johnson fight for the ball. Johnson, making his
return from a neck injury blasted against the underside of the bar with
two minutes to go

Brazilian striker Junior loses out to Sunderland's George McCartney.

DERBY [0] 0 West Ham [0] 1

Head for the exit early at Pride Park Stadium and you're likely to miss the key moment of the match. Junior headed an 88th-minute winner against Watford and Ian Taylor left it later against Sunderland only for Mart Poom to grab a sensational equaliser deep into stoppage time.

In this contest, Don Hutchison expertly volleyed home from a Wayne Quinn corner with a minute remaining to give West Ham United a 1-0 victory in a largely even contest. It was harsh on the Rams, who had been so close to stretching their unbeaten record to six games.

Chances were evenly spread on Saturday with both goalkeepers, Andy Oakes and David James, equally busy. Oakes displayed fine form denying Hammers striker David Connolly on three occasions. In front of Oakes, the back four stood up well to West Ham's probing.

Morris had caused the West Ham defence to wobble once or twice early on as he looked in the mood to add to his match-winning performance at Bradford. After he went off injured, Ian Taylor was forced forward, partnered by Tudgay. The two combined to create a clear-cut opening after 67 minutes when Tudgay picked out Taylor who headed over from an inviting position.

West Ham looked in good shape to bounce straight back to the Premiership, with much good football being played.They also have the best defensive record in the division, not something you associate with a club whose tradition is based on attractive, attacking football.

Hutchison had an eventful 20 minutes, collecting a yellow card before his decisive goal. Quinn's delivered a corner and Hutchison thumped the ball home.

The Rams still showed enough character to almost grab an equaliser when the willing Taylor met Caldwell's cross only for James to smartly smother the downward header.

Result.......Result.......Result.

DERBY ....(0) 0   WEST HAM ....(0) 1
                                              Hutchison 90

Att 22,810
Referee: M Fletcher

Stats......Stats.......Stats......Stats

DERBY				WEST HAM		
1st	2nd	Total		Total	2nd	1st
5	3	8	Corners	6	3	3
7	8	15	Fouls	11	8	3
0	1	1	Yellow cards	2	2	0
0	0	0	Red cards	0	0	0
2	1	3	Caught Offside	3	1	2
4	2	6	Shots on target	6	4	2
4	3	7	Shots off target	3	1	2
0	0	0	Hit woodwork	0	0	0
38	47	42%	Possession	58%	53	62

WEST HAM dominated the first 15 minutes but we came back well and had to change things around after losing Matt (Svensson) and Lee (Morris) to injury.

George Burley

DERBY had a lot of confidence and for spells we were on the rack a bit. I think Derby can count themselves unlucky not to get something.

Trevor Brooking

Other Div 1 Results

Burnley 3 Walsall 1, Crewe 0 Watford 1, Crystal Palace 2 Cardiff 1, Gillingham 0 West Brom 2, Ipswich 2 Rotherham 1, Millwall 2 Coventry 1, Preston 1 Wimbledon 0, Reading 2 Bradford 2, Sheff Utd 0 Sunderland 1, Stoke 2 Nottm Forest 1, Wigan 1 Norwich 1

DERBY [0] 0 West Ham [0] 1

Goalkeeper Stats: Andy Oakes
Saves: Catch 2, Round Post 1,
Crosses: Catch 2, Parry 1

Derby Player Stats		Shots on target L/R/H/Oth	Shots off target L/R/H/Oth	Caught offside	Fouls conceded	Free-kicks won	Corners taken	Clearances	Defensive blocks
3 Luciano Zavagno	1st	-/-/-/-	-/-/-/-	-	-	-	-	1	-
	2nd	-/-/-/-	-/-/-/-	-	-	1	-	-	-
23 Marcus Tudgay ▲ 59	1st	-/-/-/-	-/-/-/-	-	-	-	-	-	-
	2nd	-/-/-/-	-/-/-/-	1	-	-	-	-	-
10 Michael Johnson	1st	-/-/1/-	-/-/-/-	-	1	1	-	1	-
	2nd	-/-/-/-	-/-/-/-	-	1	1	-	5	-
11 Lee Morris ▼ 59	1st	1/-/-/-	2/-/-/-	-	-	-	-	-	-
	2nd	-/-/-/-	-/-/-/-	-	-	-	-	-	-
7 Ian Taylor	1st	-/-/-/-	-/-/-/-	-	2	-	-	-	-
	2nd	-/-/1/-	-/-/1/-	-	2	-	-	1	-
32 Gary Caldwell	1st	-/-/-/-	-/1/-/-	-	-	-	-	2	-
	2nd	-/-/-/-	-/-/-/-	-	2	-	-	-	-
12 Simo Valakari ▲ 43	1st	-/-/-/-	-/-/-/-	-	-	-	-	-	-
	2nd	-/-/-/-	-/-/-/-	-	1	-	-	1	-
8 Candido Costa	1st	-/-/-/-	-/-/-/-	-	1	-	3	-	-
	2nd	-/-/-/-	-/1/-/-	-	-	1	1	-	-
30 Lee Holmes	1st	-/-/-/-	-/-/-/-	-	1	-	2	-	-
	2nd	-/-/-/-	-/-/-/-	-	-	4	2	-	-
34 Mathias Svensson ▼ 43	1st	1/-/1/-	-/-/-/-	1	2	1	-	2	-
	2nd	-/-/-/-	-/-/-/-	-	-	-	-	-	-
1 Andy Oakes	1st	-/-/-/-	-/-/-/-	-	-	1	-	-	-
	2nd	-/-/-/-	-/-/-/-	-	-	-	-	-	-
6 Pablo Mills	1st	-/-/-/-	-/-/-/-	-	-	-	-	1	-
	2nd	-/-/-/-	-/-/-/-	-	-	1	-	2	-
29 Tom Huddlestone 68	1st	-/-/-/-	-/1/-/-	-	-	-	-	-	-
	2nd	-/1/-/-	1/-/-/-	-	2	-	-	-	-

Subs not used: Grant, Elliott, Boertien. - Formation: 4-4-2

Goalkeeper Stats: David James Saves: Catch 1, Parry 1, Crosses: Catch 8

	Player Stats	Shots on target	Shots off target	Caught offside	Fouls conceded	Free-kicks won	Corners taken	Clearances	Defensive blocks
12	Matthew Etherington	-/-/-/-	-/-/-/-	1	-	1	-	-	-
20	Niclas Alexandersson	-/-/-/-	-/1/-/-	1	2	1	4	-	-
6	Michael Carrick ▼ 83	-/-/-/-	-/-/-/-	-	-	2	-	-	-
33	Neil Mellor ▼ 71	-/-/-/-	-/1/-/-	1	2	1	-	-	-
7	Christian Dailly	-/-/-/-	-/-/-/-	-	1	3	-	1	-
5	Robert Lee ▲ 83	-/-/-/-	-/-/-/-	-	-	-	-	-	-
8	David Connolly	1/2/1/-	-/-/-/-	-	1	1	-	-	-
4	Don Hutchison ▲ 71 74	2/-/-/-	-/-/1/-	-	1	1	-	-	-
2	Tomas Repka	-/-/-/-	-/-/-/-	-	3	1	-	1	-
19	Ian Pearce	-/-/-/-	-/-/-/-	-	-	-	-	3	-
14	Wayne Quinn	-/-/-/-	-/-/-/-	-	-	2	2	3	-
16	Kevin Horlock 84	-/-/-/-	-/-/-/-	-	1	2	-	2	-

Subs not used: Bywater, Ferdinand, Garcia. - Formation: 4-4-2

Derby Played: 11 Won 3 Drawn 3 Lost 5 For 11 Against 17 Pos 20

Derby County secured a point against Wigan Athletic in an eventful contest shaped by a poor display of refereeing. Puzzled looks filled Pride Park Stadium as Mr Prosser's judgement at key moments saw the game swing one way and then the other.

The Rams could have been two up, instead found themselves two down before a spirited showing saw them claw back to 2-2.

There is certainly more fight about George Burley's team and they needed to battle after falling two goals behind to a couple of Andy Liddell free-kicks.

Oakes, so often the saviour in recent weeks, should probably have done better from the first, but could do nothing when Liddell thumped home his second from the edge of the area after 31 minutes.

Wigan's lead looked decisive. They had been miserly in their previous half dozen games, conceding only two goals, and it was not looking good for the Rams. They needed a lifeline.

When Ian Taylor appeared to run into a defensive combination of Tony Dinning and Ian Breckin, the referee stunned most people in the ground by giving a penalty and Taylor kept his nerve to beat John Filan again for his fifth goal of the season.

Then Taylor robbed Jimmy Bullard in midfield and his perfect pass split a square and stranded Wigan backline for Morris to race clear and beat Filan. That was relief for Morris, who had been unable to finish when presented with two chances in the opening three minutes of the game set up by the highly promising Lee Holmes, who went close himself with a curling free-kick in the first half.

Both teams will claim that they could have taken all three points but the best chances fell to Wigan, whose front two of Horsfield and the Nathan Ellington looked a strong partnership.

Result......Result......Result.

DERBY ....(1) 2 **WIGAN** ....(2) 2
Taylor 40(p)   Liddell 4, 31
Morris 62

Att 19,151
Referee: P Prosser

Stats......Stats.......Stats......Stats

DERBY				WIGAN		
1st	2nd	Total		Total	2nd	1st
1	2	3	Corners	4	3	1
7	11	18	Fouls	19	12	7
3	1	4	Yellow cards	2	1	1
0	0	0	Red cards	0	0	0
2	2	4	Caught Offside	1	0	1
5	4	9	Shots on target	15	9	6
3	2	5	Shots off target	5	3	2
0	0	0	Hit woodwork	0	0	0
48	55	51%	Possession	49%	45	52

THERE were a lot of decisions out there which I thought were wrong but we could not influence those, we had to remain professional.
George Burley

I'M not one to bang on about referees but something's got to be done because both George Burley and I were doing our heads in on the touchline.
Paul Jewell

Other Div 1 Results

Bradford 0 Ipswich 1, Burnley P Reading P, Gillingham P Sunderland P, Preston P Watford P, Rotherham 0 Millwall 0, Sheff Utd P Crewe P, Stoke P Crystal Palace P, Walsall P Nottm Forest P

DERBY [1] 2 Wigan [2] 2

Goalkeeper Stats: Andy Oakes
Saves: Catch 6, Round Post 1, Punch 1, Parry 1, Crosses: Catch 4, Punch 2

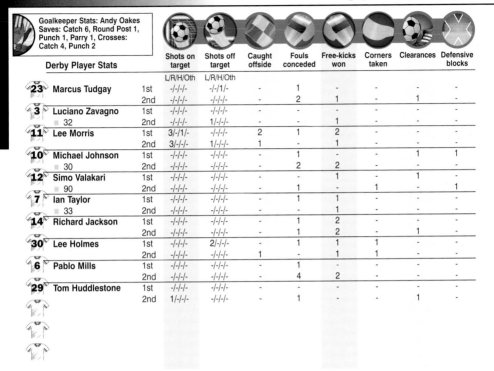

Derby Player Stats		Shots on target L/R/H/Oth	Shots off target L/R/H/Oth	Caught offside	Fouls conceded	Free-kicks won	Corners taken	Clearances	Defensive blocks
23 Marcus Tudgay	1st	-/-/-/-	-/-/1/-	-	1	-	-	-	-
	2nd	-/-/-/-	-/-/-/-	-	2	1	-	1	-
3 Luciano Zavagno	1st	-/-/-/-	-/-/-/-	-	-	-	-	-	-
■ 32	2nd	-/-/-/-	1/-/-/-	-	-	1	-	-	-
11 Lee Morris	1st	3/-/1/-	-/-/-/-	2	1	2	-	-	-
	2nd	3/-/-/-	1/-/-/-	1	-	1	-	-	-
10 Michael Johnson	1st	-/-/-/-	-/-/-/-	-	1	-	-	1	1
■ 30	2nd	-/-/-/-	-/-/-/-	-	2	2	-	-	-
12 Simo Valakari	1st	-/-/-/-	-/-/-/-	-	-	1	-	1	-
■ 90	2nd	-/-/-/-	-/-/-/-	-	1	-	1	-	1
7 Ian Taylor	1st	-/-/-/-	-/-/-/-	-	1	1	-	-	-
■ 33	2nd	-/-/-/-	-/-/-/-	-	-	1	-	-	-
14 Richard Jackson	1st	-/-/-/-	-/-/-/-	-	1	2	-	-	-
	2nd	-/-/-/-	-/-/-/-	-	1	2	-	1	-
30 Lee Holmes	1st	-/-/-/-	2/-/-/-	-	1	1	1	-	-
	2nd	-/-/-/-	-/-/-/-	1	-	1	1	-	-
6 Pablo Mills	1st	-/-/-/-	-/-/-/-	-	1	-	-	-	-
	2nd	-/-/-/-	-/-/-/-	-	4	2	-	-	-
29 Tom Huddlestone	1st	-/-/-/-	-/-/-/-	-	-	-	-	-	-
	2nd	1/-/-/-	-/-/-/-	-	1	-	-	1	-

Subs not used: Grant, Elliott, Bolder, Boertien, Labarthe. - Formation: 4-4-2

Goalkeeper Stats: John Filan Saves: Catch 1, Parry 2, Crosses: Catch 4, Punch 1

	Player Stats	Shots on target	Shots off target	Caught offside	Fouls conceded	Free-kicks won	Corners taken	Clearances	Defensive blocks
10	Lee McCulloch ▼ 83	1/2/-/-	-/-/-/-	-	2	2	-	-	-
16	Tony Dinning ▼ 72	-/-/-/-	-/-/-/-	-	2	1	-	-	-
3	Stephen McMillan	-/-/-/-	-/-/-/-	-	2	1	-	-	-
9	Nathan Ellington	-/2/1/-	-/2/-/-	-	-	2	-	-	-
6	Ian Breckin ■ 72	-/-/1/-	-/-/1/-	-	1	1	-	2	1
7	Andy Liddell ■ 34	-/5/-/-	-/-/1/-	-	2	-	-	-	-
15	Geoff Horsfield	-/2/-/-	-/-/-/-	1	5	6	-	2	-
18	Jason Jarrett ▲ 72	-/1/-/-	-/-/-/-	-	1	-	-	-	-
19	Nicky Eaden	-/-/-/-	-/-/-/-	-	1	1	-	-	-
21	Jimmy Bullard	-/-/-/-	-/-/1/-	-	-	1	4	-	-
20	Gary Teale ▲ 83	-/-/-/-	-/-/-/-	-	-	-	-	-	-
4	Matt Jackson	-/-/-/-	-/-/-/-	-	3	2	-	1	1

Subs not used: Walsh, Flynn, Baines. - Formation: 4-3-3

Derby Played: 12 Won 3 Drawn 4 Lost 5 For 13 Against 19 Pos 16

Crystal Palace [1] 1 DERBY [0] 1

14th October

Another Derby County comeback saw them take a point from a 1-1 draw against Crystal Palace at Selhurst Park. They had now lost only once in the last eight games and were unbeaten in four away matches.

Full-back Danny Butterfield fired Palace ahead at the end of a first half in which the Rams had shown little. But they improved in the second half and equalised after 74 minutes thanks to an own goal. In between, the Rams' Portuguese Under-21 international Candido Costa had failed to take two good chances.

Palace started brightly going close on a number of occasions, but Derby gradually found their feet and got back into the game.

Morris pulled a shot well wide after skipping past a couple of defenders and a Lee Holmes' strike from 25 yards was on target. Costa was seeing plenty of the ball as he floated with some menace just behind Morris, and he had a clear sight of goal after 34 minutes.

But Palace responded by taking the lead on the stroke of half time.

Black released Neil Shipperley through the middle and, with Oakes advancing, Michael Johnson did well to win the ball and Pablo Mills conceded a corner in completing the clearance. Michael Hughes took the kick, Oakes stretched to tip the ball away and Butterfield sent a beautifully controlled drive rising into the net.

Hughes was menacing for Palace but the Rams dug in.

Tudgay made an impact, Holmes and Costa worked tirelessly and the passing improved. With 74 minutes on the clock, Holmes fed Zavagno on the over-lap and he delivered a testing left-footed cross. Berthelin came to collect but Powell appeared to slice the ball against his goalkeeper and it bounced into the net.

Stung by this, Palace rallied and the game finished with the Rams hanging on for a valuable point.

Result.......Result.......Result.

CRYSTAL P ....(1) 1   DERBY ....(0) 1
Butterfield 45   Zavagno 74

Att 14,344
Referee: P Armstrong

Stats......Stats.......Stats......Stats

CRYSTAL PALACE				DERBY		
1st	2nd	Total		Total	2nd	1st
6	5	11	Corners	1	0	1
10	8	18	Fouls	12	8	4
1	1	2	Yellow cards	0	0	0
0	1	1	Red cards	0	0	0
1	3	4	Caught Offside	6	6	0
2	6	8	Shots on target	3	1	2
2	5	7	Shots off target	4	0	4
0	1	1	Hit woodwork	0	0	0
46	54	50%	Possession	50%	46	54

 WE have a knack of switching off and in the second half we let them come onto us and then we let in a sloppy goal.
Steve Kember

 WE passed the ball around better in the second half and showed good composure - in the first we couldn't pass the ball as I wanted them to.
George Burley

Other Div 1 Results

Crewe 2 Bradford 2, Ipswich 6 Burnley 1, Millwall 0 Preston 1, Nottm Forest 2 Rotherham 2, Reading 2 Gillingham 1, Sunderland 0 Cardiff 0, Watford 1 Walsall 1, West Brom 0 Sheff Utd 2, Wigan 2 Stoke 1

Crystal Palace [1] 1 DERBY [0] 1

Goalkeeper Stats: Andy Oakes Saves: Parry 1, Crosses: Catch 4

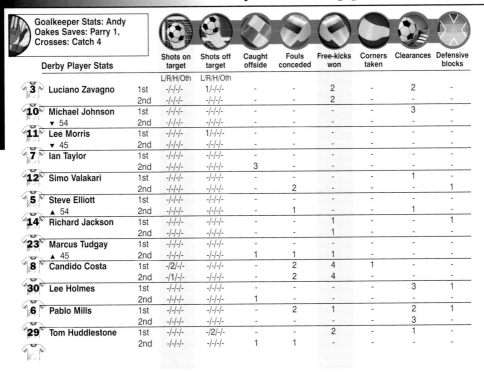

Derby Player Stats		Shots on target	Shots off target	Caught offside	Fouls conceded	Free-kicks won	Corners taken	Clearances	Defensive blocks
		L/R/H/Oth	L/R/H/Oth						
3 Luciano Zavagno	1st	-/-/-/-	1/-/-/-	-	-	2	-	2	-
	2nd	-/-/-/-	-/-/-/-	-	-	2	-	-	-
10 Michael Johnson	1st	-/-/-/-	-/-/-/-	-	-	-	-	3	-
▼ 54	2nd	-/-/-/-	-/-/-/-	-	-	-	-	-	-
11 Lee Morris	1st	-/-/-/-	1/-/-/-	-	-	-	-	-	-
▼ 45	2nd	-/-/-/-	-/-/-/-	-	-	-	-	-	-
7 Ian Taylor	1st	-/-/-/-	-/-/-/-	-	-	-	-	-	-
	2nd	-/-/-/-	-/-/-/-	3	-	-	-	-	-
12 Simo Valakari	1st	-/-/-/-	-/-/-/-	-	-	-	-	1	-
	2nd	-/-/-/-	-/-/-/-	-	2	-	-	-	1
5 Steve Elliott	1st	-/-/-/-	-/-/-/-	-	-	-	-	-	-
▲ 54	2nd	-/-/-/-	-/-/-/-	-	1	-	-	1	-
14 Richard Jackson	1st	-/-/-/-	-/-/-/-	-	-	1	-	-	1
	2nd	-/-/-/-	-/-/-/-	-	-	1	-	-	-
23 Marcus Tudgay	1st	-/-/-/-	-/-/-/-	-	-	-	-	-	-
▲ 45	2nd	-/-/-/-	-/-/-/-	1	1	1	-	-	-
8 Candido Costa	1st	-/2/-/-	-/-/-/-	-	2	4	1	-	-
	2nd	-/1/-/-	-/-/-/-	-	2	4	-	-	-
30 Lee Holmes	1st	-/-/-/-	-/-/-/-	-	-	-	-	3	1
	2nd	-/-/-/-	-/-/-/-	1	-	-	-	-	-
6 Pablo Mills	1st	-/-/-/-	-/-/-/-	-	2	1	-	2	1
	2nd	-/-/-/-	-/-/-/-	-	-	-	-	3	-
29 Tom Huddlestone	1st	-/-/-/-	-/2/-/-	-	-	2	-	1	-
	2nd	-/-/-/-	-/-/-/-	1	1	-	-	-	-

Subs not used: Grant, Bolder, Boertien. Formation: 4-3-2-1

Goalkeeper Stats: Cedric Berthelin Saves: Catch 1, Parry 2, Crosses: Catch 2

	Player Stats	Shots on target	Shots off target	Caught offside	Fouls conceded	Free-kicks won	Corners taken	Clearances	Defensive blocks
5	Kit Symons	-/-/-/-	-/-/-/-	-	-	-	-	2	-
14	Ben Watson ▲ 84	-/-/-/-	1/-/-/-	-	-	-	-	-	-
16	Tommy Black	-/1/-/-	-/-/-/-	1	-	2	1	-	-
4	Danny Butterfield	-/1/-/-	-/1/-/-	-	-	-	6	1	-
10	Shaun Derry	-/-/-/-	-/-/-/-	-	3	-	-	-	-
17	Michael Hughes ▼ 84	-/-/-/-	-/-/-/-	-	3	-	4	-	-
2	Curtis Fleming ▪ 33	-/-/-/-	-/-/-/-	-	1	2	-	-	2
11	Neil Shipperley	-/2/1/-	-/1/1/-	-	5	1	-	-	-
32	Darren Powell ▪ 7 ▪ 90	-/-/-/-	-/-/1/-	-	2	2	-	2	-
9	Dougie Freedman	1/1/1/-	-/-/-/-	3	2	2	-	-	-
22	Wayne Routledge	-/-/-/-	-/2/-/-	-	2	2	-	-	-

Subs not used: Riihilahti, Borrowdale, Williams, Cronin. - Formation: 3-4-3

Crewe [2] 3 DERBY [0] 0

Derby County's poor defending made for a miserable afternoon against Crewe Alexandra. In a strange game, the Rams had plenty of possession and created a number of promising openings without ever looking convincing in front of goal.

While County made chances and missed them, Crewe found the net on three occasions giving their manager Dario Gradi the perfect welcome back present following his heart surgery.

Crewe needed only nine minutes to take advantage. A bad mistake by Pablo Mills allowed Andrew Barrowman to race clear. Lee Grant parried his shot upwards rather than away and when Dean Ashton scuffed a cross-cum-shot, the ball fell to Barrowman who tucked it away.

The second goal on 24 minutes featured a four-man move and fine finish by Ashton. Yet the Rams had their moments in the first half.

Loan signing Danny Dichio came closest with a header and sixteen-year-olds Lee Holmes and Tom Huddlestone, operating with some purpose in the wide midfield roles, also threatened the Crewe goal.

Stung by their first-half failings, the Rams tried to make amends after the break. They pushed Crewe back and should all at least have hit the target, if not the net, from excellent positions. Crewe were edgy and looked like a team who had squandered a two-goal advantage against Bradford City only a few days earlier.

A goal for the Rams then would have made it very interesting but they were caught by a sucker-punch. Zavagno diverted the ball into the path of substitute Ben Rix who lifted his shot past Grant.

Only two defeats in the last nine games had been encouraging for the Rams but it was now four without a win and only one victory in the last seven. It meant that Burley's team sank back down to a lowly 18th in the table.

Result.......Result.......Result.

CREWE ....(2) 3   DERBY ....(0) 0
Barrowman 10
Ashton 24
Rix 78

Att 8,656
Referee: M Warren

Stats......Stats.......Stats......Stats

CREWE   DERBY

1st	2nd	Total		Total	2nd	1st
0	1	1	Corners	7	5	2
6	5	11	Fouls	17	9	8
0	0	0	Yellow cards	5	5	0
0	0	0	Red cards	1	1	0
6	2	8	Caught Offside	4	1	3
5	1	6	Shots on target	6	2	4
2	1	3	Shots off target	7	4	3
0	0	0	Hit woodwork	0	0	0
37	50	43%	Possession	57%	50	63

THE match was similar to last Tuesday's against Bradford, when we had let a two-goal lead slip, but this time we got the two goals and didn't concede.

Dario Gradi

DEFENSIVELY we were very poor and we can't carry on defending like that. We knew it was going to be a hard season but there were encouraging signs.

George Burley

Other Div 1 Results

Coventry 1 Cardiff 3, Crystal Palace 1 Rotherham 1, Ipswich 1 Stoke 0, Millwall 2 Sheff Utd 0, Nottm Forest 6 Wimbledon 0, Reading 3 Preston 2, Sunderland 1 Walsall 0, Watford 1 Bradford 0, West Brom 1 Norwich 0, West Ham 2 Burnley 2, Wigan 1 Gillingham 0

Crewe [2] 3 DERBY [0] 0

Goalkeeper Stats: Lee Grant
Saves: Catch 1, Parry 1,
Crosses: Catch 4

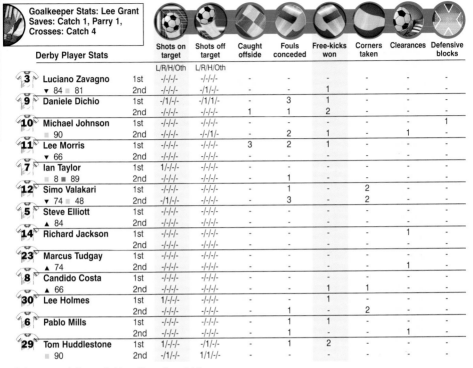

Derby Player Stats		Shots on target	Shots off target	Caught offside	Fouls conceded	Free-kicks won	Corners taken	Clearances	Defensive blocks
		L/R/H/Oth	L/R/H/Oth						
3 Luciano Zavagno	1st	-/-/-/-	-/-/-/-	-	-	-	-	-	-
▼ 84 ■ 81	2nd	-/-/-/-	-/1/-/-	-	-	1	-	-	-
9 Daniele Dichio	1st	-/1/-/-	-/1/1/-	-	3	1	-	-	-
	2nd	-/-/-/-	-/-/-/-	1	1	2	-	-	-
10 Michael Johnson	1st	-/-/-/-	-/-/-/-	-	-	-	-	-	1
■ 90	2nd	-/-/-/-	-/-/1/-	-	2	1	-	1	-
11 Lee Morris	1st	-/-/-/-	-/-/-/-	3	2	1	-	-	-
▼ 66	2nd	-/-/-/-	-/-/-/-	-	-	-	-	-	-
7 Ian Taylor	1st	1/-/-/-	-/-/-/-	-	-	-	-	-	-
■ 8 ■ 89	2nd	-/-/-/-	-/-/-/-	-	1	-	-	-	-
12 Simo Valakari	1st	-/-/-/-	-/-/-/-	-	1	-	2	-	-
▼ 74 ■ 48	2nd	-/1/-/-	-/-/-/-	-	3	-	2	-	-
5 Steve Elliott	1st	-/-/-/-	-/-/-/-	-	-	-	-	-	-
▲ 84	2nd	-/-/-/-	-/-/-/-	-	-	-	-	-	-
14 Richard Jackson	1st	-/-/-/-	-/-/-/-	-	-	-	-	1	-
	2nd	-/-/-/-	-/-/-/-	-	-	-	-	-	-
23 Marcus Tudgay	1st	-/-/-/-	-/-/-/-	-	-	-	-	-	-
▲ 74	2nd	-/-/-/-	-/-/-/-	-	-	-	-	1	-
8 Candido Costa	1st	-/-/-/-	-/-/-/-	-	-	-	-	-	-
▲ 66	2nd	-/-/-/-	-/-/-/-	-	-	1	1	-	-
30 Lee Holmes	1st	1/-/-/-	-/-/-/-	-	-	1	-	-	-
	2nd	-/-/-/-	-/-/-/-	-	1	-	2	-	-
6 Pablo Mills	1st	-/-/-/-	-/-/-/-	-	1	1	-	-	-
	2nd	-/-/-/-	-/-/-/-	-	1	-	-	1	-
29 Tom Huddlestone	1st	1/-/-/-	-/1/-/-	-	1	2	-	-	-
■ 90	2nd	-/1/-/-	1/1/-/-	-	-	-	-	-	-

Subs not used: Camp, Bolder. - Formation: 4-4-2

Goalkeeper Stats: Clayton Ince Saves: Catch 6, Parry 1, Crosses: Catch 2, Punch 2

	Player Stats	Shots on target	Shots off target	Caught offside	Fouls conceded	Free-kicks won	Corners taken	Clearances	Defensive blocks
19	Justin Cochrane ▼ 90	-/-/-/-	-/-/-/-	-	2	-	-	4	1
11	David Vaughan	-/-/-/-	-/-/-/-	-	-	-	-	1	-
3	Richard Walker	-/-/-/-	-/-/-/-	-	3	3	-	3	1
7	Neil Sorvel ▲ 45	-/-/-/-	-/-/-/-	-	-	-	-	1	-
10	Dean Ashton	-/1/-/-	-/1/-/-	5	-	1	-	1	-
9	Steve Jones	-/-/-/-	1/-/-/-	1	1	3	-	-	-
14	Ben Rix ▲ 74	1/-/-/-	-/-/-/-	-	-	-	-	1	-
4	Kenny Lunt	-/-/-/-	-/1/-/-	-	-	4	1	-	-
28	Andrew Barrowman ▼ 74	-/2/-/-	-/-/-/-	2	3	2	-	-	-
6	Stephen Foster	-/-/1/-	-/-/-/-	-	1	2	-	-	-
29	Billy Jones ▲ 90	-/-/-/-	-/-/-/-	-	-	-	-	-	-
2	David Wright	-/-/-/-	-/-/-/-	-	1	1	-	2	-
8	David Brammer ▼ 45	-/1/-/-	-/-/-/-	-	-	-	-	1	-

Subs not used: Bankole, Smart. - Formation: 4-3-3

Derby Played: 14 Won 3 Drawn 5 Lost 6 For 14 Against 23 Pos 18

Norwich [0] 2 DERBY [0] 1

Wasteful Derby County snatched defeat from the jaws of victory against 10-man Norwich City at Carrow Road after finding themselves one up through Ian Taylor's penalty around the hour mark.

A first win in five games was beckoning the Rams but they somehow managed to throw the points away. County had played some of their best football of the season and created a stack of chances. However, when they did hit the target, goalkeeper Robert Green produced two or three marvellous saves.

Danny Dichio was proving a handful and was a coat of paint away from giving the Rams the lead after nine minutes. He turned Malky Mackay only to see his firm shot thud against the post with Green beaten.

Zavagno was also at the centre of things. It was he who burst into the area from Dichio's lay-off, forcing McVeigh to give away a penalty. Taylor stepped forward to smash his penalty high into the net.

Green kept out Dichio's fine downward header with a brilliant save and then Norwich grabbed an equaliser from an 81st-minute penalty. Dichio was judged to have handled a Mulryne corner but Grant looked to have saved the day by diving to his right to keep out Roberts' spot-kick. However, an eagle-eyed assistant referee flagged to say Grant had moved and Roberts accepted the chance to redeem himself by blasting home his second effort.

Still the Rams had chances to win it. Candido Costa was guilty of a glaring miss when he sliced his shot wide when through on goal and Green then leapt to his left to turn away Taylor's volley.

Grant also punched and caught well under pressure but the Rams keeper was left exposed on Norwich's winning goal. The defending was poor and the marking non-existent as the ball reached Mulryne in the area and he turned to sweep a low shot beyond Grant.

Result.......Result.......Result.

NORWICH ....(0) 2   DERBY ....(0) 1
Roberts 81(p)   Taylor 61(p)
Mulryne 90

Att 16,346
Referee: R Beeby

Stats......Stats.......Stats......Stats

NORWICH						DERBY
1st	2nd	Total		Total	2nd	1st
0	5	5	Corners	10	7	3
10	3	13	Fouls	20	8	12
1	1	2	Yellow cards	4	3	1
1	0	1	Red cards	0	0	0
2	2	4	Caught Offside	3	1	2
3	5	8	Shots on target	13	7	6
5	1	6	Shots off target	6	3	3
0	0	0	Hit woodwork	1	0	1
37	46	42%	Possession	58%	54	63

"I don't know whether the penalty should have been retaken or not. I was just relieved to see the linesman with his flag across his chest.

Nigel Worthington "

"IF a goalkeeper's going to try to save a penalty can he help being two inches off his line? They'll say 'that's the rules' but I say it's an impossibility.

George Burley "

Other Div 1 Results

Crewe 2 Preston 1, Crystal Palace 3 Ipswich 4, Reading 0 Walsall 1, Sunderland 0 Rotherham 0, Watford 1 Coventry 1, West Brom 0 Wimbledon 1, Wigan 1 Sheff Utd 1

Goalkeeper Stats: Lee Grant
Saves: Catch 3, Parry 1, Crosses:
Catch 6, Round Post 1, Punch 1 ▪ 81

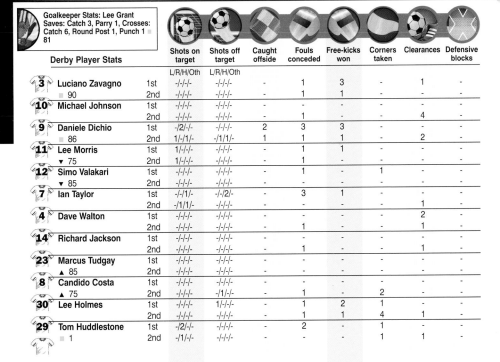

Derby Player Stats		Shots on target L/R/H/Oth	Shots off target L/R/H/Oth	Caught offside	Fouls conceded	Free-kicks won	Corners taken	Clearances	Defensive blocks
3 Luciano Zavagno	1st	-/-/-	-/-/-	-	1	3	-	1	-
▪ 90	2nd	-/-/-	-/-/-	-	1	1	-	-	-
10 Michael Johnson	1st	-/-/-	-/-/-	-	-	-	-	-	-
	2nd	-/-/-	-/-/-	-	1	-	-	4	-
9 Daniele Dichio	1st	-/2/-	-/-/-	2	3	3	-	-	-
▪ 86	2nd	1/-/1/-	-/1/1/-	1	1	1	-	2	-
11 Lee Morris	1st	1/-/-	-/-/-	-	1	1	-	-	-
▼ 75	2nd	1/-/-	-/-/-	-	1	-	-	-	-
12 Simo Valakari	1st	-/-/-	-/-/-	-	1	-	1	-	-
▼ 85	2nd	-/-/-	-/-/-	-	-	-	-	-	-
7 Ian Taylor	1st	-/-/1/-	-/-/2/-	-	3	1	-	-	-
	2nd	-/1/1/-	-/-/-	-	-	-	-	1	-
4 Dave Walton	1st	-/-/-	-/-/-	-	-	-	-	2	-
	2nd	-/-/-	-/-/-	-	1	-	-	1	-
14 Richard Jackson	1st	-/-/-	-/-/-	-	-	-	-	-	-
	2nd	-/-/-	-/-/-	-	1	-	-	1	-
23 Marcus Tudgay	1st	-/-/-	-/-/-	-	-	-	-	-	-
▲ 85	2nd	-/-/-	-/-/-	-	-	-	-	-	-
8 Candido Costa	1st	-/-/-	-/-/-	-	-	-	-	-	-
▲ 75	2nd	-/-/-	-/1/-/-	-	1	-	2	-	-
30 Lee Holmes	1st	-/-/-	1/-/-/-	-	1	2	1	-	-
	2nd	-/-/-	-/-/-	-	1	1	4	1	-
29 Tom Huddlestone	1st	-/2/-/-	-/-/-	-	2	-	1	-	-
▪ 1	2nd	-/1/-/-	-/-/-	-	-	-	1	1	-

Subs not used: Camp, Elliott, Bolder. - Formation: 4-4-2

Goalkeeper Stats: Robert Green Saves: Catch 1, Crosses: Catch 6, Parry 1, Round Post 1

	Player Stats	Shots on target	Shots off target	Caught offside	Fouls conceded	Free-kicks won	Corners taken	Clearances	Defensive blocks
9	Iwan Roberts ▲ 74	-/-/-	-/-/-	1	-	-	-	-	-
4	Malky Mackay	-/-/-	-/-/-	1	3	3	-	4	-
25	Peter Crouch ▼ 74	-/-/1/-	-/1/-/-	-	1	1	-	-	-
20	Damien Francis ▪ 11	-/1/-/-	-/-/-	-	2	3	-	1	2
18	Paul McVeigh ▼ 74	-/1/1/-	-/1/-/-	-	1	-	3	-	-
15	Mark Rivers ▼ 74 ▪ 52	-/-/-	-/-/1/-	2	1	-	-	-	-
5	Craig Fleming	-/-/-	-/-/-	-	1	1	-	3	-
17	Marc Edworthy	-/-/-	-/-/-	-	1	2	1	5	-
3	Adam Drury	-/-/-	-/-/-	-	1	2	-	4	1
23	Ryan Jarvis ▲ 74	-/1/-/-	-/-/-	-	-	1	-	1	-
8	Gary Holt	-/-/-	-/-/-	-	-	5	-	1	1
7	Phillip Mulryne ▲ 74	-/1/-/-	-/1/-/-	-	-	-	1	-	-
26	Kevin Harper ▪ 45	1/-/-/-	1/1/-/-	-	2	1	-	-	-

Subs not used: Lewis, Easton. - Formation: 4-4-2

Derby Played: 15 Won 3 Drawn 5 Lost 7 For 15 Against 25 Pos 19

DERBY [0] 1 Coventry [2] 3

Derby County's new owners took their places in the comfort of the directors' box with some eagerness and excitement about this game. But their first look at the team was memorable for all the wrong reasons and they will have left Pride Park Stadium in no doubt about the size of the task facing them both on and off the field.

The Rams slumped 3-1 to a Coventry City side that came into the game short of points and confidence. But the visitors created a dozen good openings and could have doubled their margin of victory.

If the defending at Crewe a week earlier had been sloppy, against Coventry it was woeful. There should have been little danger when Andrew Whing hoisted a hopeful cross into the area after 11 minutes, but Walton misjudged his header to leave Jackson and Grant stranded and Stephen Warnock with the chance to steer home a firm shot.

A brief rally saw Danny Dichio's header disallowed for offside and a goal for the Rams at that stage may have changed the course of the game. Instead, Coventry went two up after 38 minutes, courtesy of more calamitous defending.

This time Jackson's poor clearance struck Suffo who had the simple task of finding the empty net.

Whatever was said at the interval had the desired effect and the Rams enjoyed their best 15 minutes. Dichio's diving header was saved before 16-year-old Lee Holmes reduced the deficit with his first senior goal.

However, it was Coventry who wrestled back control and the chances started to come thick and fast for the visitors. Cameroon international Suffo made up for missing an earlier chance by scoring Coventry's third with 10 minutes remaining.

It was not the best way to end a week in which the club had teetered on the brink of financial ruin and spent a brief spell in receivership before the new owners moved in.

Result.......Result.......Result.

DERBY ....(0) 1   **COVENTRY**....(2) 3
Holmes 52   Warnock 11
                              Suffo 38, 80

Att 21,641
Referee: R Pearson

Stats......Stats.......Stats......Stats

DERBY					COVENTRY	
1st	2nd	Total		Total	2nd	1st
2	1	3	Corners	5	4	1
3	4	7	Fouls	9	2	7
1	2	3	Yellow cards	2	0	2
0	0	0	Red cards	0	0	0
4	1	5	Caught Offside	5	3	2
4	3	7	Shots on target	6	3	3
3	0	3	Shots off target	6	4	2
0	0	0	Hit woodwork	0	0	0
40	50	45%	Possession	55%	50	60

IT was a day when we didn't play at all and that was extremely disappointing. We didn't pass the ball well or create enough chances.
George Burley

WE were extremely strong, brave and determined and created chances for the whole 90 minutes. We came out all guns blazing and fully deserved to win.
Eric Black

Other Div 1 Results

Bradford 1 Nottm Forest 2, Burnley 1 Millwall 1, Cardiff 0 West Ham 0, Gillingham 1 Crystal Palace 0, Norwich 1 Sunderland 0, Preston 1 Ipswich 1, Rotherham 0 West Brom 3, Stoke 1 Crewe 1, Walsall 2 Wigan 0, Wimbledon 1 Watford 3

Goalkeeper Stats: Lee Grant
Saves: Tip Over 1, Catch 1,
Crosses: Catch 2

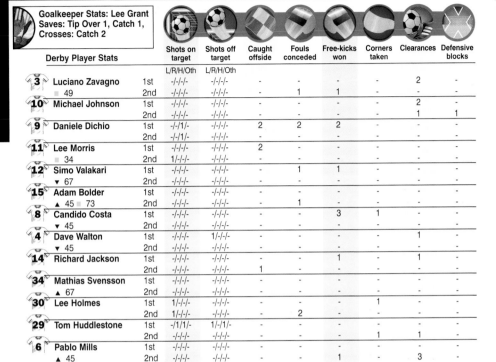

Derby Player Stats		Shots on target	Shots off target	Caught offside	Fouls conceded	Free-kicks won	Corners taken	Clearances	Defensive blocks
		L/R/H/Oth	L/R/H/Oth						
3 Luciano Zavagno	1st	-/-/-/-	-/-/-/-	-	-	-	-	2	-
49	2nd	-/-/-/-	-/-/-/-	-	1	1	-	-	-
10 Michael Johnson	1st	-/-/-/-	-/-/-/-	-	-	-	-	2	-
	2nd	-/-/-/-	-/-/-/-	-	-	-	-	1	1
9 Daniele Dichio	1st	-/-/1/-	-/-/-/-	2	2	2	-	-	-
	2nd	-/-/1/-	-/-/-/-	-	-	-	-	-	-
11 Lee Morris	1st	-/-/-/-	-/-/-/-	2	-	-	-	-	-
34	2nd	1/-/-/-	-/-/-/-	-	-	-	-	-	-
12 Simo Valakari	1st	-/-/-/-	-/-/-/-	-	1	1	-	-	-
▼ 67	2nd	-/-/-/-	-/-/-/-	-	-	-	-	-	-
15 Adam Bolder	1st	-/-/-/-	-/-/-/-	-	-	-	-	-	-
▲ 45 73	2nd	-/-/-/-	-/-/-/-	-	1	-	-	-	-
8 Candido Costa	1st	-/-/-/-	-/-/-/-	-	-	3	1	-	-
▼ 45	2nd	-/-/-/-	-/-/-/-	-	-	-	-	-	-
4 Dave Walton	1st	-/-/-/-	1/-/-/-	-	-	-	-	1	-
▼ 45	2nd	-/-/-/-	-/-/-/-	-	-	-	-	-	-
14 Richard Jackson	1st	-/-/-/-	-/-/-/-	-	-	1	-	1	-
	2nd	-/-/-/-	-/-/-/-	1	-	-	-	-	-
34 Mathias Svensson	1st	-/-/-/-	-/-/-/-	-	-	-	-	-	-
▲ 67	2nd	-/-/-/-	-/-/-/-	-	-	-	-	-	-
30 Lee Holmes	1st	1/-/-/-	-/-/-/-	-	-	-	1	-	-
	2nd	1/-/-/-	-/-/-/-	-	2	-	-	-	-
29 Tom Huddlestone	1st	-/1/1/-	1/-/1/-	-	-	-	-	-	-
	2nd	-/-/-/-	-/-/-/-	-	-	-	1	1	-
6 Pablo Mills	1st	-/-/-/-	-/-/-/-	-	-	-	-	-	-
▲ 45	2nd	-/-/-/-	-/-/-/-	-	-	1	-	3	-

Subs not used: Camp, Boertien. - Formation: 4-4-2

Goalkeeper Stats: Pegguy Arphexad Saves: Catch 1, Punch 1, Crosses: Catch 4

	Player Stats	Shots on target	Shots off target	Caught offside	Fouls conceded	Free-kicks won	Corners taken	Clearances	Defensive blocks
17	Michael Doyle	-/-/-/-	1/-/-/-	-	-	-	-	-	-
7	Craig Pead ▲ 89	-/-/-/-	-/-/-/-	-	-	-	-	-	-
5	Richard Shaw ■ 31	-/-/-/-	-/-/-/-	-	1	-	-	3	1
8	Patrick Suffo	1/2/-/-	1/1/1/-	2	1	1	-	1	-
9	Dele Adebola ▲ 83	-/-/-/-	-/-/-/-	1	-	-	-	-	-
6	Youssef Safri ▼ 89	-/1/-/-	-/-/-/-	-	1	1	2	1	-
18	Steve Staunton ▼ 79	-/-/-/-	-/-/-/-	-	1	-	-	2	-
11	Graham Barrett	1/-/-/-	-/1/-/-	2	-	1	3	-	-
26	Stephen Warnock	1/-/-/-	-/-/-/-	-	2	-	-	1	-
2	Andrew Whing	-/-/-/-	-/-/-/-	-	-	1	-	1	1
12	Andrew Morrell ▼ 83	-/-/-/-	-/-/-/-	-	1	1	-	-	-
4	Muhamed Konjic ■ 26	-/-/-/-	-/-/1/-	-	2	2	-	5	-
35	Yazid Mansouri ▲ 79	-/-/-/-	-/-/-/-	-	-	-	-	-	-

Subs not used: Shearer, Davenport. - Formation: 4-4-2

...October Team Stats.....Team Stats......Team Stats......Team S

League table at the end of October

		HOME					AWAY						
	P	W	D	L	F	A	W	D	L	F	A	Pts	Df
West Brom	15	6	0	2	13	6	4	1	2	10	7	31	10
Wigan	16	5	3	0	9	4	3	3	2	12	9	30	8
Norwich	15	7	0	0	14	5	1	4	3	7	10	28	6
Sheff Utd	15	4	1	2	14	7	4	2	2	10	9	27	8
Sunderland	15	5	2	1	10	4	3	1	3	9	7	27	8
West Ham	15	3	5	0	10	5	4	1	2	8	5	27	8
Ipswich	16	5	2	1	18	8	3	1	4	11	14	27	7
Nottm Forest	15	4	2	2	17	7	3	1	3	11	11	24	10
Reading	15	4	2	2	13	9	3	1	3	10	9	24	5
Millwall	16	5	2	1	12	5	1	4	3	8	11	24	4
Cardiff	15	4	2	1	15	3	2	3	3	11	12	23	11
Crewe	15	5	1	2	12	8	1	2	4	5	11	21	-2
Preston	15	4	1	2	12	8	2	1	5	8	11	20	1
Walsall	15	4	2	1	12	6	1	2	5	5	10	19	1
Coventry	14	3	2	2	10	9	2	2	3	11	12	19	0
Burnley	15	3	1	3	11	10	2	3	3	12	18	19	-5
Stoke	15	3	3	1	10	7	1	1	6	7	13	16	-3
Crystal Palace	15	2	3	3	11	12	2	1	4	9	12	16	-4
Watford	15	2	4	2	10	9	2	0	5	6	11	16	-4
Gillingham	15	3	1	3	8	10	1	3	4	6	13	16	-9
Derby	16	1	2	5	9	16	2	3	3	7	12	14	-12
Rotherham	16	2	3	3	5	9	0	4	4	5	16	13	-15
Bradford	15	1	1	6	7	15	2	2	3	7	10	12	-11
Wimbledon	15	1	1	5	10	18	1	0	7	5	19	7	-22

October matches table

	P	W	D	L	F	A	Pts
Ipswich	6	5	1	0	15	6	16
Watford	6	3	2	1	7	6	11
Coventry	6	3	1	2	9	7	10
Reading	5	3	1	1	9	7	10
West Ham	6	2	4	0	8	4	10
Preston	6	3	1	2	7	6	10
Wigan	6	2	3	1	7	7	9
West Brom	5	3	0	2	6	3	9
Nottm Forest	6	2	2	2	12	7	8
Crewe	6	2	2	2	8	7	8
Cardiff	5	2	2	1	7	3	8
Millwall	5	2	2	1	5	3	8
Norwich	5	2	2	1	5	4	8
Sunderland	5	2	2	1	2	1	8
Walsall	5	2	1	2	5	5	7
Burnley	4	1	2	1	7	10	5
Crystal Palace	6	1	2	3	7	11	5
Stoke	4	1	1	2	4	5	4
Sheff Utd	5	1	1	3	4	6	4
Rotherham	6	0	4	2	4	8	4
Gillingham	4	1	0	3	2	5	3
Wimbledon	5	1	0	4	2	11	3
Bradford	5	0	2	3	5	8	2
Derby	6	0	2	4	5	12	2

October team stats details

Club Name	Ply	Shots On	Shots Off	Corners	Hit W'work	Caught Offside	Offside Trap	Fouls	Yellow Cards	Red Cards	Pens Awarded	Pens Con
Bradford	5	30	22	27	0	15	7	85	9	0	- (-)	-
Burnley	4	23	25	27	5	15	19	39	4	0	- (-)	-
Cardiff	5	26	24	14	1	22	21	59	11	2	1 (1)	1
Coventry	6	51	39	43	4	12	26	74	14	0	1 (1)	1
Crewe	6	35	23	32	4	23	19	61	2	0	- (-)	-
Crystal Palace	6	36	33	44	3	17	26	77	10	1	2 (1)	1
Derby	6	44	32	32	1	25	28	89	17	1	2 (2)	2
Gillingham	4	24	13	25	0	13	9	66	7	1	- (-)	1
Ipswich	6	53	39	53	1	21	23	69	10	0	3 (2)	3
Millwall	5	16	21	24	1	23	10	99	11	3	1 (1)	-
Norwich	5	35	16	25	1	21	7	63	8	1	1 (1)	-
Nottm Forest	6	32	37	49	1	22	13	71	3	0	1 (1)	-
Preston	6	40	44	35	1	23	6	97	11	2	1 (1)	2
Reading	6	40	30	35	2	16	14	56	5	0	1 (1)	-
Rotherham	6	19	31	30	1	20	14	67	12	3	- (-)	1
Sheff Utd	5	45	14	34	0	18	22	69	13	0	- (-)	1
Stoke	4	14	22	22	2	15	19	62	6	0	- (-)	-
Sunderland	5	33	29	26	1	16	27	75	6	2	- (-)	-
Walsall	5	20	16	18	0	19	30	60	8	1	- (-)	-
Watford	6	34	40	42	1	19	8	69	7	1	- (-)	-
West Brom	5	29	20	42	0	20	16	56	4	0	- (-)	-
West Ham	6	45	25	34	4	23	19	72	12	0	- (-)	-
Wigan	6	49	34	24	0	21	26	88	5	0	1 (1)	1
Wimbledon	5	24	15	22	1	2	32	57	12	2	- (-)	1

...October Player Stats..... Player Stats...... Player Stats......Pla

Monthly Top scorers

Delroy Facey (Burnley)	5
Pablo Counago (Ipswich)	4
Scott Fitzgerald (Watford)	3
Marlon Harewood (West Ham)	3
Geoff Horsfield (Wigan)	3
Andy Reid (Nottm Forest)	3
Andy Liddell (Wigan)	3
Dean Ashton (Crewe)	2
Steve Jones (Crewe)	2
Richard Naylor (Ipswich)	2

Penalties scored

2 Pablo Counago (Ipswich), Ian Taylor (Derby)

Assists

Andy Reid (Nottm Forest)	4
Nicholas Shorey (Reading)	3
Jim Magilton (Ipswich)	3
Kris Commons (Stoke)	2
Danny Butterfield (Crystal Palace)	2
Tony Craig (Millwall)	2
Robert Earnshaw (Cardiff)	2

Quickest goals

3:29 mins - Andy Liddell (Derby vs Wigan)

3:31 mins - Vincent Samways (Reading vs Walsall)

3:41 mins - Delroy Facey (Burnley vs Walsall)

3:46 mins - Geoff Horsfield (Wigan vs Sheff Utd)

4:08 mins - Steven Sidwell (Reading vs Bradford)

Top Keeper

	Mins	Gls
Mart Poom (Sunderland)	480	1
Russell Hoult (West Brom)	477	3
Tony Warner (Millwall)	476	3
Neil Alexander (Cardiff)	475	3
David James (West Ham)	572	4
Robert Green (Norwich)	478	4
Alec Chamberlain (Watford)	112	1
Jonathan Gould (Preston)	575	6

Shots on target

Jimmy Bullard (Wigan)	12
Dougie Freedman (Crystal P)	11
Lee Morris (Leicester)	11
Jermain Defoe (West Ham)	11
Michael Tonge (Sheff Utd)	10
Patrick Suffo (Coventry)	10
Pablo Counago (Ipswich)	10
Andy Liddell (Wigan)	10
Marcus Stewart (Sunderland)	9
David Connolly (West Ham)	9

Shots off target

Marlon Harewood (West Ham)	13
Tom Huddlestone (Derby)	9
Paul Devlin (Watford)	9
Dean Ashton (Crewe)	9
Paul Ifill (Millwall)	8
Steven Sidwell (Reading)	8
Kevin Kyle (Sunderland)	8
Jim Magilton (Ipswich)	7
Pablo Counago (Ipswich)	7
Nicky Forster (Reading)	7

Caught offside

Pablo Counago (Ipswich)	15
Dean Ashton (Crewe)	14
Darren Byfield (Sunderland)	14
Marlon Harewood (West Ham)	12
Geoff Horsfield (Wigan)	12
Nicky Forster (Reading)	11
Noel Whelan (Millwall)	10
Kevin Kyle (Sunderland)	10
Dougie Freedman (Crystal P)	9

Free-kicks won

Pablo Counago (Ipswich)	22
Wayne Routledge (Crystal P)	21
Geoff Horsfield (Wigan)	21
Shefki Kuqi (Ipswich)	16
Andrew Johnson (Crystal P)	16
Ashley Ward (Sheff Utd)	15
Matt Jackson (Wigan)	14
Paul Devlin (Watford)	14
Justin Cochrane (Crewe)	13

Derby v Wigan

Fouls conceded

Ashley Ward (Sheff Utd)	20
Neil Shipperley (Crystal Palace)	18
Bob Peeters (Millwall)	18
Geoff Horsfield (Wigan)	16
Andy Gray (Sheff Utd)	16
Kevin Kyle (Sunderland)	15
Youssef Safri (Coventry)	15
Paul Robinson (Millwall)	14
Gareth Williams (Nottm Forest)	13

Fouls without a card

Bob Peeters (Millwall)	18
Geoff Horsfield (Wigan)	16
Kevin Kyle (Sunderland)	15
Paul Robinson (Millwall)	14
Gareth Williams (Nottm Forest)	13
Paul McKenna (Preston)	13
Gary Birch (Walsall)	10
David Wetherall (Bradford)	10
Gareth Taylor (Nottm Forest)	10

Pictured here is Lee Morris on a charge through the opposition defence. County's poor defending made for a miserable afternoon against Crewe, resulting in Burley's men slipping down to 18th place.

16 year old Tom Huddlestone had another strong game in midfield despite seeing his side losing 3-1 to Coventry. Fellow youngster Lee Holmes grabbed a consolation for the Rams in the 52nd minute.

Lee Morris tackles Wigan's Matt Jackson and later goes on to score Derby's equaliser. This was after he missed two chances early on in the game.

Marcus Tudgay outjumps a crowd of Wigan defenders to challenge
John Filan for the ball.

Preston [1] 3 DERBY [0] 0

Derby County's fourth consecutive defeat stretched their winless run to a deeply worrying seven matches. A miserable October spilt over into November as Preston North End emerged as 3-0 winners from a poor quality contest at Deepdale.

The scoreline did flatter the home team but a run of two points from a possible 21 was hardly encouraging as the season continued to pass them by.

There was no faulting the players' endeavour. They enjoyed some good spells of possession, created a number of openings and won plenty of corners but when they did find the target, the agility of Preston goalkeeper Jonathan Gould denied them.

Adam Bolder and Youl Mawene made their first starts of the season, Mawene as part of a completely different back four from the previous game against Coventry City. Steve Elliott also came in at centre-back and he gave away the penalty for Preston's opener after 21 minutes.

Referee Paul Robinson pointed to the spot when Elliott slid in on Fuller. Graham Alexander drilled his penalty past Lee Grant and then Michael Keane and Fuller were both inches away from doubling Preston's lead.

But Preston had Gould to thank for keeping their lead intact either side of half-time. First, he dived to his right to tip Elliott's deflected volley round the post and then brilliantly clawed away an effort from Lee Morris when he looked certain to score.

Candido Costa replaced the quiet Lee Holmes and the Rams, now on top, decided to switch to a back three as they went in search of the equaliser.

Instead it was Preston who capitalised. They raided down both flanks to score two goals in five minutes and leave what looked to be a confused defence in tatters. Fuller scored twice, one with a header and one with a neat finish after good work from Lewis.

Result.......Result.......Result.

PRESTON............(1) 3   DERBY ....(0) 0
Alexander 22(p)
Healy 68
Fuller 72

Att 12,839
Referee: P Robinson

Stats......Stats.......Stats......Stats

PRESTON				DERBY		
1st	2nd	Total		Total	2nd	1st
1	1	2	Corners	8	4	4
7	5	12	Fouls	14	3	11
0	0	0	Yellow cards	3	2	1
0	0	0	Red cards	0	0	0
1	6	7	Caught Offside	1	0	1
3	3	6	Shots on target	3	2	1
3	2	5	Shots off target	6	2	4
1	0	1	Hit woodwork	0	0	0
45	53	49%	Possession	51%	47	55

> I think the result flattered us a little. I feel sorry for George Burley. They didn't deserve to lose 3-0. But we've got the hang of clean sheets.
>
> **Craig Brown**

> I am disappointed. This was never a 3-0 game. I think we had more possession, more chances than Preston and they are a good side.
>
> **George Burley**

Other Div 1 Results

Burnley 1 Cardiff 1, Coventry 1 West Ham 1, Crewe 1 Reading 0, Ipswich 3 Gillingham 4, Millwall 1 Nottm Forest 0, Stoke 2 Sheff Utd 2, Walsall 1 Norwich 3, Watford 1 Rotherham 0, West Brom 0 Sunderland 0, Wigan 5 Crystal Palace 0, Wimbledon 2 Bradford 1

Preston [1] 3 DERBY [0] 0

Goalkeeper Stats: Lee Grant
Crosses: Catch 2

Derby Player Stats

#	Player		Shots on target L/R/H/Oth	Shots off target L/R/H/Oth	Caught offside	Fouls conceded	Free-kicks won	Corners taken	Clearances	Defensive blocks
11	Lee Morris ▼ 84	1st	-/-/-/-	1/-/-/-	1	1	-	-	-	-
		2nd	-/1/-/-	-/-/-/-	-	1	-	-	-	-
9	Daniele Dichio ⬛ 35	1st	-/-/-/-	-/-/1/-	-	7	3	-	-	-
		2nd	-/-/-/-	-/-/2/-	-	1	-	-	-	-
12	Simo Valakari	1st	-/-/-/-	-/-/-/-	-	1	-	-	-	-
		2nd	-/-/-/-	-/-/-/-	-	1	1	-	-	-
5	Steve Elliott ⬛ 69	1st	1/-/-/-	-/-/1/-	-	1	-	-	2	1
		2nd	-/1/-/-	-/-/-/-	-	1	-	-	1	-
16	Youl Mawene	1st	-/-/-/-	-/-/-/-	-	-	3	-	2	-
		2nd	-/-/-/-	-/-/-/-	-	-	-	-	-	-
19	Nathan Doyle	1st	-/-/-/-	-/-/-/-	-	-	-	-	-	-
		2nd	-/-/-/-	-/-/-/-	-	-	1	-	-	-
23	Marcus Tudgay ▲ 84	1st	-/-/-/-	-/-/-/-	-	-	-	-	-	-
		2nd	-/-/-/-	-/-/-/-	-	-	-	-	-	-
17	Paul Boertien ▲ 76	1st	-/-/-/-	-/-/-/-	-	-	-	-	-	-
		2nd	-/-/-/-	-/-/-/-	-	-	1	-	-	-
15	Adam Bolder	1st	-/-/-/-	-/-/-/-	-	-	-	-	-	-
		2nd	-/-/-/-	-/-/-/-	-	-	-	-	-	-
8	Candido Costa ▲ 57 ⬛ 69	1st	-/-/-/-	-/-/-/-	-	-	-	-	-	-
		2nd	-/-/-/-	-/-/-/-	-	-	1	-	-	-
30	Lee Holmes ▼ 57	1st	-/-/-/-	-/-/-/-	-	-	1	-	-	-
		2nd	-/-/-/-	-/-/-/-	-	-	-	-	-	-
32	Peter Kennedy ▼ 76	1st	-/-/-/-	1/-/-/-	-	1	-	4	1	-
		2nd	-/-/-/-	-/-/-/-	-	-	-	4	-	-
6	Pablo Mills	1st	-/-/-/-	-/-/-/-	-	-	-	-	-	1
		2nd	-/-/-/-	-/-/-/-	-	-	-	-	1	-

Subs not used: Camp, Walton. - Formation: 4-4-2

PRESTON NORTH END FC

Goalkeeper Stats: Jonathan Gould Saves: Round Post 1, Parry 1, Crosses: Catch 5

#	Player Stats	Shots on target	Shots off target	Caught offside	Fouls conceded	Free-kicks won	Corners taken	Clearances	Defensive blocks
25	Richard Cresswell ▼ 76	-/-/-/-	-/-/-/-	2	2	1	-	2	1
34	Simon Lynch ▲ 76	-/-/-/-	-/-/1/-	-	-	-	-	-	-
2	Graham Alexander	-/1/-/-	-/1/-/-	-	1	-	1	1	-
22	Claude Davis	-/-/-/-	-/-/-/-	-	2	2	-	2	-
7	Lee Cartwright ▲ 86	-/-/-/-	-/-/-/-	-	1	-	-	-	-
19	Michael Keane	-/-/-/-	1/-/-/-	-	1	3	-	1	1
3	Brian O'Neil ▼ 65	-/-/-/-	-/-/-/-	-	-	-	-	-	-
11	David Healy ▼ 86	-/1/-/-	-/-/-/-	3	-	-	-	-	-
5	Michael Jackson	-/-/-/-	-/-/-/-	-	1	1	-	1	-
20	Chris Lucketti	-/-/-/-	-/-/-/-	-	3	4	-	6	-
9	Ricardo Fuller	1/1/1/-	-/1/-/-	1	1	3	-	-	-
16	Paul McKenna	-/-/-/-	-/-/-/-	1	-	-	-	1	-
17	Eddie Lewis ▲ 65	-/-/-/-	1/-/-/-	-	-	-	1	-	-

Subs not used: Lonergan, Edwards. - Formation: 3-3-3

Derby Played: 17 Won 3 Drawn 5 Lost 9 For 16 Against 31 Pos 21

DERBY [2] 2 Ipswich [0] 2

George Burley watched his Derby County team produce an encouraging display, and yet extend their damaging run without a win to eight games. They matched and, at times, stretched Ipswich Town to breaking point, building a two-goal interval lead before being pegged back.

While both sides could have won, they could also have lost as chances went begging in the last quarter of an enthralling encounter.

After goals from loan players Peter Kennedy and Danny Dichio, a win looked well within reach. Kennedy marked his home debut by curling a delicious free-kick from 30 yards beyond the despairing dive of Kelvin Davis and into the top corner.

Within a minute, the advantage had been doubled. A pass from Lee Holmes exposed a static and square Ipswich back line to release Dichio, who coolly lifted the ball past Davis for his first goal in five games. Skipper Ian Taylor was back after suspension and was an influence, while Lee Grant looked sharper and more assured in goal, a fact acknowledged by the supporters.

The Rams may have been ahead but the general feeling was that they were far from home and dry. Ipswich emerged from the break as a far more focussed team and the scores were level within 20 minutes.

Tommy Miller beat Grant with a firmly-struck penalty after Pablo Mills' clumsy challenge had halted Ian Westlake's venture into the area. Then the defensive weakness in wide areas was highlighted again when Jermaine Wright skipped past an isolated Kennedy and his pinpoint cross was headed home by Bent.

The smart money was suddenly back on an Ipswich victory and Shefki Kuqi wasted two opportunities to inflict a fifth consecutive defeat.

This was a big improvement on the shocking home showing against Coventry City and the gap between the Rams and Ipswich appears to have closed on the pitch if not in the table.

Result.......Result.......Result.

DERBY ....(2) 2   **IPSWICH**........(0) 2
Dichio 45   Miller 56(p)
Kennedy 45   Bent 65

Att 19,976
Referee: K Hill

Stats......Stats.......Stats......Stats

DERBY					IPSWICH		
1st	2nd	Total			Total	2nd	1st
1	3	4	Corners		7	3	4
7	9	16	Fouls		13	5	8
0	3	3	Yellow cards		3	2	1
0	0	0	Red cards		0	0	0
3	1	4	Caught Offside		3	1	2
6	0	6	Shots on target		7	4	3
2	3	5	Shots off target		5	5	0
0	0	0	Hit woodwork		0	0	0
49	52	51%	Possession		49%	48	51

BEFORE the game we might have been saying a point wouldn't be a bad result. But after the way we started, we're disappointed to lose two points.
George Burley

WE can score goals from nowhere. But we haven't got a clean sheet in us, and I'm sick of having to say that. We need to work defensively.
Joe Royle

Other Div 1 Results

Bradford 1 Walsall 1, Cardiff 3 Stoke 1, Crystal Palace 1 Preston 1, Gillingham 2 Crewe 0, Norwich 3 Millwall 1, Nottm Forest 1 Watford 1, Reading 1 Wigan 0, Rotherham 3 Wimbledon 1, Sheff Utd 1 Burnley 0, Sunderland 0 Coventry 0, West Ham 3 West Brom 4

DERBY [2] 2 Ipswich [0] 2

Goalkeeper Stats: Lee Grant Saves: Catch 1, Crosses: Catch 4 ■ 59

Derby Player Stats		Shots on target L/R/H/Oth	Shots off target L/R/H/Oth	Caught offside	Fouls conceded	Free-kicks won	Corners taken	Clearances	Defensive blocks
10 Michael Johnson	1st	-/-/-	-/-/-	-	-	-	-	-	2
	2nd	-/-/-	-/-/-	-	-	1	-	4	-
11 Lee Morris	1st	2/-/-	-/-/-	-	-	2	-	-	-
	2nd	-/-/-	-/1/-	1	1	1	-	-	-
13 Lee Grant ■ 59	1st	-/-/-	-/-/-	-	-	-	-	-	-
	2nd	-/-/-	-/-/-	-	-	1	-	-	-
9 Daniele Dichio	1st	-/2/-	-/1/-	3	3	2	-	-	-
	2nd	-/-/-	-/-/-	-	1	-	-	-	-
7 Ian Taylor	1st	-/-/1/-	-/-/-	-	1	1	-	1	-
	2nd	-/-/-	-/-/1/-	-	1	-	-	-	-
12 Simo Valakari ▼ 80 ■ 66	1st	-/-/-	-/-/-	-	-	-	-	-	-
	2nd	-/-/-	-/-/-	-	2	-	-	-	-
16 Youl Mawene	1st	-/-/-	-/-/-	-	1	2	-	2	-
	2nd	-/-/-	-/-/1/-	-	1	-	-	1	1
8 Candido Costa ▲ 80	1st	-/-/-	-/-/-	-	-	-	-	-	-
	2nd	-/-/-	-/-/-	-	-	1	1	-	-
32 Peter Kennedy	1st	1/-/-	-/-/-	-	1	1	1	-	-
	2nd	-/-/-	-/-/-	-	-	-	2	-	2
30 Lee Holmes ■ 52	1st	-/-/-	-/1/-	-	-	-	-	-	-
	2nd	-/-/-	-/-/-	-	1	1	-	-	-
29 Tom Huddlestone	1st	-/-/-	-/-/-	-	-	-	-	-	1
	2nd	-/-/-	-/-/-	-	-	-	-	-	-
6 Pablo Mills	1st	-/-/-	-/-/-	-	1	-	-	2	-
	2nd	-/-/-	-/-/-	-	2	-	-	4	-

Subs not used: Camp, Elliott, Bolder, Tudgay. - Formation: 4-4-2

Goalkeeper Stats: Kelvin Davis Saves: Catch 2, Crosses: Catch 4

	Player Stats	Shots on target	Shots off target	Caught offside	Fouls conceded	Free-kicks won	Corners taken	Clearances	Defensive blocks
11	Jermaine Wright	-/-/-	-/-/-	-	-	1	-	1	-
32	Shefki Kuqi ▼ 90	-/1/1/-	1/1/1/-	2	-	4	-	-	-
15	Georges Santos ■ 90	-/-/-	-/-/-	-	1	3	-	5	-
18	Darren Bent ■ 58	-/2/1/-	-/-/-	1	1	-	-	-	-
2	Fabian Wilnis ■ 41	-/-/-	-/-/-	-	2	2	-	-	1
33	Ian Westlake	-/1/-/-	-/1/-/-	-	2	3	-	1	-
14	Matthew Richards	-/-/-	-/-/-	-	1	-	-	1	-
9	Pablo Counago ▼ 34	-/-/-	-/-/-	-	2	1	-	-	-
7	Jim Magilton	-/-/-	-/-/-	-	1	-	7	1	-
8	Tommy Miller	-/-/-	-/-/-	-	1	1	-	-	-
17	Dean Bowditch ▼ 77 ▲ 34	-/-/-	-/1/-/-	-	2	-	-	-	-
10	Alun Armstrong ▲ 77	-/-/-	-/-/-	-	-	-	-	-	-
21	Scott Mitchell ▲ 90	-/-/-	-/-/-	-	-	-	-	-	-

Subs not used: Price, McGreal. - Formation: 4-3-3

Relief swept around Pride Park Stadium as Derby County brought their barren run to an end with a welcome 2-0 victory over Burnley in what was a must win game.

The Rams had not won in the previous eight games, not kept a clean sheet in 12 and had failed to record a home victory for two months. But three points swept those statistics aside and lifted the team to 19th in the table after spending an uncomfortable week in the dreaded drop zone.

Lee Morris' cool finish put the Rams ahead after 20 minutes and skipper Ian Taylor slammed home a stoppage-time penalty for his seventh goal of the season and his fourth from the spot.

The visitors saw plenty of the ball but the Rams were in no mood to let another lead slip and silly mistakes were replaced by a spirited determination to dig in and hold on.

Goalkeeper Lee Grant performed well to deny Burnley with fine saves at key moments. He reacted sharply to turn over Gareth Farrelly's deflected cross in the opening minutes and dived athletically to keep out a glancing header from David May that looked bound for the bottom corner.

And Taylor was outstanding in midfield, making tackles, getting forward and looking likely to grab a goal. His importance to the team became clearer by the week.

The lead came when Burnley's offside trap failed, allowing a grateful Morris to race clear from Taylor's pass. The striker kept his head and, with Brian Jensen committing himself slightly early, he coolly lifted the call over the keeper for his fourth goal of the season.

The victory was secured in a frantic spell of stoppage time. First, Burnley were reduced to 10 men when Arthur Gnohere hauled back Dichio as he was about to move clear on goal, and referee Uriah Rennie pointed to the spot.

Taylor had led by example throughout and stepped forward to secure the win and calm the nerves.

Result.......Result.......Result.

DERBY ....(1) 2   **BURNLEY** ......(0) 0
Morris 20
Taylor 90(p)

Att 21,960
Referee: U Rennie

Stats......Stats.......Stats......Stats

DERBY						BURNLEY
1st	2nd	Total		Total	2nd	1st
3	4	7	Corners	8	2	6
6	4	10	Fouls	15	12	3
1	0	1	Yellow cards	2	2	0
0	0	0	Red cards	1	1	0
2	1	3	Caught Offside	5	3	2
3	7	10	Shots on target	5	2	3
3	2	5	Shots off target	5	4	1
0	1	1	Hit woodwork	0	0	0
53	52	52%	Possession	48%	48	47

LAST weekend we were two goals up against Ipswich and drew 2-2 but the key in this game was that we didn't make the individual mistakes.

George Burley

ARTHUR Gnohere's sending off is a cause for concern because it was a straight red and the wrong decision. Uriah Rennie certainly gets himself noticed.

Stan Ternent

Other Div 1 Results

Bradford P West Brom P, Crystal Palace P Crewe P, Gillingham 1 Wimbledon 2, Norwich 1 Watford 2, Nottm Forest P Ipswich P, Reading 1 Millwall 0, Rotherham P Coventry P, Sheff Utd P Walsall P, Sunderland P Wigan P, West Ham P Stoke P

DERBY [1] 2 Burnley [0] 0

Goalkeeper Stats: Lee Grant Saves: Parry 1, Crosses: Tip Over 1, Catch 5, Round Post 1

Derby Player Stats		Shots on target L/R/H/Oth	Shots off target L/R/H/Oth	Caught offside	Fouls conceded	Free-kicks won	Corners taken	Clearances	Defensive blocks
9 Daniele Dichio	1st	-/-/-/-	-/-/1/-	-	-	-	-	1	-
	2nd	-/-/-/-	-/-/1/-	-	1	5	-	1	-
10 Michael Johnson ▪ 37	1st	-/-/-/-	-/-/-/-	-	2	1	-	5	-
	2nd	-/-/-/-	-/-/-/-	-	1	-	-	1	-
11 Lee Morris	1st	2/-/-/-	-/-/-/-	1	-	-	-	-	-
	2nd	-/-/-/-	-/-/-/-	1	-	2	-	-	-
7 Ian Taylor	1st	-/-/1/-	-/-/1/-	-	-	-	-	-	-
	2nd	-/-/1/-	-/-/-/-	-	-	-	-	-	-
12 Simo Valakari ▲ 86	1st	-/-/-/-	-/-/-/-	-	-	-	-	-	-
	2nd	-/1/-/-	-/-/-/-	-	1	-	1	-	-
14 Richard Jackson	1st	-/-/-/-	-/-/-/-	-	-	-	-	-	1
	2nd	-/-/-/-	-/-/-/-	-	-	-	-	1	-
16 Youl Mawene ▼ 37	1st	-/-/-/-	-/-/-/-	-	1	-	-	1	-
	2nd	-/-/-/-	-/-/-/-	-	-	-	-	-	-
17 Paul Boertien ▲ 69	1st	-/-/-/-	-/-/-/-	-	-	-	-	-	-
	2nd	-/-/-/-	-/-/-/-	-	-	1	-	-	-
8 Candido Costa ▼ 86	1st	-/-/-/-	-/-/-/-	-	2	1	-	-	-
	2nd	-/1/-/-	-/-/-/-	-	-	-	-	-	-
32 Peter Kennedy	1st	-/-/-/-	-/-/-/-	-	-	1	3	-	-
	2nd	2/-/-/-	-/-/-/-	-	1	1	3	-	-
30 Lee Holmes ▼ 69	1st	-/-/-/-	1/-/-/-	1	-	-	-	-	-
	2nd	-/-/-/-	1/-/-/-	-	-	-	-	-	-
29 Tom Huddlestone	1st	-/-/-/-	-/-/-/-	-	1	-	-	1	-
	2nd	-/1/-/-	-/-/-/-	-	-	-	-	1	-
6 Pablo Mills ▲ 37	1st	-/-/-/-	-/-/-/-	-	-	-	-	-	-
	2nd	-/-/-/-	-/-/-/-	-	-	3	-	1	-

Subs not used: Camp, Tudgay. - Formation: 4-4-2

Goalkeeper Stats: Brian Jensen Saves: Catch 1, Round Post 2, Crosses: Catch 2, Punch 2

	Player Stats	Shots on target	Shots off target	Caught offside	Fouls conceded	Free-kicks won	Corners taken	Clearances	Defensive blocks
7	Glen Little ▪ 64	-/-/-/-	1/-/-/-	-	2	1	3	-	-
12	Tony Grant	-/-/-/-	-/-/-/-	-	1	1	-	2	-
2	Lee Roche ▲ 75	-/-/-/-	-/-/-/-	-	1	-	-	-	-
10	Ian Moore	-/-/-/-	-/1/1/-	1	1	2	-	-	-
15	Dean West ▼ 75	-/-/-/-	-/-/-/-	-	-	1	-	-	-
20	Richard Chaplow ▪ 7	-/1/-/-	-/-/1/-	-	2	1	-	-	-
16	Gareth Farrelly ▼ 57	1/-/-/-	-/-/-/-	-	-	-	3	1	-
3	Mohammed Camara	-/-/-/-	-/-/-/-	-	-	1	-	-	1
8	Robert Blake	-/-/-/-	-/1/-/-	2	-	3	2	-	-
6	Graham Branch ▲ 57	-/-/1/-	-/-/-/-	2	2	-	-	-	-
17	Arthur Gnohere ▪ 90	-/-/1/-	-/-/-/-	-	5	-	-	3	2
5	David May	-/-/1/-	-/-/-/-	-	-	-	-	2	-

Subs not used: McGregor, O'Neill, Pilkington. - Formation: 4-4-2

Millwall [0] 0 DERBY [0] 0

Points were proving more important than performances for Derby County. Their unbeaten run was stretched to three games when they followed a nervy victory over Burnley with a battling goalless draw at Millwall.

Escaping from the Lions' Den with a point will be seen as a good result but they were indebted to goalkeeper Lee Grant. His agility, mixed with a little luck and some spirited defending from central pair Youl Mawene and Michael Johnson, earned the draw.

They showed character in clawing out a second consecutive clean sheet from a difficult afternoon but much of their performance was instantly forgettable. They failed to register a single shot of note and won only two corners, the first coming after 67 minutes.

There was plenty of endeavour in midfield but no creativity or service to the front two and Lee Holmes needs the ball if he is to offer width. The opening half-hour of the contest was dreadful and the only incident worthy of mention was a decent Grant save from Cahill.

Grant's duel with Cahill and the lively Paul Ifill eventually became a running theme. He smothered Ifill's testing low drive, parried a powerful shot from the same player and then went full stretch to push away an effort from Peter Sweeney.

On the one occasion that Grant was beaten, Mawene saved the day with a wonderful goal-line clearance from David Livermore two minutes before half-time.

So the Rams emerged with a valuable point against a team who boasted a more than useful home record of six victories and only one defeat in their 10 outings. However, the reward for their efforts was to drop a place to 20th in the table.

Result.......Result.......Result.

MILLWALL ....(0) 0   DERBY ....(0) 0
Att 10,308
Referee: P Danson

Stats......Stats.......Stats......Stats

MILLWALL				DERBY		
1st	2nd	Total		Total	2nd	1st
3	7	10	Corners	2	2	0
5	7	12	Fouls	9	7	2
1	0	1	Yellow cards	0	0	0
0	0	0	Red cards	0	0	0
2	2	4	Caught Offside	2	1	1
8	5	13	Shots on target	2	0	2
0	2	2	Shots off target	0	0	0
1	0	1	Hit woodwork	0	0	0
43	53	48%	Possession	52%	47	57

> I need a new striker, simple as that. Until we get someone who can poach a few goals we won't be able to take the team to the next level.
>
> **Dennis Wise**

> LEE Grant has great potential. He's only 20 but was outstanding and can go all the way. It was his fabulous saves that got us a point
>
> **George Burley**

Other Div 1 Results

Burnley 1 Rotherham 1, Coventry 2 Gillingham 2, Crewe 3 Sunderland 0, Ipswich 3 Sheff Utd 0, Preston 0 Norwich 0, Stoke 1 Bradford 0, Walsall 0 Crystal Palace 0, Watford 0 West Ham 0, West Brom 0 Reading 0, Wigan 2 Nottm Forest 2, Wimbledon 0 Cardiff 1

Goalkeeper Stats: Lee Grant
Saves: Round Post 1, Parry 5, Crosses: Catch 4, Parry 1

Derby Player Stats		Shots on target L/R/H/Oth	Shots off target L/R/H/Oth	Caught offside	Fouls conceded	Free-kicks won	Corners taken	Clearances	Defensive blocks
22 Lee Bradbury	1st	-/-/-/	-/-/-/	1	-	-	-	-	1
▼ 90	2nd	-/-/-/	-/-/-/	-	1	1	-	3	-
10 Michael Johnson	1st	-/-/-/	-/-/-/	-	-	-	-	3	-
	2nd	-/-/-/	-/-/-/	-	1	2	-	3	-
11 Lee Morris	1st	1/-/-/	-/-/-/	-	-	-	-	-	-
	2nd	-/-/-/	-/-/-/	1	1	-	-	-	-
7 Ian Taylor	1st	-/-/-/	-/-/-/	-	1	-	-	-	-
	2nd	-/-/-/	-/-/-/	-	-	-	-	1	-
12 Simo Valakari	1st	-/-/-/	-/-/-/	-	1	1	-	-	-
▼ 64	2nd	-/-/-/	-/-/-/	-	2	-	-	-	-
14 Richard Jackson	1st	-/-/-/	-/-/-/	-	-	-	-	-	1
	2nd	-/-/-/	-/-/-/	-	-	-	-	-	-
16 Youl Mawene	1st	-/-/-/	-/-/-/	-	-	1	-	1	-
	2nd	-/-/-/	-/-/-/	-	2	-	-	2	2
23 Marcus Tudgay	1st	-/-/-/	-/-/-/	-	-	-	-	-	-
▲ 90	2nd	-/-/-/	-/-/-/	-	-	-	-	-	-
17 Paul Boertien	1st	-/-/-/	-/-/-/	-	-	-	-	-	-
▲ 45	2nd	-/-/-/	-/-/-/	-	1	-	-	1	-
15 Adam Bolder	1st	-/-/-/	-/-/-/	-	-	-	-	-	-
▲ 64	2nd	-/-/-/	-/-/-/	-	-	-	-	-	-
30 Lee Holmes	1st	-/-/-/	-/-/-/	-	-	2	-	-	-
▼ 45	2nd	-/-/-/	-/-/-/	-	-	-	-	-	-
32 Peter Kennedy	1st	1/-/-/	-/-/-/	-	-	1	-	-	1
	2nd	-/-/-/	-/-/-/	-	1	-	2	-	2
29 Tom Huddlestone	1st	-/-/-/	-/-/-/	-	-	-	-	-	-
	2nd	-/-/-/	-/-/-/	-	-	1	-	2	-

Subs not used: Camp, Mills. - Formation: 4-4-2

Goalkeeper Stats: Tony Warner Saves: Catch 1, Crosses: Catch 4

	Player Stats	Shots on target	Shots off target	Caught offside	Fouls conceded	Free-kicks won	Corners taken	Clearances	Defensive blocks
26	Peter Sweeney	2/-/-/	1/-/-/	-	1	1	9	-	-
16	Aboubaka Fofana ▲ 7	-/-/-/	-/-/-/	-	-	1	-	-	-
7	Paul Ifill	1/3/-/	-/-/-/	2	2	2	-	-	-
22	Kevin Braniff ▲ 90	-/-/-/	-/-/-/	-	-	-	-	-	-
4	Tim Cahill ▼ 90 ■ 45	-/1/3/	-/-/-/	2	5	2	-	-	-
3	Robert Ryan	-/-/-/	-/-/-/	-	-	-	1	2	-
17	Kevin Muscat	-/-/-/	-/-/-/	-	1	-	-	-	-
12	Darren Ward	-/-/-/	-/-/-/	-	1	-	-	2	-
2	Matthew Lawrence	-/-/-/	-/-/-/	-	2	1	-	2	1
29	Bob Peeters ▼ 7	-/-/-/	-/-/-/	-	-	-	-	-	-
8	David Livermore	2/-/-/	-/1/-/	-	-	2	-	-	-
14	Andy Roberts	1/-/-/	-/-/-/	-	-	-	-	2	-

Subs not used: Gueret, Nethercott, Wise. - Formation: 4-4-2

Derby Played: 20 Won 4 Drawn 7 Lost 9 For 20 Against 33 Pos 20

DERBY [1] 3 Wimbledon [1] 1

Derby County were breathing a little easier after three scrappy goals brought three crucial points against bottom club Wimbledon.

This was a must-win fixture and the Rams eventually delivered to stretch their unbeaten run to four matches meaning November had proved a fairly good month following a deeply-worrying October.

But they were certainly not given an easy ride by Wimbledon and it needed two second-half goals in the space of a minute from Marcus Tudgay and Lee Holmes to end the game as a contest.

The Rams were handed a 13th-minute lead when hapless German defender Nico Herzig made a complete hash of clearing Candido Costa's low cross and sent a header arcing into his own net off a post. But Wimbledon drew level seven minutes later when they picked their way through some poor challenges for Nigel Reo-Coker to coolly beat Lee Grant from 12 yards.

The shape of the game quickly changed. With the Rams now edgy and their passing ragged, the Dons controlled the rest of the first half and should have gone ahead. Manager George Burley must have said the right things and certainly made the right decisions at the interval as Derby emerged re-energised.

But the Rams still needed a helping hand and Wimbledon obliged after 52 minutes. Jamie Darlington dithered deep in his own area and allowed Tudgay to charge the ball down and score with a shot that entered the net off the unfortunate Herzig.

Tudgay, in for the injured Lee Morris, had barely finished celebrating his first senior goal when the Rams made it 3-1. Wimbledon's goalkeeper and defenders were sucked underneath Costa's cross and Holmes bundled home at the back post with the ball having crossed the line before Herzig cleared.

The two-goal blast settled the Rams and flattened the visitors, and the margin of victory would have been greater had Ian Taylor and Lee Bradbury not squandered clear-cut chances.

Result.......Result.......Result.

DERBY ....(1) 3   **WIMBLEDON** (1) 1
Herzig 13 (og)   Reo-Coker 20
Tudgay 52
Holmes 53

Att 22,025
Referee: T Parkes

Stats......Stats.......Stats......Stats

DERBY				WIMBLEDON		
1st	2nd	Total		Total	2nd	1st
2	4	6	Corners	4	0	4
10	6	16	Fouls	8	5	3
1	2	3	Yellow cards	0	0	0
0	0	0	Red cards	0	0	0
3	2	5	Caught Offside	2	1	1
1	5	6	Shots on target	3	1	2
2	2	4	Shots off target	5	2	3
0	0	0	Hit woodwork	0	0	0
45	47	46%	Possession	54%	53	55

 THIS win was so important because there's no doubt this was a six-pointer and it gives us a little bit of breathing space.
George Burley

WE'VE given the game away. The only way they were going to score was by us making a mistake so what do we do? We make two.

Stuart Murdoch

Other Div 1 Results

Bradford 3 Millwall 2, Cardiff 2 Ipswich 3, Crystal Palace 1 Coventry 1, Gillingham 3 Stoke 1, Norwich 1 Crewe 0, Nottm Forest 0 West Brom 3, Reading 2 Watford 1, Rotherham 2 Walsall 0, Sheff Utd 2 Preston 0, Sunderland 1 Burnley 1, West Ham 4 Wigan 0

DERBY [1] 3 Wimbledon [1] 1

Goalkeeper Stats: Lee Grant Saves: Parry 1, Crosses: Catch 2

Derby Player Stats		Shots on target	Shots off target	Caught offside	Fouls conceded	Free-kicks won	Corners taken	Clearances	Defensive blocks
		L/R/H/Oth	L/R/H/Oth						
22 Lee Bradbury	1st	-/-/-/-	-/-/-/-	3	2	1	-	-	-
■ 90	2nd	-/1/-/-	-/-/-/-	-	2	-	-	-	-
3 Luciano Zavagno	1st	-/-/-/-	-/-/-/-	-	-	-	-	-	-
▲ 72	2nd	-/-/-/-	-/-/-/-	-	-	-	-	-	1
10 Michael Johnson	1st	-/-/-/-	-/-/-/-	-	1	-	-	1	-
▼ 63	2nd	-/-/-/-	-/-/-/-	-	-	-	-	-	-
7 Ian Taylor	1st	-/-/-/-	-/-/-/-	-	2	-	-	2	-
■ 40	2nd	-/-/-/-	-/-/1/-	-	1	1	1	1	-
14 Richard Jackson	1st	-/-/-/-	-/-/-/-	-	1	-	-	-	-
	2nd	-/-/-/-	-/-/-/-	-	-	-	-	-	-
16 Youl Mawene	1st	-/-/-/-	-/-/-/-	-	1	-	-	3	-
	2nd	-/-/-/-	-/-/-/-	-	-	-	-	2	-
23 Marcus Tudgay	1st	-/-/-/-	-/-/1/-	-	1	-	-	-	-
■ 84	2nd	1/1/-/-	-/-/-/-	1	2	-	-	-	-
15 Adam Bolder	1st	-/-/-/-	-/-/-/-	-	-	-	-	-	-
▲ 45	2nd	-/-/-/-	-/-/-/-	-	-	1	-	-	-
8 Candido Costa	1st	-/-/-/-	-/-/-/-	-	1	1	2	-	-
	2nd	-/-/-/-	-/-/-/-	-	1	2	3	-	-
30 Lee Holmes	1st	-/-/-/-	-/-/-/-	-	-	-	-	-	-
▼ 72	2nd	1/-/-/-	1/-/-/-	1	-	-	-	1	-
32 Peter Kennedy	1st	-/-/-/-	-/-/-/-	-	1	1	-	-	-
	2nd	1/-/-/-	-/-/-/-	-	-	1	-	-	-
29 Tom Huddlestone	1st	-/1/-/-	1/-/-/-	-	-	-	-	-	-
▼ 45	2nd	-/-/-/-	-/-/-/-	-	-	-	-	-	-
6 Pablo Mills	1st	-/-/-/-	-/-/-/-	-	-	-	-	-	-
▲ 63	2nd	-/-/-/-	-/-/-/-	-	-	-	-	1	-

Subs not used: Camp, McLeod. - Formation: 4-4-2

Goalkeeper Stats: Steve Banks Saves: Catch 3, Parry 1, Crosses: Catch 1

	Player Stats	Shots on target	Shots off target	Caught offside	Fouls conceded	Free-kicks won	Corners taken	Clearances	Defensive blocks
21	Nico Herzig ▼ 61	-/-/-/-	-/-/-/-	-	-	1	-	-	-
17	Adam Nowland	-/-/-/-	-/2/-/-	-	1	3	3	-	-
10	Dean Holdsworth ▲ 80	-/-/-/-	-/-/-/-	-	-	-	-	-	-
26	Nigel Reo-Coker	-/1/-/-	-/-/-/-	1	2	1	-	2	-
11	Patrick Agyemang ▼ 80	-/-/-/-	-/1/-/-	-	1	1	-	-	-
18	Wayne Gray ▲ 61	-/-/-/-	-/-/-/-	-	-	-	-	-	-
7	Joel McAnuff	-/1/-/-	-/-/-/-	-	1	1	1	-	-
8	Wade Small ▼ 88	1/-/-/-	-/-/-/-	1	1	4	-	-	-
6	Darren Holloway ▲ 88	-/-/-/-	-/-/-/-	-	-	-	-	-	-
19	Ben Chorley	-/-/-/-	-/1/-/-	-	1	2	-	1	-
20	Mikele Leigertwood	-/-/-/-	-/-/1/-	-	-	2	-	2	-
24	Jermaine Darlington	-/-/-/-	-/-/-/-	-	-	1	-	1	1
25	Dean Lewington	-/-/-/-	-/-/-/-	-	1	-	-	1	-

Subs not used: Worgan, Gier. - Formation: 4-5-1

Derby Played: 21 Won 5 Drawn 7 Lost 9 For 23 Against 34 Pos 20

...November Team Stats.....Team Stats......Team Stats......Team S

League table at the end of November

		HOME					AWAY						
	P	W	D	L	F	A	W	D	L	F	A	Pts	Df
West Brom	20	6	2	2	13	6	6	2	2	18	11	40	14
Norwich	21	9	1	1	20	9	2	5	3	10	11	39	10
Sheff Utd	20	7	1	2	19	7	4	3	3	12	14	37	10
Ipswich	20	6	2	2	24	12	4	2	4	16	18	34	10
Wigan	20	6	4	0	16	6	3	3	4	12	14	34	8
Reading	21	7	2	2	17	10	3	2	5	10	13	34	4
West Ham	20	4	5	1	17	9	4	4	2	10	7	33	11
Sunderland	20	5	4	1	11	5	4	2	4	12	11	33	7
Cardiff	20	5	3	2	21	8	3	4	3	13	13	31	13
Preston	20	6	2	2	17	9	2	2	6	9	14	28	3
Millwall	21	6	3	1	13	5	1	4	6	11	18	28	1
Crewe	20	7	1	2	16	8	1	2	7	5	16	27	-3
Nottm Forest	20	4	3	3	18	11	3	2	5	14	18	26	3
Gillingham	21	5	1	5	15	16	2	4	4	12	18	26	-7
Coventry	20	3	5	2	13	12	2	5	3	13	14	25	0
Burnley	21	4	3	3	16	12	2	4	5	13	22	25	-5
Walsall	20	5	3	2	17	10	1	3	6	6	13	24	0
Watford	21	3	5	2	11	9	3	1	7	11	17	24	-4
Crystal Palace	20	2	5	3	13	14	3	2	5	10	17	22	-8
Derby	21	3	3	5	16	19	2	4	4	7	15	22	-11
Stoke	20	4	4	2	13	10	1	1	8	9	19	20	-7
Rotherham	20	4	3	3	10	10	0	5	5	6	18	20	-12
Bradford	20	2	2	6	11	18	2	3	5	8	13	17	-12
Wimbledon	21	2	2	6	13	21	0	2	9	9	26	14	-25

November matches table

	P	W	D	L	F	A	Pts
Norwich	6	3	2	1	9	5	11
Gillingham	6	3	1	2	13	11	10
Sheff Utd	5	3	1	1	7	5	10
Reading	6	3	1	2	4	5	10
West Brom	5	2	3	0	8	4	9
Cardiff	5	2	2	1	8	6	8
Derby	5	2	2	1	7	6	8
Preston	5	2	2	1	6	4	8
Watford	6	2	2	2	6	6	8
Ipswich	4	2	1	1	11	8	7
Wimbledon	6	2	1	3	7	10	7
Rotherham	4	2	1	1	6	3	7
West Ham	5	1	3	1	9	6	6
Burnley	6	1	3	2	6	6	6
Coventry	6	0	6	0	5	5	6
Sunderland	5	1	3	1	4	5	6
Crewe	5	2	0	3	4	5	6
Crystal Palace	5	1	3	1	3	7	6
Walsall	5	1	2	2	6	7	5
Bradford	5	1	2	2	5	6	5
Wigan	4	1	1	2	7	7	4
Stoke	5	1	1	3	5	9	4
Millwall	5	1	1	3	4	7	4
Nottm Forest	5	0	2	3	4	11	2

November team stats details

Club Name	Ply	Shots On	Shots Off	Corners	Hit W'work	Caught Offside	Offside Trap	Fouls	Yellow Cards	Red Cards	Pens Awarded	Pens Con
Bradford	5	20	18	26	0	17	13	57	5	0	- (-)	-
Burnley	6	28	30	42	2	24	28	64	7	1	- (-)	1
Cardiff	5	41	27	30	2	9	10	38	7	0	2 (2)	-
Coventry	6	39	42	34	1	15	21	60	10	0	1 (1)	1
Crewe	5	28	30	16	1	8	22	40	4	1	- (-)	1
Crystal Palace	5	23	12	29	1	6	19	48	11	0	- (-)	1
Derby	5	27	20	27	1	15	18	65	10	0	1 (1)	1
Gillingham	6	44	30	43	2	21	12	61	6	0	- (-)	-
Ipswich	4	33	21	29	0	10	15	56	7	0	3 (3)	3
Millwall	5	43	14	30	1	15	14	69	7	0	- (-)	1
Norwich	6	49	33	40	2	29	4	83	11	2	- (-)	-
Nottm Forest	5	30	32	21	1	17	13	70	7	0	- (-)	-
Preston	5	36	33	39	2	14	7	63	3	0	1 (1)	1
Reading	6	21	41	43	1	29	22	57	10	0	1 (1)	-
Rotherham	4	20	18	25	2	18	19	42	2	1	- (-)	-
Sheff Utd	5	44	36	35	3	14	10	50	6	0	3 (3)	2
Stoke	5	36	34	30	0	15	5	68	7	1	- (-)	-
Sunderland	5	50	36	39	2	18	26	61	5	0	- (-)	-
Walsall	5	21	30	18	1	17	24	57	8	2	- (-)	-
Watford	6	43	23	36	0	22	28	76	6	0	1 (1)	1
West Brom	5	19	21	22	0	15	12	59	7	0	- (-)	-
West Ham	5	35	21	34	0	35	10	51	4	1	1 (1)	-
Wigan	4	27	22	11	1	18	21	43	3	3	1 (1)	1
Wimbledon	6	27	21	24	0	8	36	69	4	1	- (-)	-

...November Player Stats..... Player Stats...... Player Stats......Pla

Monthly Top scorers

Paul Shaw (Sheff Utd)	4
Ian Henderson (Norwich)	4
Darren Wrack (Walsall)	3
Robert Earnshaw (Cardiff)	3
Brian Deane (West Ham)	3
Steve Jones (Crewe)	3
Nathan Ellington (Wigan)	3
Jason Koumas (West Brom)	3
David Healy (Preston)	3
Paul McVeigh (Norwich)	2

Penalties scored

2 Robert Earnshaw (Cardiff), Jack Lester (Sheff Utd), Tommy Miller (Ipswich)

Assists

Dean Windass (Bradford)	3
Andy Hessenthaler (Gillingham)	3
Darren Huckerby (Norwich)	3
John Oster (Sunderland)	2
Peter Sweeney (Millwall)	2
Shefki Kuqi (Ipswich)	2
John Robinson (Cardiff)	2

Quickest goals

0:41 mins - Jermain Defoe (West Ham vs West Brom)

3:13 mins - Gifton Noel-Williams (Stoke vs Sheff Utd)

3:36 mins - Kevin Horlock (West Ham vs Wigan)

4:01 mins - Robert Blake (Burnley vs Reading)

4:05 mins - Michael Branch (Bradford vs Walsall)

Top Keeper

	Mins	Gls
P Arphexad (Coventry)	235	1
G Montgomery (Rotherham)	286	2
Jonathan Gould (Preston)	479	4
Russell Hoult (West Brom)	475	4
Robert Green (Norwich)	576	5
M Hahnemann (Reading)	575	5
Lenny Pidgeley (Watford)	577	6
Michael Pollitt (Rotherham)	96	1

Shots on target

Stewart Downing (Sunderland)	14
Steve Jones (Crewe)	12
David Healy (Preston)	11
Robert Earnshaw (Cardiff)	10
Paul Shaw (Sheff Utd)	10
Michael Tonge (Sheff Utd)	10
Scott Fitzgerald (Watford)	10
Danny Webber (Watford)	9
Nathan Ellington (Wigan)	9
Nicky Forster (Reading)	9

Shots off target

Dean Ashton (Crewe)	11
Andy Reid (Nottm Forest)	10
Steven Sidwell (Reading)	10
Darren Huckerby (Norwich)	10
Shefki Kuqi (Ipswich)	9
Youssef Safri (Coventry)	8
Scott Fitzgerald (Watford)	8
Patrick Suffo (Coventry)	8
Daniele Dichio (Millwall)	7
Michael Doyle (Coventry)	7

Caught offside

Darren Huckerby (Norwich)	20
Nicky Forster (Reading)	19
Marlon Harewood (West Ham)	13
Brian Deane (West Ham)	13
David Connolly (West Ham)	13
Geoff Horsfield (Wigan)	12
Rob Hulse (West Brom)	11
Scott Fitzgerald (Watford)	9
Danny Webber (Watford)	8

Free-kicks won

Darren Huckerby (Norwich)	16
Daniele Dichio (Millwall)	16
Gavin Gordon (Cardiff)	15
Ashley Ward (Sheff Utd)	13
Georges Santos (Ipswich)	13
Andy Gray (Sheff Utd)	12
David Healy (Preston)	12
Ian Westlake (Ipswich)	12
Paul Devlin (Watford)	12

Preston v Derby

Fouls conceded

Gareth Taylor (Nottm Forest)	20
Peter Crouch (Norwich)	16
Richard Cresswell (Preston)	15
Daniele Dichio (Millwall)	15
Arthur Gnohere (QPR)	14
Paul Devlin (Watford)	13
Tim Cahill (Millwall)	13
Andy Gray (Sheff Utd)	12
Graham Branch (Burnley)	12

Fouls without a card

Andy Gray (Sheff Utd)	12
Graham Branch (Burnley)	12
Chris Morgan (Sheff Utd)	11
Richard Barker (Rotherham)	10
Nigel Reo-Coker (West Ham)	10
Christian Dailly (West Ham)	9
Paolo Vernazza (Watford)	9
Marlon Harewood (West Ham)	8
Adam Nowland (West Ham)	8

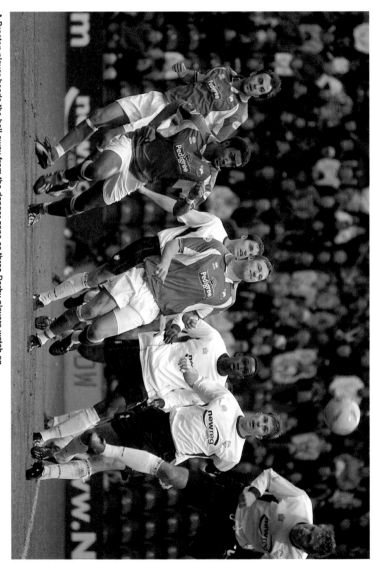

A Preston player heads the ball away from the danger zone as three Derby players watch on.

Tom Huddlestone takes the ball past a despairing Ipswich defender. Derby went on to secure a draw against George Burley's former club. County had now gone eight games without a win.

Ipswich [1] 2 DERBY [0] 1

Derby County's generosity had cost them dear already during the season and did so again in this game. The first gift arrived after only 26 seconds, the other with around 20 minutes remaining and manager George Burley's emotional return to Portman Road ended in a 2-1 defeat.

Marcus Tudgay pulled a goal back, his second in as many games, but this first defeat in five left Burley's team hovering above the Division One relegation zone with a tough looking festive programme looming.

Burley received a wonderful welcome from the Ipswich supporters who recognised his achievements during 22 years as player and manager at the club.

However, he had barely took his seat in the visiting dug-out when his team fell behind. Ian Westlake lifted the ball over a dozing defence to release Darren Bent and he coolly lobbed Lee Grant from 20 yards. Grant was not overly worked after that and so it was bitterly disappointing when Ipswich, top scorers in the division, were handed a second goal after 69 minutes.

Simo Valakari, playing his 50th game for the club, played a pass blind, straight into the path of Bent, and he raced clear. Grant did well to parry the shot and Mawene, racing back and unable to break his stride, saw the ball rebound off him and into his own net. It was a comedy of errors and there was plenty of scratching of heads when the Rams pulled a goal back four minutes later.

Luciano Zavagno, also making his 50th appearance, crossed, John McGreal headed clear but only for Bolder to return the ball. Tudgay, looking yards offside but played on by left-back Matt Richards, hoisted the ball high over the advancing Davis and into the net.

Result.......Result.......Result.

IPSWICH..............(1) 2   DERBY ....(0) 1
Bent 1   Tudgay 73
Mawene 69 (og)

Att 25,018
Referee: M Messias

Stats......Stats.......Stats......Stats

IPSWICH | | | | | | **DERBY**

1st	2nd	Total		Total	2nd	1st
4	1	5	Corners	3	2	1
5	7	12	Fouls	14	6	8
1	2	3	Yellow cards	2	2	0
0	0	0	Red cards	0	0	0
0	1	1	Caught Offside	1	1	0
3	3	6	Shots on target	8	5	3
2	3	5	Shots off target	3	2	1
0	0	0	Hit woodwork	0	0	0
51	52	51%	Possession	49%	48	49

> **❝**I don't think we had too many problems, although we weren't at our best going forward. I'll take that result when we were so depleted.
>
> **Joe Royle** **❞**

> **❝**CHRISTMAS came early for Ipswich. I can't believe how many errors we managed to make in the opening 24 seconds of a football match.
>
> **George Burley** **❞**

Other Div 1 Results

Burnley 3 Sheff Utd 2, Crewe 1 Gillingham 1, Millwall 0 Norwich 0, Preston 4 Crystal Palace 1, Stoke 2 Cardiff 3, Walsall 1 Bradford 0, Watford 1 Nottm Forest 1, West Brom 1 West Ham 1, Wigan 0 Reading 2, Wimbledon 1 Rotherham 2

Goalkeeper Stats: Lee Grant
Saves: Catch 1, Crosses: Catch 1

Derby Player Stats		Shots on target	Shots off target	Caught offside	Fouls conceded	Free-kicks won	Corners taken	Clearances	Defensive blocks
		L/R/H/Oth	L/R/H/Oth						
3 Luciano Zavagno	1st	-/-/-/-	-/-/-/-	-	-	-	-	1	1
	2nd	-/-/-/-	-/-/-/-	-	-	-	-	-	-
22 Lee Bradbury	1st	1/-/-/-	-/-/-/-	-	3	1	-	1	1
▪ 76	2nd	-/-/-/-	-/-/-/-	1	1	-	-	-	-
10 Michael Johnson	1st	-/-/-/-	-/-/-/-	-	-	-	-	-	-
▼ 8	2nd	-/-/-/-	-/-/-/-	-	-	-	-	-	-
12 Simo Valakari	1st	-/-/-/-	-/-/-/-	-	1	1	-	-	-
▼ 78	2nd	-/1/-/-	-/-/-/-	-	-	-	-	-	-
7 Ian Taylor	1st	-/1/-/-	-/1/-/-	-	-	-	-	-	-
▪ 77	2nd	-/1/-/-	-/-/-/-	-	2	1	-	-	1
14 Richard Jackson	1st	-/-/-/-	-/-/-/-	-	-	-	-	-	-
	2nd	-/-/-/-	-/-/-/-	-	-	1	-	1	-
16 Youl Mawene	1st	-/-/-/-	-/-/-/-	-	1	-	-	-	-
	2nd	-/-/-/-	-/-/-/-	-	-	1	-	1	-
23 Marcus Tudgay	1st	-/1/-/-	-/-/-/-	-	-	2	-	1	-
▼ 87	2nd	-/1/-/-	-/-/-/-	-	-	1	-	1	-
18 Izale McLeod	1st	-/-/-/-	-/-/-/-	-	-	-	-	-	-
▲ 87	2nd	-/-/-/-	-/-/-/-	-	-	-	-	-	-
15 Adam Bolder	1st	-/-/-/-	-/-/-/-	-	2	1	-	-	-
	2nd	-/1/-/-	-/-/-/-	-	-	1	-	-	-
8 Candido Costa	1st	-/-/-/-	-/-/-/-	-	-	-	1	-	-
	2nd	-/1/-/-	-/1/-/-	-	1	2	2	-	-
30 Lee Holmes	1st	-/-/-/-	-/-/-/-	-	-	-	-	-	-
▲ 78	2nd	-/-/-/-	-/1/-/-	-	1	-	-	-	-
6 Pablo Mills	1st	-/-/-/-	-/-/-/-	-	1	-	-	1	-
▲ 8	2nd	-/-/-/-	-/-/-/-	-	1	-	-	-	-

Subs not used: Camp, Boertien. - Formation: 4-4-2

Goalkeeper Stats: Kelvin Davis Saves: Catch 2, Crosses: Catch 2 ▪ 76

	Player Stats	Shots on target	Shots off target	Caught offside	Fouls conceded	Free-kicks won	Corners taken	Clearances	Defensive blocks
11	Jermaine Wright	-/-/-/-	-/-/-/-	-	2	-	-	1	-
33	Ian Westlake	-/-/-/-	-/1/-/-	-	3	-	-	-	-
23	Chris Bart-Williams ▪ 43	-/1/-/-	-/-/-/-	-	-	5	-	1	-
14	Matthew Richards	-/-/-/-	-/-/-/-	-	1	-	-	-	1
4	John McGreal	-/-/-/-	-/-/-/-	-	-	4	-	2	-
12	Richard Naylor ▼ 22	-/-/-/-	-/-/-/-	-	-	-	1	1	-
8	Tommy Miller	-/1/-/-	-/-/-/-	-	-	1	-	-	-
7	Jim Magilton	-/2/-/-	1/-/-/-	-	-	-	2	-	-
32	Shefki Kuqi ▪ 78	-/-/-/-	-/1/-/-	-	1	2	-	2	-
18	Darren Bent	1/1/-/-	1/-/-/-	1	-	1	-	-	-
25	Alan Mahon ▲ 22	-/-/-/-	1/-/-/-	-	4	1	2	-	-

Subs not used: Price, Bowditch, Counago, Reuser. - Formation: 4-4-2

Rotherham [0] 0 DERBY [0] 0

A hard-earned point from a goalless draw against Rotherham United brought little more than cold comfort for Derby County. For all their first-half endeavour and second-half improvement, the Rams sank back into the Division One drop zone with the season at its halfway stage.

The point taken from Millmoor was just about deserved and was possible thanks mainly to the sterling contributions of central defenders David Walton and Youl Mawene. Joining Walton and Mawene in the queue for praise was skipper Ian Taylor whose value to the team had grown over the months. Battered and bruised from a physical encounter, he limped off in the closing minutes with an ankle injury.

The first half belonged to Rotherham as the Rams invited pressure. Paul Warne went close when his volley from 25 yards dropped narrowly wide and Lee Grant held a Martin McIntosh header before tipping a free-kick from the same player round the post.

The Rams somehow reached the interval level even if they rarely ventured forward, the only opening falling to Candido Costa. He was released by Taylor's measured pass but his first touch and speed of thought was not good enough and he was crowded out.

The Rams were never likely to prosper by trying to match Rotherham's style and needed reminding that moving the ball and getting it in wide areas was a better option. When they did this, there was more purpose about their play and belief blossomed. Luciano Zavagno, who stuck to his task throughout and Lee Holmes started to threaten down the left.

Adam Bolder became involved in midfield and there suddenly looked to be more space on Millmoor's narrow pitch. Mike Pollitt dived bravely among the flying boots after a Marcus Tudgay cross had caused confusion.

Holmes, back in after the strange decision to leave him out at Ipswich, followed up and was unluckily booked especially as a Rotherham player appeared to take a liking to his shirt and refused to let go.

Lee Bradbury, in need of a goal, shot straight at Pollitt with 15 minutes to go and for all their improved play, it was the Rams' only strike of note on target.

They may have kept three clean sheets in the last five games but the absence of a cutting edge remained a problem.

Result.......Result.......Result.

ROTHERHAM ......(0) 0   DERBY ....(0) 0
Att 7,320
Referee: P Dowd

Stats......Stats.......Stats......Stats

ROTHERHAM				DERBY		
1st	2nd	Total		Total	2nd	1st
2	5	7	Corners	3	2	1
5	2	7	Fouls	19	10	9
0	0	0	Yellow cards	3	2	1
0	0	0	Red cards	0	0	0
1	1	2	Caught Offside	4	1	3
3	3	6	Shots on target	2	2	0
2	1	3	Shots off target	2	1	1
0	0	0	Hit woodwork	0	0	0
49	51	50%	Possession	50%	49	51

 WE needed a goal and if we'd got it we would've gone on to get three or four. If the lads give their all every week we'll survive.

Ronnie Moore

 WE just didn't play in the first half but in the second we got on top and could've won the game. The squad is still not strong enough.

George Burley

Other Div 1 Results

Burnley 1 Coventry 2, Crystal Palace 1 Nottm Forest 0, Gillingham 0 Preston 1, Millwall 0 Ipswich 0, Norwich 4 Cardiff 1, Sheff Utd 2 Watford 2, Stoke 3 Reading 0, West Brom 2 Crewe 2, West Ham 3 Sunderland 2, Wigan 1 Bradford 0, Wimbledon 0 Walsall 1

Rotherham [0] 0 DERBY [0] 0

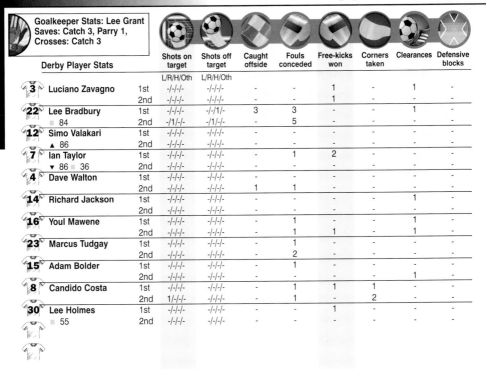

Goalkeeper Stats: Lee Grant
Saves: Catch 3, Parry 1,
Crosses: Catch 3

Derby Player Stats		Shots on target	Shots off target	Caught offside	Fouls conceded	Free-kicks won	Corners taken	Clearances	Defensive blocks
		L/R/H/Oth	L/R/H/Oth						
3 Luciano Zavagno	1st	-/-/-/-	-/-/-/-	-	-	1	-	1	-
	2nd	-/-/-/-	-/-/-/-	-	-	1	-	-	-
22 Lee Bradbury	1st	-/-/-/-	-/-/1/-	3	3	-	-	1	-
▪ 84	2nd	-/1/-/-	-/1/-/-	-	5	-	-	-	-
12 Simo Valakari	1st	-/-/-/-	-/-/-/-	-	-	-	-	-	-
▲ 86	2nd	-/-/-/-	-/-/-/-	-	-	-	-	-	-
7 Ian Taylor	1st	-/-/-/-	-/-/-/-	-	1	2	-	-	-
▼ 86 ▪ 36	2nd	-/-/-/-	-/-/-/-	-	-	-	-	-	-
4 Dave Walton	1st	-/-/-/-	-/-/-/-	-	-	-	-	-	-
	2nd	-/-/-/-	-/-/-/-	1	1	-	-	-	-
14 Richard Jackson	1st	-/-/-/-	-/-/-/-	-	-	-	-	1	-
	2nd	-/-/-/-	-/-/-/-	-	-	-	-	-	-
16 Youl Mawene	1st	-/-/-/-	-/-/-/-	-	1	-	-	1	-
	2nd	-/-/-/-	-/-/-/-	-	1	1	-	1	-
23 Marcus Tudgay	1st	-/-/-/-	-/-/-/-	-	1	-	-	-	-
	2nd	-/-/-/-	-/-/-/-	-	2	-	-	-	-
15 Adam Bolder	1st	-/-/-/-	-/-/-/-	-	1	-	-	-	-
	2nd	-/-/-/-	-/-/-/-	-	-	-	-	1	-
8 Candido Costa	1st	-/-/-/-	-/-/-/-	-	1	1	1	-	-
	2nd	1/-/-/-	-/-/-/-	-	1	-	2	-	-
30 Lee Holmes	1st	-/-/-/-	-/-/-/-	-	-	1	-	-	-
▪ 55	2nd	-/-/-/-	-/-/-/-	-	-	-	-	-	-

Subs not used: Camp, McLeod, Mills, Boertien. - Formation: 4-4-2

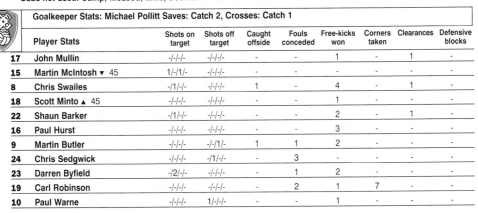

Goalkeeper Stats: Michael Pollitt Saves: Catch 2, Crosses: Catch 1

	Player Stats	Shots on target	Shots off target	Caught offside	Fouls conceded	Free-kicks won	Corners taken	Clearances	Defensive blocks
17	John Mullin	-/-/-/-	-/-/-/-	-	-	1	-	1	-
15	Martin McIntosh ▼ 45	1/-/1/-	-/-/-/-	-	-	-	-	-	-
8	Chris Swailes	-/1/-/-	-/-/-/-	1	-	4	-	1	-
18	Scott Minto ▲ 45	-/-/-/-	-/-/-/-	-	-	1	-	-	-
22	Shaun Barker	-/1/-/-	-/-/-/-	-	-	2	-	1	-
16	Paul Hurst	-/-/-/-	-/-/-/-	-	-	3	-	-	-
9	Martin Butler	-/-/-/-	-/-/1/-	1	1	2	-	-	-
24	Chris Sedgwick	-/-/-/-	-/1/-/-	-	3	-	-	-	-
23	Darren Byfield	-/2/-/-	-/-/-/-	-	1	2	-	-	-
19	Carl Robinson	-/-/-/-	-/-/-/-	-	2	1	7	-	-
10	Paul Warne	-/-/-/-	1/-/-/-	-	-	1	-	-	-

Subs not used: Hoskins, Montgomery, R Barker, Talbot. - Formation: 4-4-2

Derby Played: 23 Won 5 Drawn 8 Lost 10 For 24 Against 36 Pos 22

West Brom [0] 1 DERBY [0] 1

The Christmas present Derby County craved was cruelly snatched from their grasp by West Bromwich Albion at the Hawthorns. Only four minutes remained when Candido Costa fired home a low drive from 18 yards to record his first goal for club.

But they were robbed of the victory they deserved when defender Thomas Gaardsoe headed a dramatic stoppage-time equaliser for Albion.

Before that, Derby out-fought, out-thought and out-played Albion from start to finish. They created and squandered a stack of chances and were denied by their former goalkeeper, Russell Hoult, on other occasions.

Lee Morris, who had missed three games with a calf strain, was back on the left side and set the tone early on. Having twisted and turned Bernt Haas and Sean Gregan, his teasing low cross struck the shin of Lee Bradbury and bobbled a yard wide.

The Rams' fine start had seen them take the game by the scruff of the neck, leaving goalkeeper Lee Grant with little more to do than keep himself warm. Therefore, his sharp reactions after 23 minutes deserved praise as he dropped to his right to turn a firm, low shot from Haas behind.

While there was a slight improvement from Albion after the break, the Rams continued to stretch and open up their hosts.

So there was little argument when Rams took the lead in the 86th minute. A run from Morris ended with the ball falling for Costa on the edge of the area. He steadied himself and sent a low shot skidding beyond the dive of Hoult and into the bottom corner.

A first away win in eight was within reach but the Rams have been guilty of conceding late goals this season and the Albion equaliser came with 90 minutes on the clock. Hulse headed on a Jason Koumas corner and Gaardsoe, sent forward, stooped to head home from a yard out.

Result......Result......Result.

WEST BROM ......(0) 1   **DERBY** ....(0) 1
Gaardsoe 90   Costa 86

Att 26,412
Referee: G Cain

Stats......Stats.......Stats......Stats

WEST BROM				DERBY		
1st	2nd	Total		Total	2nd	1st
2	3	5	Corners	8	2	6
5	3	8	Fouls	5	4	1
0	0	0	Yellow cards	0	0	0
0	0	0	Red cards	0	0	0
4	1	5	Caught Offside	3	2	1
2	2	4	Shots on target	7	5	2
0	2	2	Shots off target	8	3	5
0	0	0	Hit woodwork	0	0	0
45	45	45%	Possession	55%	55	55

> Individually, a lot of players were as poor as I've ever seen them and collectively that was as poor a performance as I've seen since I've been here.
>
> **Gary Megson**

> THE people who were at The Hawthorns must have gone home wondering how Derby didn't win that game. It was a game we dominated by 80 or 90%.
>
> **George Burley**

Other Div 1 Results

Cardiff 0 Walsall 1, Coventry 0 Sheff Utd 1, Crewe 3 Burnley 1, Crystal Palace 0 Millwall 1, Gillingham 1 Watford 0, Norwich 1 Nottm Forest 0, Reading 0 Wimbledon 3, Stoke 1 Preston 1, Sunderland 3 Bradford 0, West Ham 1 Ipswich 2, Wigan 1 Rotherham 2

West Brom [0] 1 DERBY [0] 1

Goalkeeper Stats: Lee Grant
Saves: Catch 1, Parry 1, Round
Post 1, Crosses: Catch 1, Punch 1

Derby Player Stats		Shots on target	Shots off target	Caught offside	Fouls conceded	Free-kicks won	Corners taken	Clearances	Defensive blocks
		L/R/H/Oth	L/R/H/Oth						
22 Lee Bradbury	1st	-/-/-/-	-/-/-/-	1	-	-	-	-	-
	2nd	-/-/-/-	-/-/-/-	2	2	-	-	-	-
3 Luciano Zavagno	1st	-/-/-/-	-/-/-/-	-	1	-	-	1	1
	2nd	1/-/-/-	1/-/-/-	-	-	-	-	1	-
10 Michael Johnson	1st	-/-/-/-	-/-/-/-	-	-	2	-	-	-
	2nd	-/-/-/-	-/-/-/-	-	1	-	-	-	-
11 Lee Morris	1st	-/-/1/-	-/2/-/-	-	-	-	4	-	-
	2nd	1/-/-/-	-/-/-/-	-	-	1	1	-	-
7 Ian Taylor	1st	-/-/-/-	1/1/-/-	-	-	-	-	-	-
	2nd	-/-/-/-	1/-/-/-	-	-	-	-	-	-
14 Richard Jackson	1st	-/-/-/-	-/-/-/-	-	-	-	-	-	-
	2nd	-/-/-/-	-/-/-/-	-	-	-	-	-	-
16 Youl Mawene	1st	-/-/-/-	-/-/-/-	-	-	3	-	-	-
	2nd	-/-/-/-	-/-/-/-	-	-	1	-	2	-
23 Marcus Tudgay	1st	-/-/1/-	1/-/-/-	-	-	-	-	-	-
▼ 67	2nd	-/-/1/-	-/-/-/-	-	-	-	-	1	-
15 Adam Bolder	1st	-/-/-/-	-/-/-/-	-	-	-	2	-	-
	2nd	-/1/-/-	1/-/-/-	-	-	-	-	-	-
8 Candido Costa	1st	-/-/-/-	-/-/-/-	-	-	-	-	-	-
▲ 67	2nd	-/1/-/-	-/-/-/-	-	-	1	-	-	-
29 Tom Huddlestone	1st	-/-/-/-	-/-/-/-	-	-	-	-	-	-
	2nd	-/-/-/-	-/-/-/-	-	1	-	1	-	-

Subs not used: Camp, Mills, Holmes, Boertien. - Formation: 4-3-3

Goalkeeper Stats: Russell Hoult Saves: Catch 2, Punch 1, Crosses: Catch 6, Round Post 1

	Player Stats	Shots on target	Shots off target	Caught offside	Fouls conceded	Free-kicks won	Corners taken	Clearances	Defensive blocks
12	Scott Dobie ▲ 79	-/-/-/-	-/-/-/-	-	-	-	-	-	-
20	Artim Sakiri ▲ 53	-/-/-/-	-/-/-/-	1	-	2	1	-	-
24	Thomas Gaardsoe	-/-/1/-	-/-/-/-	2	1	-	-	-	-
15	Rob Hulse ▲ 53	1/-/-/-	-/1/1/-	-	-	-	-	-	-
4	James O'Connor ▼ 53	-/-/-/-	-/-/-/-	-	1	-	-	-	-
6	Phil Gilchrist	-/-/-/-	-/-/-/-	-	-	1	-	7	-
34	Geoff Horsfield ▼ 79	-/-/-/-	-/-/-/-	-	1	-	-	-	-
2	Bernt Haas	-/1/-/-	-/-/-/-	-	1	-	1	4	1
19	Lee Hughes ▼ 53	-/-/-/-	-/-/-/-	1	2	1	-	-	-
18	Jason Koumas	-/-/-/-	-/-/-/-	1	-	-	2	-	-
14	Sean Gregan	-/-/-/-	-/-/-/-	-	-	-	1	-	-
10	Andy Johnson	1/-/-/-	-/-/-/-	-	1	1	-	2	-
33	Paul Robinson	-/-/-/-	-/-/-/-	-	1	-	-	3	-

Subs not used: Murphy, Moore. - Formation: 5-3-2

DERBY [0] 0 Norwich [0] 4

Derby County slipped deeper into relegation trouble when they were swept aside 4-0 by Division One leaders Norwich City. All the renewed hope from a fully-deserved Boxing Day draw against West Bromwich Albion was blown away on a blustery afternoon at Pride Park Stadium.

Derby had matched Norwich in the opening period only for the match to turn in a key moment seven minutes after the break. Lee Grant, who had already made a handful of smart saves, failed to collect a hanging cross from Paul McVeigh while under severe pressure.

Derby claimed the goalkeeper was fouled, referee Graham Laws disagreed and centre-back Craig Fleming drove home the loose ball. Norwich then capitalised on Derby's disorganisation , adding three more goals through Malky Mackay, the excellent McVeigh and a Leon McKenzie penalty to run out comfortable winners.

Grant had spilt a corner a minute before coming for McVeigh's cross on 52 minutes. There were plenty of bodies in there and contact but, unfortunately for Derby, everything fell for Norwich and Fleming scored with a controlled finish.

Norwich's greater quality took over from that moment and they looked what they are, a good bet to win promotion to the Premiership. McVeigh rattled the bar with a stunning 20-yard volley after Grant had punched away Adam Drury's free-kick but it was 2-0 after 78 minutes.

McVeigh, now involved in everything, curled a free-kick to the back post where Mackay arrived and had little trouble in heading past Grant.

Norwich made it three only minutes later. Jackson's last-ditch tackle prevented McKenzie from scoring but McVeigh did with the outside of his right foot from Gary Holt's cross. They rounded off the win when Youl Mawene's challenge from behind on McKenzie brought a penalty.

Result......Result.......Result.

DERBY ....(0) 0   NORWICH......(0) 4

Fleming 51
Mackay 78
McVeigh 81
McKenzie 88(p)

Att 23,783
Referee: G Laws

Stats.....Stats.......Stats......Stats

DERBY				NORWICH		
1st	2nd	Total		Total	2nd	1st
2	3	5	Corners	10	8	2
8	7	15	Fouls	21	9	12
0	2	2	Yellow cards	2	1	1
0	0	0	Red cards	0	0	0
0	0	0	Caught Offside	3	2	1
2	2	4	Shots on target	11	7	4
2	4	6	Shots off target	6	3	3
0	0	0	Hit woodwork	1	1	0
42	48	45%	Possession	55%	52	58

THE scoreline doesn't help at all but goals change games and I thought the referee's decision ahead of the first goal was terrible, disgraceful.
George Burley

IT was a very close game in the first half when we had two or three half-chances but then Rob Green's had to make a big save.
Nigel Worthington

Other Div 1 Results

Bradford 1 Coventry 0, Burnley 0 Stoke 1, Ipswich 1 Crystal Palace 3, Millwall 1 Gillingham 2, Nottm Forest 0 West Ham 2, Preston 0 Crewe 0, Rotherham 0 Sunderland 2, Sheff Utd 1 Wigan 1, Walsall 1 Reading 1, Watford 2 Cardiff 1

DERBY [0] 0 Norwich [0] 4

Goalkeeper Stats: Lee Grant Saves: Catch 1, Punch 1, Round Post 1, Crosses: Fumble 1, Punch 1

Derby Player Stats		Shots on target L/R/H/Oth	Shots off target L/R/H/Oth	Caught offside	Fouls conceded	Free-kicks won	Corners taken	Clearances	Defensive blocks
3 Luciano Zavagno	1st	-/-/-/-	-/-/-/-	-	1	2	-	1	-
59	2nd	-/-/-/-	-/-/-/-	-	3	2	-	-	-
10 Michael Johnson	1st	-/-/-/-	-/-/-/-	-	1	-	-	2	-
	2nd	-/-/-/-	-/-/-/-	-	-	-	-	5	1
11 Lee Morris	1st	-/-/-/-	1/-/-/-	-	-	1	-	-	-
	2nd	-/-/-/-	-/-/-/-	-	-	2	-	1	-
7 Ian Taylor	1st	-/-/-/-	-/-/-/-	-	-	-	-	-	-
89	2nd	-/-/-/-	-/1/-/-	-	1	-	-	1	-
14 Richard Jackson	1st	-/-/-/-	-/-/-/-	-	1	2	-	1	-
	2nd	-/-/-/-	-/-/-/-	-	-	-	-	-	-
16 Youl Mawene	1st	-/-/-/-	-/-/-/-	-	2	1	-	1	-
	2nd	-/-/1/-	-/-/-/-	-	1	2	-	-	-
23 Marcus Tudgay	1st	-/1/-/-	-/-/-/-	-	1	1	-	-	-
	2nd	-/-/-/-	-/1/-/-	-	1	2	-	-	-
18 Izale McLeod	1st	-/-/-/-	-/-/-/-	-	-	-	-	-	-
▲ 78	2nd	-/-/-/-	-/-/1/-	-	1	-	-	-	-
15 Adam Bolder	1st	-/-/-/-	-/-/-/-	-	1	-	1	-	-
	2nd	1/-/-/-	-/1/-/-	-	-	-	1	1	-
8 Candido Costa	1st	-/-/-/-	-/-/-/-	-	-	-	-	-	-
▲ 64	2nd	-/-/-/-	-/-/-/-	-	-	-	1	-	-
30 Lee Holmes	1st	-/-/-/-	-/-/-/-	-	1	2	1	-	-
▼ 78	2nd	-/-/-/-	-/-/-/-	-	-	-	1	-	-
29 Tom Huddlestone	1st	-/1/-/-	-/1/-/-	-	-	-	-	-	-
▼ 64	2nd	-/-/-/-	-/-/-/-	-	-	1	-	-	-

Subs not used: Camp, Mills, Boertien. - Formation: 4-4-2

Goalkeeper Stats: Robert Green Saves: Catch 2, Punch 1, Round Post 1, Crosses: Catch 5, Round Post 1, Punch 1

	Player Stats	Shots on target	Shots off target	Caught offside	Fouls conceded	Free-kicks won	Corners taken	Clearances	Defensive blocks
9	Iwan Roberts ▲ 86	-/-/-/-	-/-/-/-	-	-	-	-	-	-
20	Damien Francis	1/-/-/-	-/-/1/-	1	3	1	-	-	-
14	Leon McKenzie ▼ 90	1/1/-/-	2/-/1/-	-	5	3	-	1	-
4	Malky Mackay	-/-/2/-	-/-/1/-	1	1	1	-	6	-
11	Jim Brennan ▲ 45	-/-/-/-	-/-/-/-	1	-	-	-	-	-
18	Paul McVeigh ■ 83	-/4/-/-	-/-/-/-	-	2	3	9	-	-
19	Mathias Svensson ▼ 86	-/-/-/-	-/1/-/-	-	2	3	-	-	-
5	Craig Fleming	1/-/-/-	-/-/-/-	-	1	-	-	5	-
3	Adam Drury ■ 24	-/-/-/-	-/-/-/-	-	2	1	-	-	-
23	Ryan Jarvis ▲ 90	-/-/-/-	-/-/-/-	-	-	-	-	-	-
17	Marc Edworthy	-/-/-/-	-/-/-/-	-	2	2	-	3	-
8	Gary Holt	-/-/-/-	-/-/-/-	-	1	-	-	-	-
22	Ian Henderson ▼ 45	-/-/-/-	-/-/-/-	-	2	1	1	-	-

Subs not used: Crichton, Easton. - Formation: 4-4-2

Derby Played: 25 Won 5 Drawn 9 Lost 11 For 25 Against 41 Pos 22

...December Team Stats.....Team Stats......Team Stats......Team S

League table at the end of December

		HOME					AWAY					Pts	Df
	P	W	D	L	F	A	W	D	L	F	A		
Norwich	26	11	1	1	25	10	4	6	3	16	11	52	20
West Brom	26	6	5	2	17	10	7	3	3	19	12	47	14
Sheff Utd	25	8	3	2	24	10	5	3	4	15	17	45	12
Sunderland	26	7	5	1	17	7	5	3	5	17	15	44	12
Ipswich	26	7	2	4	27	18	5	4	4	19	20	42	8
Wigan	26	7	4	2	18	10	4	5	4	17	18	42	7
West Ham	26	5	5	3	21	14	5	6	2	14	9	41	12
Preston	26	8	3	2	26	13	3	4	6	13	17	40	9
Reading	26	7	2	4	17	16	4	3	6	13	17	38	-3
Millwall	26	6	5	2	14	7	3	4	6	15	19	36	3
Crewe	26	8	2	3	22	13	2	4	7	10	19	36	0
Cardiff	26	5	4	4	24	14	4	4	5	18	21	35	7
Walsall	26	6	5	2	20	12	3	3	7	8	15	35	1
Stoke	26	5	5	3	19	14	4	1	8	14	20	33	-1
Gillingham	25	6	1	6	16	17	3	5	4	15	20	33	-6
Rotherham	26	5	4	4	12	12	3	5	5	12	20	33	-8
Coventry	26	4	6	3	15	14	3	5	5	15	19	32	-2
Crystal Palace	26	3	5	5	15	18	5	2	6	17	22	31	-8
Watford	26	4	6	3	15	14	3	2	8	13	20	29	-6
Nottm Forest	25	4	4	4	19	14	3		7	15	21	28	-1
Burnley	26	5	3	5	20	17	2	4	7	17	30	28	-10
Derby	25	3	3	6	16	23	2	6	5	9	18	24	-16
Bradford	26	3	2	8	12	21	2	3	8	8	18	20	-19
Wimbledon	26	2	3	8	14	24	3	0	10	13	28	18	-25

December matches table

	P	W	D	L	F	A	Pts
Norwich	5	4	1	0	11	1	13
Stoke	6	4	1	1	11	5	13
Rotherham	6	4	1	1	8	4	13
Preston	6	3	3	0	13	7	12
Sunderland	6	3	2	1	11	6	11
Walsall	6	3	2	1	5	4	11
Crewe	6	2	3	1	11	8	9
Crystal Palace	6	3	0	3	9	9	9
Sheff Utd	5	2	2	1	8	6	8
West Ham	6	2	2	2	8	7	8
Wigan	6	2	2	2	7	8	8
Ipswich	6	2	2	2	6	8	8
Millwall	5	2	2	1	5	3	8
West Brom	6	1	4	1	5	5	7
Gillingham	4	2	1	1	4	3	7
Coventry	6	2	1	3	4	6	7
Watford	5	1	2	2	6	8	5
Cardiff	6	1	1	4	8	14	4
Wimbledon	5	1	1	3	5	5	4
Reading	5	1	1	3	3	10	4
Burnley	5	1	0	4	8	13	3
Bradford	6	1	0	5	1	8	3
Nottm Forest	5	0	2	3	2	6	2
Derby	4	0	2	2	2	7	2

December team stats details

Club Name	Ply	Shots On	Shots Off	Corners	Hit W'work	Caught Offside	Offside Trap	Fouls	Yellow Cards	Red Cards	Pens Awarded	Pens Con
Bradford	6	22	21	26	2	20	10	72	15	1	- (-)	-
Burnley	5	35	32	58	2	5	21	72	9	1	3 (3)	2
Cardiff	6	51	27	27	2	18	16	49	6	0	- (-)	-
Coventry	6	36	44	43	0	28	20	83	9	0	2 (1)	1
Crewe	6	24	24	28	0	18	14	41	5	0	- (-)	1
Crystal Palace	6	39	28	43	5	9	31	70	6	1	1 (-)	1
Derby	4	21	19	19	0	8	8	53	7	0	- (-)	-
Gillingham	4	23	28	34	1	12	9	58	5	0	1 (1)	-
Ipswich	6	35	32	24	0	24	21	72	12	1	1 (1)	1
Millwall	5	26	21	23	1	17	23	66	14	1	- (-)	1
Norwich	5	34	22	30	3	28	6	82	5	0	1 (1)	1
Nottm Forest	5	36	24	24	0	17	17	68	7	1	- (-)	-
Preston	6	58	33	38	1	16	4	89	11	1	2 (1)	1
Reading	5	29	21	34	1	27	15	47	1	0	- (-)	1
Rotherham	6	29	23	27	3	18	14	74	7	0	1 (1)	2
Sheff Utd	5	29	30	33	1	16	22	56	4	1	2 (2)	2
Stoke	6	39	29	34	2	14	9	84	11	2	2 (2)	-
Sunderland	6	37	40	25	5	20	37	77	10	2	3 (3)	2
Walsall	6	23	19	27	0	16	19	79	7	0	- (-)	-
Watford	5	24	17	20	1	18	15	69	10	1	- (-)	2
West Brom	6	37	30	35	0	19	17	60	6	0	- (-)	-
West Ham	6	29	28	32	2	16	26	53	6	1	- (-)	-
Wigan	6	49	45	41	0	19	29	85	7	1	- (-)	1
Wimbledon	5	21	22	26	1	15	15	46	6	0	1 (1)	1

DECEMBER STATS

Monthly Top scorers

Peter Thorne (Cardiff)	7
Ricardo Fuller (Preston)	5
Andrew Johnson (Crystal Palace)	5
Steve Jones (Crewe)	5
Ade Akinbiyi (Stoke)	4
David Healy (Preston)	4
Jermain Defoe (West Ham)	4
Dean Ashton (Crewe)	3
Jason De Vos (Ipswich)	2
Scott Fitzgerald (Watford)	2

Penalties scored

3 Robert Blake (Burnley), **2** Jack Lester (Sheff Utd), Marcus Stewart (Sunderland)

Assists

Kenny Lunt (Crewe)	5
Ricardo Fuller (Preston)	3
Tim Cahill (Millwall)	3
John Eustace (Stoke)	3
Richard Chaplow (Burnley)	2
Darren Wrack (Walsall)	2
Gifton Noel-Williams (Stoke)	2

Quickest goals

0:24 mins - Darren Bent (Ipswich vs Derby)
2:13 mins - Ricardo Fuller (Gillingham vs Preston)
3:03 mins - Jason McAteer (West Ham vs Sunderland)
3:33 mins - Heidar Helguson (Watford vs Stoke)
4:31 mins - Andy Roberts (Cardiff vs Millwall)

Top Keeper

	Mins	Gls
Robert Green (Norwich)	477	1
Nico Vaesen (Gillingham)	190	1
Patrick Kenny (Sheff Utd)	190	1
Robert Kozluk (Sheff Utd)	359	2
Tony Warner (Millwall)	479	3
Michael Pollitt (Rotherham)	569	4
Alan Combe (Bradford)	283	2
James Walker (Walsall)	565	4

Shots on target

Robert Earnshaw (Cardiff)	16
Ricardo Fuller (Preston)	15
Lee McCulloch (Wigan)	14
Eddie Lewis (Preston)	14
David Healy (Preston)	13
Peter Thorne (Cardiff)	12
Robert Blake (Burnley)	11
Jason Koumas (West Brom)	11
Ade Akinbiyi (Stoke)	10
Nathan Ellington (Wigan)	10

Shots off target

Nathan Ellington (Wigan)	15
Patrick Suffo (Coventry)	10
Shefki Kuqi (Ipswich)	9
John Oster (Sunderland)	9
John Eustace (Stoke)	9
Rob Hulse (West Brom)	9
Kevin Kyle (Sunderland)	8
Gary Teale (Wigan)	8
Ricardo Fuller (Preston)	8
Dean Windass (Bradford)	7

Caught offside

Nicky Forster (Reading)	18
Marlon King (Nottm Forest)	13
Julian Joachim (Coventry)	12
Patrick Agyemang (Gillingham)	9
Ade Akinbiyi (Stoke)	9
Leon McKenzie (Norwich)	9
Nick Chadwick (Millwall)	9
Darren Byfield (Sunderland)	8
Dean Ashton (Crewe)	8

Free-kicks won

Gifton Noel-Williams (Stoke)	19
Richard Langley (Cardiff)	19
Ricardo Fuller (Preston)	14
Tim Cahill (Millwall)	14
Peter Thorne (Cardiff)	14
Marlon Harewood (West Ham)	14
Mamady Sidibe (Gillingham)	14
Jack Lester (Sheff Utd)	13
Dean Ashton (Crewe)	13

Ipswich v Derby

Fouls conceded

Arthur Gnohere (QPR)	15
Jeff Whitley (Sunderland)	15
Jason De Vos (Ipswich)	14
Nathan Ellington (Wigan)	14
Lee Bradbury (Derby)	14
Paul Warne (Rotherham)	14
Gifton Noel-Williams (Stoke)	14
Gary Birch (Walsall)	14
Richard Cresswell (Preston)	13

Fouls without a card

Jeff Whitley (Sunderland)	15
Nathan Ellington (Wigan)	14
Paul Warne (Rotherham)	14
Gary Birch (Walsall)	14
Leon McKenzie (Norwich)	12
Steven Sidwell (Reading)	12
Gareth Williams (Nottm Forest)	10
Tony Grant (Burnley)	10
Paul Devlin (Watford)	10

An unchallenged Marcus Tudgay heads the ball during Derby's first game in December. He scored in the 73rd minute but it was not enough to prevent a defeat and the threat of relegation remained.

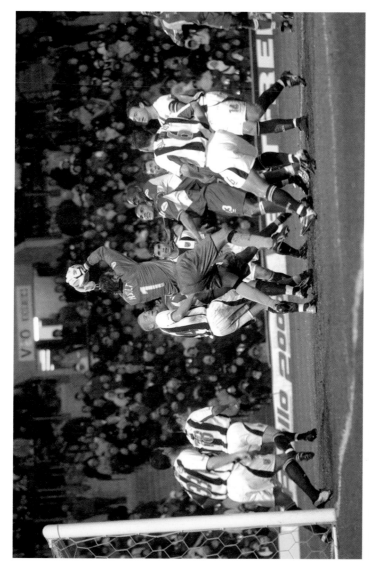

West Brom 'keeper Russel Hoult in action. Derby were robbed of a well-deserved victory when Thomas Gaardsoe headed in a dramatic stoppage-time equaliser for Albion.

Lee Holmes is surrounded by Rotherham players. Another point gained, but still no win for Burely's men.

Ian Taylor nicks the ball away from two West Brom defenders during the hard-fought 1-1 draw.

For the second game running, Derby folded in the second half and suffered another heavy defeat. Ipswich Town struck three goals after the break to win Saturday's FA Cup third round tie 3-0 at Portman Road.

The Rams played well at West Bromwich Albion on Boxing Day and in patches against Norwich and Ipswich but the cold facts are that they had not won in five games and scored only two goals.

The one plus from their third meeting with Ipswich in two months was the debut display of Spanish striker Manel. He offered a physical presence, looked confident in possession and proved a handful for the home defence.

When Ipswich were two-up, Manel saw a looping header bounce back off the bar with Kelvin Davis nowhere and then the Spaniard, released by Ian Taylor, was denied by the Ipswich goalkeeper's fine diving save.

But scoring goals had been a problem all season. Leading marksman Ian Taylor had not scored from open play in his last 16 appearances and Morris had only one in his last 11 games.

The closest Ipswich came in a first half lacking quality was when Tommy Miller's shot flashed narrowly over and Pablo Counago headed wide with Lee Grant stranded. Magilton's first contribution was to deliver a free-kick onto the head of the unchallenged Naylor who gave Grant no chance from six yards.

Counago set Kuqi away in acres of space down the right and his galloping stride took him into the area before he pulled the ball back for Miller to sweep a low shot from 12 yards wide of Grant.

Derby were also found wanting in the build up to the third goal. Dean Bowditch was too quick for Huddlestone and the foul brought him a yellow card. Reuser sent the resulting free-kick skidding towards goal, Grant's howler saw him spill the ball and then push it in the direction of the net before Kuqi wheeled away claiming that he had tapped the ball over the line.

Result.......Result.......Result.

IPSWICH..............(0) 3   DERBY ....(0) 0
Naylor 54, Miller 69
Kuqi 89
Att 16,159
Referee: P Crossley

Stats......Stats.......Stats.....Stats

IPSWICH				DERBY		
1st	2nd	Total		Total	2nd	1st
2	0	2	Corners	3	0	3
5	5	10	Fouls	14	6	8
1	0	1	Yellow cards	1	1	0
0	0	0	Red cards	0	0	0
0	3	3	Caught Offside	1	1	0
5	5	10	Shots on target	3	2	1
5	3	8	Shots off target	8	3	5
0	0	0	Hit woodwork	1	1	0
41	49	45%	Possession	55%	51	59

SHEFKI has had his critics but today he ran behind their defence and chased for the team. It's nice when substitutions work out so well.

Joe Royle

THE first goal cost us the tie. It would have been a big bonus if we'd got a result at Ipswich and I don't think anyone expected it.

George Burley

Other FA Cup Round 3 Results

Accrington S 0 Colchester 0, Barnsley 0 Scunthorpe 0, Birmingham 4 Blackburn 0, Bradford 1 Luton 2, Cardiff 0 Sheff U 1, Coventry 2 Peterboro 1, Crewe 0 Telford 1, Everton 3 Norwich 1, Gillingham 3 Charlton 2, Kidderminster 1 Wolverhampton 1, Man City 2 Leicester 2, Mansfield 0 Burnley 2, Middlesbrough 2 Notts C 0, Millwall 2 Walsall 1, Northampton 1 Rotherham 1, Nottm Forest 1 West Brom 0, Portsmouth 2 Blackpool 1, Preston 3 Reading 3, Southampton 0 Newcastle 3, Southend 1 Scarboro 1, Sunderland 1 Hartlepool 0, Swansea 2 Macclesfield 1, Tottenham 3 Crystal P 0, Tranmere 1 Bolton 1, Watford 2 Chelsea 0, Wigan 1 West Ham 2, Wimbledon 1 Stoke 1

Ipswich [0] 3 DERBY [0] 0

Goalkeeper Stats: Lee Grant Saves: Catch 2, Crosses: Catch 5

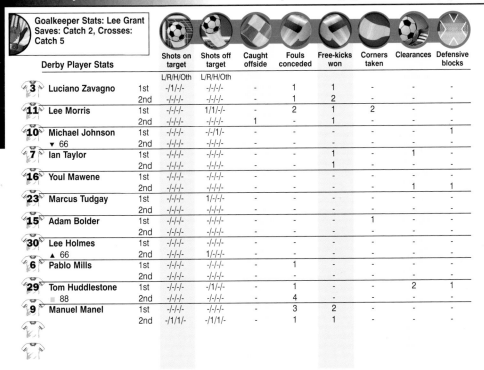

Derby Player Stats		Shots on target L/R/H/Oth	Shots off target L/R/H/Oth	Caught offside	Fouls conceded	Free-kicks won	Corners taken	Clearances	Defensive blocks
3 Luciano Zavagno	1st	-/1/-/-	-/-/-/-	-	1	1	-	-	-
	2nd	-/-/-/-	-/-/-/-	-	1	2	-	-	-
11 Lee Morris	1st	-/-/-/-	1/1/-/-	-	2	1	2	-	-
	2nd	-/-/-/-	-/-/-/-	1	-	1	-	-	-
10 Michael Johnson ▼ 66	1st	-/-/-/-	-/-/1/-	-	-	-	-	-	1
	2nd	-/-/-/-	-/-/-/-	-	-	-	-	-	-
7 Ian Taylor	1st	-/-/-/-	-/-/-/-	-	-	1	-	1	-
	2nd	-/-/-/-	-/-/-/-	-	-	1	-	-	-
16 Youl Mawene	1st	-/-/-/-	-/-/-/-	-	-	-	-	-	-
	2nd	-/-/-/-	-/-/-/-	-	-	-	-	1	1
23 Marcus Tudgay	1st	-/-/-/-	1/-/-/-	-	-	-	-	-	-
	2nd	-/-/-/-	-/-/-/-	-	-	-	-	-	-
15 Adam Bolder	1st	-/-/-/-	-/-/-/-	-	-	-	1	-	-
	2nd	-/-/-/-	-/-/-/-	-	-	-	-	-	-
30 Lee Holmes ▲ 66	1st	-/-/-/-	-/-/-/-	-	-	-	-	-	-
	2nd	-/-/-/-	1/-/-/-	-	-	-	-	-	-
6 Pablo Mills	1st	-/-/-/-	-/-/-/-	-	1	-	-	-	-
	2nd	-/-/-/-	-/-/-/-	-	-	-	-	-	-
29 Tom Huddlestone ■ 88	1st	-/-/-/-	-/1/-/-	-	1	-	-	2	1
	2nd	-/-/-/-	-/-/-/-	-	4	-	-	-	-
9 Manuel Manel	1st	-/-/-/-	-/-/-/-	-	3	2	-	-	-
	2nd	-/1/1/-	-/1/1/-	-	1	1	-	-	-

Subs not used: Labarthe Tome, McLeod, Boertien, Camp. - Formation: 4-3-3

Goalkeeper Stats: Kelvin Davis Saves: Catch 1, Parry 1, Round Post 2, Crosses: Catch 5

	Player Stats	Shots on target	Shots off target	Caught offside	Fouls conceded	Free-kicks won	Corners taken	Clearances	Defensive blocks
11	Jermaine Wright	-/1/-/-	1/-/-/-	-	1	-	-	-	-
23	Chris Bart-Williams ▼ 53	-/-/-/-	-/1/-/-	-	-	1	-	-	-
12	Richard Naylor	-/-/1/-	-/-/-/-	-	1	2	-	4	-
32	Shefki Kuqi ▲ 51	-/1/-/-	-/1/-/-	2	1	1	-	-	-
18	Darren Bent ▼ 51	-/-/-/-	-/1/1/-	-	-	1	-	1	-
2	Fabian Wilnis ■ 45	-/-/-/-	-/-/-/-	-	2	2	-	-	-
14	Matthew Richards	-/-/-/-	-/-/-/-	-	-	-	-	-	-
4	John McGreal	-/-/-/-	-/-/-/-	-	2	3	-	5	-
9	Pablo Counago ▼ 75	-/2/-/-	-/-/1/-	-	1	2	-	-	-
7	Jim Magilton ▲ 53	-/-/-/-	-/-/-/-	-	-	-	-	-	-
8	Tommy Miller	-/1/-/-	1/1/-/-	-	2	1	-	1	-
30	Martijn Reuser	-/2/-/-	-/-/-/-	1	-	-	2	-	-
17	Dean Bowditch ▲ 75	-/1/-/-	-/-/-/-	-	-	1	-	-	-

Subs not used: Abbey, Santos. - Formation: 4-4-2

Stoke [1] 2 DERBY [1] 1

The alarm bells were ringing as Derby County dug themselves deeper into relegation trouble. They had now gone five games without a League victory following the 2-1 defeat by a predictable Stoke City team.

There was a shortage of goals at one end - only three in the last five games - while they were once again leaking like a sieve at the other. A perfect start provided by Lee Morris' goal in the second minute was wasted as schoolboy defending handed Stoke two goals and the three points.

There was real hope of a first away win in more than three months when Morris struck to give them an unexpected early lead. Bolder's shot looped up off Gerry Taggart and an alert Morris, playing his 100th game for the club, took advantage of Stoke's hesitation to finish neatly from close range.

But the defence was tested by the muscle of Ade Akinbiyi and Gifton Noel-Williams, whose regular supply line was provided by the impressive Peter Hoekstra.

Lee Grant saved at the feet of Akinbiyi before the striker pulled Stoke level after 29 minutes. Goalkeeper Ed de Goey launched a free-kick downfield. The Rams' dithering defence allowed it to bounce through them and a grateful Akinbiyi volleyed low past the exposed Grant.

Noel-Williams then saw his drive turned round the post by Grant but the Rams could have gone in ahead at the break had Bolder not pulled his shot wide from inside the area.

Stoke's winning goal came from an unsurprising source eight minutes into the second half. The decision to give a free-kick against Luciano Zavagno was harsh and John Eustace delivered from the right. Grant and his defenders watched, rather than dealt with, the ball, and Taggart headed home unchallenged at the back post.

The Rams response to falling behind was spirited and committed but Stoke completed a double over the Rams and had now won five of their last six League games.

Result.......Result.......Result.

STOKE ....(1) 2   DERBY ....(1) 1
Akinbiyi 29   Morris 1
Taggart 53

Att 16,402
Referee: A Kaye

Stats......Stats.......Stats.....Stats

STOKE				DERBY		
1st	2nd	Total		Total	2nd	1st
4	2	6	Corners	1	1	0
7	6	13	Fouls	15	7	8
1	1	2	Yellow cards	2	1	1
0	0	0	Red cards	0	0	0
5	0	5	Caught Offside	1	0	1
3	2	5	Shots on target	7	2	5
3	2	5	Shots off target	5	2	3
0	0	0	Hit woodwork	1	1	0
44	55	49%	Possession	51%	45	56

 I had been emphasising all week how big this game was as a difference in going six points or 12 points above the danger zone is massive.

Tony Pulis

 IT'S going to be very hard from now until the end of the season, but the players are up for a fight and we'll give it our best shot.

George Burley

Other Div 1 Results

Cardiff 3 Rotherham 2, Coventry 0 Watford 0, Crewe 1 Wimbledon 0, Crystal Palace 0 Burnley 0, Gillingham 0 Sheff Utd 3, Norwich 0 Bradford 1, Reading 1 Ipswich 1, Sunderland 1 Nottm Forest 0, West Ham 1 Preston 2, Wigan 0 Millwall 0

Goalkeeper Stats: Lee Grant Saves: Parry 1, Crosses: Catch 1, Punch 2

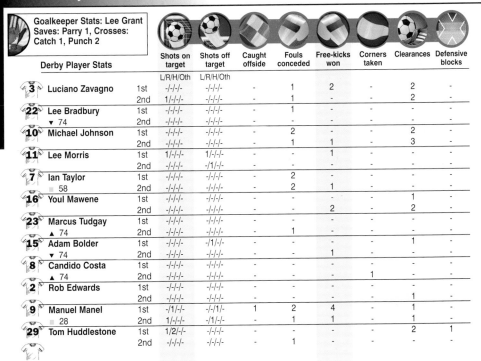

Derby Player Stats		Shots on target L/R/H/Oth	Shots off target L/R/H/Oth	Caught offside	Fouls conceded	Free-kicks won	Corners taken	Clearances	Defensive blocks
3 Luciano Zavagno	1st	-/-/-/-	-/-/-/-	-	1	2	-	2	-
	2nd	1/-/-/-	-/-/-/-	-	1	-	-	2	-
22 Lee Bradbury ▼ 74	1st	-/-/-/-	-/-/-/-	-	1	-	-	-	-
	2nd	-/-/-/-	-/-/-/-	-	-	-	-	-	-
10 Michael Johnson	1st	-/-/-/-	-/-/-/-	-	2	-	-	2	-
	2nd	-/-/-/-	-/-/-/-	-	1	1	-	3	-
11 Lee Morris	1st	1/-/-/-	1/-/-/-	-	-	1	-	-	-
	2nd	-/-/-/-	-/1/-/-	-	-	-	-	-	-
7 Ian Taylor ▪ 58	1st	-/-/-/-	-/-/-/-	-	2	-	-	-	-
	2nd	-/-/-/-	-/-/-/-	-	2	1	-	-	-
16 Youl Mawene	1st	-/-/-/-	-/-/-/-	-	-	-	-	1	-
	2nd	-/-/-/-	-/-/-/-	-	-	2	-	2	-
23 Marcus Tudgay ▲ 74	1st	-/-/-/-	-/-/-/-	-	-	-	-	-	-
	2nd	-/-/-/-	-/-/-/-	-	1	-	-	-	-
15 Adam Bolder ▼ 74	1st	-/-/-/-	-/1/-/-	-	-	-	-	1	-
	2nd	-/-/-/-	-/-/-/-	-	-	1	-	-	-
8 Candido Costa ▲ 74	1st	-/-/-/-	-/-/-/-	-	-	-	-	-	-
	2nd	-/-/-/-	-/-/-/-	-	-	-	1	-	-
2 Rob Edwards	1st	-/-/-/-	-/-/-/-	-	-	-	-	-	-
	2nd	-/-/-/-	-/-/-/-	-	-	-	-	1	-
9 Manuel Manel ▪ 28	1st	-/1/-/-	-/-/1/-	1	2	4	-	1	-
	2nd	1/-/-/-	-/1/-/-	-	1	1	-	1	-
29 Tom Huddlestone	1st	1/2/-/-	-/-/-/-	-	-	-	-	2	1
	2nd	-/-/-/-	-/-/-/-	-	1	-	-	-	-

Subs not used: Camp, Valakari, Boertien. - Formation: 4-4-2

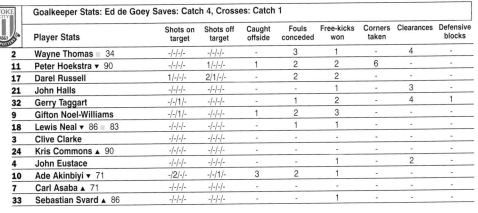

Goalkeeper Stats: Ed de Goey Saves: Catch 4, Crosses: Catch 1

	Player Stats	Shots on target	Shots off target	Caught offside	Fouls conceded	Free-kicks won	Corners taken	Clearances	Defensive blocks
2	Wayne Thomas ▪ 34	-/-/-/-	-/-/-/-	-	3	1	-	4	-
11	Peter Hoekstra ▼ 90	-/-/-/-	1/-/-/-	1	2	2	6	-	-
17	Darel Russell	1/-/-/-	2/1/-/-	-	2	2	-	-	-
21	John Halls	-/-/-/-	-/-/-/-	-	-	1	-	3	-
32	Gerry Taggart	-/-/1/-	-/-/-/-	-	1	2	-	4	1
9	Gifton Noel-Williams	-/-/1/-	-/-/-/-	1	2	3	-	-	-
18	Lewis Neal ▼ 86 ▪ 83	-/-/-/-	-/-/-/-	-	1	1	-	-	-
3	Clive Clarke	-/-/-/-	-/-/-/-	-	-	-	-	-	-
24	Kris Commons ▲ 90	-/-/-/-	-/-/-/-	-	-	-	-	-	-
4	John Eustace	-/-/-/-	-/-/-/-	-	-	1	-	2	-
10	Ade Akinbiyi ▼ 71	-/2/-/-	-/-/1/-	3	2	1	-	-	-
7	Carl Asaba ▲ 71	-/-/-/-	-/-/-/-	-	-	-	-	-	-
33	Sebastian Svard ▲ 86	-/-/-/-	-/-/-/-	-	-	1	-	-	-

Subs not used: Cutler, Hall. - Formation: 4-4-2

DERBY [1] 2 Gillingham [0] 1

New faces brought new hope for Derby County in their battle to beat the drop. An excellent free-kick from debutant left-back Jamie Vincent and a first appearance of real promise and quality from German Marco Reich helped to deliver a much-needed victory.

The win may not have altered their league-position but the light could now be seen at the end of the tunnel.

But only the sharp reflexes of goalkeeper Lee Grant prevented the Rams from going two down in the opening 10 minutes and from being pegged back when only one up.

After Grant had twice denied the lively Patrick Agyemang with smart saves, Vincent settled himself and his new Rams team-mates by grabbing the opening goal on 13 minutes. From a free-kick on the angle of the area and in a perfect position for a left-footer, he curled the ball beautifully round the wall, beyond the bemused Nico Vaesen and into the corner of the net.

Reich, quiet on the left side of midfield until that moment, suddenly emerged as a key figure. His quality and pace stood out. He was positive, skipped past players with ease and was always looking to cross or shoot.

The Rams' second goal arrived soon after. Rob Edwards struck a low shot and the ball clearly deflected off Tudgay to beat Vaesen and nestle in the bottom corner

This was a must-win game and, with the three points in sight, the Rams became edgy. Tommy Johnson did not help matters when he struck a peach of a goal from 25 yards to throw Gillingham a lifeline with 20 minutes to go. It was sweet moment for the former Rams favourite, who had earlier been denied an equaliser when Grant kept out his header.

Gillingham were reduced to nine men when Cox picked up two bookings for fouls in the space of three minutes but they still pushed forward, making for a hectic closing few minutes. Taylor looked to have scored a third for the Rams only for his thumping header to be disallowed, presumably for pushing.

Result.......Result.......Result.

DERBY ....(1) 2 GILLINGHAM (0) 1
Vincent 14   T Johnson 69
Edwards 61

Att 20,473
Referee: K Wright

Stats......Stats.......Stats......Stats

DERBY						GILLINGHAM
1st	2nd	Total		Total	2nd	1st
4	6	10	Corners	3	2	1
6	6	12	Fouls	18	7	11
0	0	0	Yellow cards	4	2	2
0	0	0	Red cards	2	1	1
2	1	3	Caught Offside	5	4	1
5	7	12	Shots on target	5	3	2
3	4	7	Shots off target	2	1	1
0	0	0	Hit woodwork	0	0	0
49	60	54%	Possession	46%	40	51

I didn't think Gillingham could argue with the second sending off, but I thought the first one was very harsh.
George Burley

WE tried to talk to the ref when he was coming off and during the match but he wouldn't even take any questions, he just dismissed them.
Wayne Jones

Other Div 1 Results

Bradford 0 Cardiff 1, Burnley 1 West Brom 1, Ipswich 6 Crewe 4, Millwall 2 Sunderland 1, Nottm Forest 0 Reading 1, Preston 2 Wigan 4, Rotherham 4 Norwich 4, Sheff Utd 3 West Ham 3, Walsall 1 Coventry 6, Watford 1 Crystal Palace 5, Wimbledon 0 Stoke 1

DERBY [1] 2 Gillingham [0] 1

Goalkeeper Stats: Lee Grant
Saves: Catch 2

Derby Player Stats		Shots on target	Shots off target	Caught offside	Fouls conceded	Free-kicks won	Corners taken	Clearances	Defensive blocks
		L/R/H/Oth	L/R/H/Oth						
31 G Labarthe Tome	1st	-/-/-	-/-/-	-	-	-	-	-	-
▲ 84	2nd	-/-/-	-/-/-	-	-	-	-	-	-
10 Michael Johnson	1st	-/-/-	-/-/-	-	2	-	-	-	-
	2nd	-/-/-	-/-/1/-	-	-	2	-	1	-
7 Ian Taylor	1st	-/1/-/-	-/-/-	1	2	-	-	-	-
	2nd	-/-/1/-	-/-/1/-	-	2	1	-	-	-
16 Youl Mawene	1st	-/-/-	-/-/-	-	-	-	-	-	-
	2nd	-/-/-	-/-/-	-	1	-	-	1	1
23 Marcus Tudgay	1st	-/-/-	-/1/-/-	-	1	1	-	-	-
	2nd	-/-/-	-/-/-	1	1	-	-	-	-
15 Adam Bolder	1st	-/-/-	-/-/-	-	-	-	-	-	-
▲ 90	2nd	-/-/-	-/-/-	-	-	-	-	-	-
8 Candido Costa	1st	-/1/-/-	-/-/-	-	1	4	1	-	-
▼ 90	2nd	-/-/-	-/-/-	-	-	1	4	-	1
22 Marco Reich	1st	-/1/-/-	-/1/-/-	-	-	3	3	-	-
	2nd	-/-/-	-/1/-/-	-	-	1	2	-	-
3 Jamie Vincent	1st	1/-/-/-	1/-/-/-	-	-	2	-	-	-
	2nd	1/-/-/-	1/-/-/-	-	1	-	-	-	-
2 Rob Edwards	1st	-/-/-	-/-/-	-	-	-	-	-	-
	2nd	-/1/-/-	-/-/-	-	-	1	-	1	-
9 Manuel Manel	1st	-/-/-	-/-/-	1	-	1	-	-	-
▼ 84	2nd	1/3/-/-	-/-/-	-	1	-	-	-	-
29 Tom Huddlestone	1st	-/1/-/-	-/-/-	-	-	-	-	-	-
	2nd	-/-/-	-/-/-	-	1	-	-	-	-

Subs not used: Camp, Jackson, Holmes. - Formation: 4-4-2

Goalkeeper Stats: Nico Vaesen Saves: Catch 1, Round Post 1, Crosses: Tip Over 1, Catch 8

	Player Stats	Shots on target	Shots off target	Caught offside	Fouls conceded	Free-kicks won	Corners taken	Clearances	Defensive blocks
15	Mark Saunders	-/-/-	-/-/-	-	2	-	-	1	-
17	Andrew Crofts ▲ 82	-/-/-	-/-/-	-	1	-	-	-	-
6	Ian Cox ■ 7 ■ 79	-/-/-	-/-/-	-	2	1	-	2	2
8	Andy Hessenthaler ▲ 62 ▼ 90	-/-/-	-/-/-	-	1	1	-	-	-
2	Nyron Nosworthy	-/-/-	-/1/-/-	-	1	1	-	1	-
18	Chris Hope	-/-/-	-/-/-	-	1	3	-	1	2
22	Danny Spiller ▼ 62	-/-/-	-/-/-	-	3	-	2	1	-
11	Tommy Johnson ▼ 82 ■ 39	1/1/1/-	-/1/-/-	-	1	-	-	-	-
4	Paul Smith	-/-/-	-/-/-	-	2	2	1	5	-
10	Patrick Agyemang	1/1/-/-	-/-/-	5	2	1	-	-	-
3	John Hills ■ 1 ■ 39	-/-/-	-/-/-	-	2	1	-	2	-
14	Leon Johnson ▲ 39	-/-/-	-/-/-	-	-	-	-	1	-
9	Darius Henderson ▼ 39	-/-/-	-/-/-	-	1	-	-	-	-

Subs not used: Bossu, James. - Formation: 4-4-2

DERBY [0] 2 Sheff Utd [0] 0

Derby County beat the big freeze and promotion-chasing Sheffield United to climb out of the Division One relegation zone. And to cap a rare joyous night for the Rams, their great rivals and neighbours Nottingham Forest took their place in the bottom three.

Two goals in the final 20 minutes from Marcus Tudgay and substitute Izale McLeod brought a deserved 2-0 victory at Pride Park Stadium.

There were a number of uplifting individual performances. Youl Mawene was excellent at the back and the young central midfield pairing of Huddlestone and Osman played with a maturity well beyond their years.

Marcus Tudgay once again gave his all up front while Candido Costa and Marco Reich offered good width and the first goal on 70 minutes was created from out wide. Reich stepped inside and his fine right-footed cross picked out Tudgay who headed home from close range.

The second came deep into injury time and from a goalkeeping blunder from Paddy Kenny. He received a back-pass from Chris Morgan and in trying to make a return pass, he played the ball against the incoming McLeod who won the chase for the loose ball and turned it into the empty net from a tight angle.

Sheffield United had a glut of strikers to choose from and went for former Rams frontman Dean Sturridge alongside Wayne Allison. Going into the game unbeaten in eight and sitting third in the table, it was not surprising to see the visitors start in a confident manner.

Derby, however, carried more of goal threat and twice went close from first-half free kicks. The first was 25 yards out and in Jamie Vincent territory.Instead, Reich flashed a shot around the wall and the ball brushed the side-netting with Kenny stranded and rather relieved.

Reich again made an impact and received a standing ovation when he was replaced four minutes from time.

Result.......Result.......Result.

DERBY ....(0) 2   SHEFF UTD ..(0) 0
Tudgay 70
McLeod 90

Att 23,603
Referee: D Crick

Stats......Stats.......Stats......Stats

DERBY				SHEFF UTD		
1st	2nd	Total		Total	2nd	1st
2	2	4	Corners	1	0	1
11	3	14	Fouls	14	5	9
2	0	2	Yellow cards	1	0	1
0	0	0	Red cards	0	0	0
0	2	2	Caught Offside	6	3	3
2	3	5	Shots on target	2	0	2
4	5	9	Shots off target	5	2	3
0	0	0	Hit woodwork	0	0	0
34	44	39%	Possession	61%	56	66

THE fact that we've been able to bring in new personnel in the last few weeks has given us more quality and more experience.
George Burley

I think we were still at the hotel, wondering whether the game was going to go ahead. Our performance was like the weather - damp and miserable.
Neil Warnock

Other Div 1 Results

No Other games

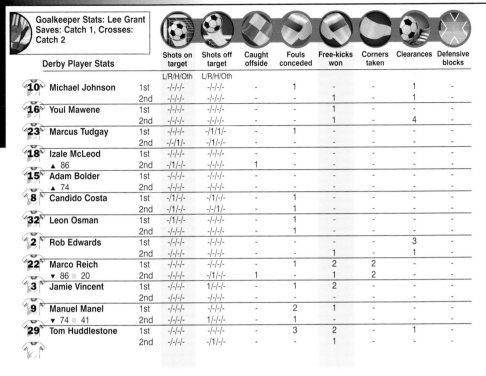

Goalkeeper Stats: Lee Grant
Saves: Catch 1, Crosses: Catch 2

Derby Player Stats		Shots on target L/R/H/Oth	Shots off target L/R/H/Oth	Caught offside	Fouls conceded	Free-kicks won	Corners taken	Clearances	Defensive blocks
10 Michael Johnson	1st	-/-/-/-	-/-/-/-	-	1	-	-	1	-
	2nd	-/-/-/-	-/-/-/-	-	-	1	-	1	-
16 Youl Mawene	1st	-/-/-/-	-/-/-/-	-	-	1	-	-	-
	2nd	-/-/-/-	-/-/-/-	-	-	1	-	4	-
23 Marcus Tudgay	1st	-/-/-/-	-/1/1/-	-	1	-	-	-	-
	2nd	-/-/1/-	-/1/-/-	-	-	-	-	-	-
18 Izale McLeod ▲ 86	1st	-/-/-/-	-/-/-/-	-	-	-	-	-	-
	2nd	-/1/-/-	-/-/-/-	1	-	-	-	-	-
15 Adam Bolder ▲ 74	1st	-/-/-/-	-/-/-/-	-	-	-	-	-	-
	2nd	-/-/-/-	-/-/-/-	-	-	-	-	-	-
8 Candido Costa	1st	-/1/-/-	-/1/-/-	-	1	-	-	-	-
	2nd	-/1/-/-	-/-/1/-	-	1	-	-	-	-
32 Leon Osman	1st	-/1/-/-	-/-/-/-	-	1	-	-	-	-
	2nd	-/-/-/-	-/-/-/-	-	1	-	-	-	-
2 Rob Edwards	1st	-/-/-/-	-/-/-/-	-	-	-	-	3	-
	2nd	-/-/-/-	-/-/-/-	-	-	1	-	1	-
22 Marco Reich ▼ 86 ■ 20	1st	-/-/-/-	-/-/-/-	-	1	2	2	-	-
	2nd	-/-/-/-	-/1/-/-	1	-	1	2	-	-
3 Jamie Vincent	1st	-/-/-/-	1/-/-/-	-	1	2	-	-	-
	2nd	-/-/-/-	-/-/-/-	-	-	-	-	-	-
9 Manuel Manel ▼ 74 ■ 41	1st	-/-/-/-	-/-/-/-	-	2	1	-	-	-
	2nd	-/-/-/-	1/-/-/-	-	1	-	-	-	-
29 Tom Huddlestone	1st	-/-/-/-	-/-/-/-	-	3	2	-	1	-
	2nd	-/-/-/-	-/1/-/-	-	-	1	-	-	-

Subs not used: Camp, Jackson, Holmes. - Formation: 4-4-2

Goalkeeper Stats: Patrick Kenny Saves: Catch 2, Crosses: Catch 3

	Player Stats	Shots on target	Shots off target	Caught offside	Fouls conceded	Free-kicks won	Corners taken	Clearances	Defensive blocks
18	Michael Tonge	-/-/-/-	-/-/-/-	-	2	1	-	-	-
22	Alan Wright	-/-/-/-	-/-/-/-	-	-	1	-	2	-
19	Dean Sturridge ▼ 68	-/-/-/-	-/-/-/-	1	3	3	-	-	-
32	Jonathan Forte ▲ 73	-/-/-/-	1/-/-/-	-	1	-	-	-	-
21	Mark Rankine ▼ 73	-/-/1/-	-/-/-/-	-	4	1	-	-	-
7	Paul Shaw	-/1/-/-	-/1/-/-	-	1	1	-	-	-
4	Nick Montgomery	-/-/-/-	-/2/-/-	-	-	3	1	-	-
14	Wayne Allison	-/-/-/-	-/-/1/-	4	1	1	-	-	-
10	Paul Peschisolido ▲ 68	-/-/-/-	-/-/-/-	1	-	-	-	-	-
6	Robert Page	-/-/-/-	-/-/-/-	-	1	-	-	4	-
5	Chris Morgan	-/-/-/-	-/-/-/-	-	-	2	-	8	-
2	Robert Kozluk ■ 18	-/-/-/-	-/-/-/-	-	1	1	-	3	-

Subs not used: Whitlow, Jagielka, Boussatta. Formation: 4-3-2-1

Derby Played: 28 Won 7 Drawn 9 Lost 12 For 30 Against 44 Pos 21

Reading [2] 3 DERBY [0] 1

Derby County remained in deep trouble following their 13th League defeat of the season. Another harsh lesson on the road saw their mini revival blown off course in the blustery, wet conditions at Reading's Madejski Stadium.

The 3-1 reverse saw the gap between themselves and third-bottom Nottingham Forest close to a point as the survival scramble took on greater urgency with each passing game. But even after going three down, there was a collection of players who had no thoughts of throwing in the towel.

They saw plenty of the ball in the second period, created a number of promising situations, tested the goalkeeper, hit the woodwork, scored through Michael Johnson and had what looked a perfectly good second goal disallowed.

But the Rams shot themselves in the foot after only two minutes. Johnson fouled the awkward Lloyd Owusu and Shaun Goater moved across a static defence, got up above Youl Mawene and headed Nicky Shorey's free kick past Lee Grant.

There was a good energy about Reading's play. Owusu and Goater looked hungry and strong, while Andy Hughes and John Salako provided useful width.

And their second goal arrived after 41 minutes. Steve Sidwell found himself in a central position 22 yards out and had the time to crack a low shot just inside the right post. Grant got his hand to the ball but could not keep it out.

At the other end, Noel Whelan led the line well on his debut. He was involved in a fine move four minutes after the break as the Rams went agonisingly close to grasping a lifeline. Leon Osman finished the neat passage of play with a low shot from 15 yards. It rebounded off the post with Marcus Hahnemann beaten.

That proved a turning point, as Goater punished more loose defending minutes later by shooting low past Grant from 20 yards for his second and Reading's third goal.

Johnson reduced the deficit around the hour mark when he dived to head home Vincent's cross and Osman had a header ruled out with seven minutes of normal time remaining.

Result.......Result.......Result.

READING ....(2) 3   DERBY ....(0) 1
Goater 2, 51   Johnson 59
Sidwell 41

Att 14,382
Referee: M Cowburn

Stats......Stats.......Stats......Stats

READING					DERBY	
1st	2nd	Total		Total	2nd	1st
2	1	3	Corners	7	4	3
7	6	13	Fouls	12	7	5
0	1	1	Yellow cards	2	1	1
0	0	0	Red cards	0	0	0
0	3	3	Caught Offside	3	2	1
3	3	6	Shots on target	8	5	3
3	1	4	Shots off target	3	1	2
0	0	0	Hit woodwork	1	1	0
40	46	43%	Possession	57%	54	60

THE two-week break gave us time to do some real practice, but if games come thick and fast, all you are doing is trying to recover.
Steve Coppell

LEON OSMAN hit an upright and if that had gone in at 2-1 it might have been a different game. I don't know why we had a goal disallowed.
George Burley

Other Div 1 Results

Cardiff 0 Nottm Forest 0, Coventry 1 Ipswich 1, Crewe 1 Millwall 2, Crystal Palace 3 Wimbledon 1, Gillingham 1 Bradford 0, Norwich 1 Sheff Utd 0, Stoke 3 Walsall 2, Sunderland P Preston P, West Brom 3 Watford 1, West Ham 2 Rotherham 1, Wigan 0 Burnley 0

Goalkeeper Stats: Lee Grant
Saves: Catch 1, Round Post 1, Crosses: Round Post 1

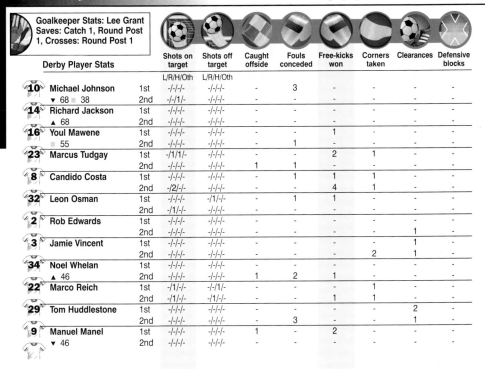

Derby Player Stats		Shots on target	Shots off target	Caught offside	Fouls conceded	Free-kicks won	Corners taken	Clearances	Defensive blocks
		L/R/H/Oth	L/R/H/Oth						
10 Michael Johnson	1st	-/-/-/-	-/-/-/-	-	3	-	-	-	-
▼ 68 ■ 38	2nd	-/-/1/-	-/-/-/-	-	-	-	-	-	-
14 Richard Jackson	1st	-/-/-/-	-/-/-/-	-	-	-	-	-	-
▲ 68	2nd	-/-/-/-	-/-/-/-	-	-	-	-	-	-
16 Youl Mawene	1st	-/-/-/-	-/-/-/-	-	-	1	-	-	-
■ 55	2nd	-/-/-/-	-/-/-/-	-	1	-	-	-	-
23 Marcus Tudgay	1st	-/1/1/-	-/-/-/-	-	-	2	1	-	-
	2nd	-/-/-/-	-/-/-/-	1	1	-	-	-	-
8 Candido Costa	1st	-/-/-/-	-/-/-/-	-	1	1	1	-	-
	2nd	-/2/-/-	-/-/-/-	-	-	4	1	-	-
32 Leon Osman	1st	-/-/-/-	-/1/-/-	-	1	1	-	-	-
	2nd	-/1/-/-	-/-/-/-	-	-	-	-	-	-
2 Rob Edwards	1st	-/-/-/-	-/-/-/-	-	-	-	-	-	-
	2nd	-/-/-/-	-/-/-/-	-	-	-	-	1	-
3 Jamie Vincent	1st	-/-/-/-	-/-/-/-	-	-	-	-	1	-
	2nd	-/-/-/-	-/-/-/-	-	-	-	2	1	-
34 Noel Whelan	1st	-/-/-/-	-/-/-/-	-	-	-	-	-	-
▲ 46	2nd	-/-/-/-	-/-/-/-	1	2	1	-	-	-
22 Marco Reich	1st	-/1/-/-	-/-/1/-	-	-	-	1	-	-
	2nd	-/1/-/-	-/1/-/-	-	-	1	1	-	-
29 Tom Huddlestone	1st	-/-/-/-	-/-/-/-	-	-	-	-	2	-
	2nd	-/-/-/-	-/-/-/-	-	3	-	-	1	-
9 Manuel Manel	1st	-/-/-/-	-/-/-/-	1	-	2	-	-	-
▼ 46	2nd	-/-/-/-	-/-/-/-	-	-	-	-	-	-

Subs not used: Camp, Bolder, McLeod. - Formation: 4-4-2

Goalkeeper Stats: Marcus Hahnemann Saves: Tip Over 1, Catch 1, Round Post 2, Crosses: Catch 5, Punch 1

	Player Stats	Shots on target	Shots off target	Caught offside	Fouls conceded	Free-kicks won	Corners taken	Clearances	Defensive blocks
11	Andy Hughes ■ 82	-/1/-/-	-/-/-/-	-	1	1	-	-	-
4	Kevin Watson ▼ 70	-/-/-/-	-/-/-/-	-	1	-	1	-	-
14	Steven Sidwell	-/2/-/-	-/-/-/-	-	2	1	-	-	-
9	Shaun Goater	1/1/1/-	-/1/-/-	1	-	1	-	1	-
2	Graeme Murty	-/-/-/-	-/-/-/-	-	1	-	-	4	-
17	John Salako	-/-/-/-	-/-/-/-	-	3	-	-	-	-
15	James Harper ▲ 70	-/-/-/-	-/-/-/-	-	-	-	-	-	-
3	Nicholas Shorey	-/-/-/-	1/-/-/-	-	1	1	2	-	-
5	Steve Brown	-/-/-/-	-/-/-/-	-	3	2	-	3	-
31	Lloyd Owusu	-/-/-/-	-/-/2/-	2	1	5	-	1	-
8	Adrian Williams	-/-/-/-	-/-/-/-	-	-	-	-	-	-

Subs not used: Kitson, Ingimarsson, Young, Morgan. - Formation: 4-4-2

Derby Played: 29 Won 7 Drawn 9 Lost 13 For 31 Against 47 Pos 21

...January Team Stats.....Team Stats......Team Stats......Team S

League table at the end of January

		HOME					AWAY					Pts	Df
	P	W	D	L	F	A	W	D	L	F	A		
Norwich	29	12	1	2	26	11	4	7	3	20	15	56	20
West Brom	29	8	5	2	22	11	7	4	3	20	13	54	18
Sheff Utd	29	8	4	2	27	13	6	3	6	18	20	49	12
Sunderland	28	8	5	1	18	7	5	3	6	18	17	47	12
Ipswich	29	8	2	4	33	22	5	6	4	21	22	47	10
Wigan	29	7	6	2	18	10	5	5	4	21	20	47	9
West Ham	29	6	5	4	24	17	5	7	2	17	12	45	12
Reading	29	8	3	4	21	18	5	3	6	14	17	45	0
Preston	28	8	3	3	28	17	4	4	6	15	18	43	8
Millwall	29	7	5	2	16	8	4	5	6	17	20	43	5
Cardiff	29	6	5	4	27	16	5	4	5	19	21	42	9
Stoke	29	7	5	3	24	17	5	1	8	15	20	42	2
Crystal Palace	30	4	6	5	18	19	7	2	6	24	24	41	-1
Crewe	29	9	2	4	24	15	2	4	8	14	25	39	-2
Coventry	29	4	8	3	16	15	4	5	5	21	19	37	3
Gillingham	28	7	1	7	17	20	3	5	5	16	22	36	-9
Walsall	29	6	5	3	21	18	3	3	9	10	20	35	-7
Rotherham	29	5	5	4	16	16	3	5	7	15	25	34	-10
Burnley	29	5	4	5	21	18	2	6	7	17	30	31	-10
Watford	29	4	6	4	16	19	3	3	9	14	23	30	-12
Derby	29	5	3	6	20	24	2	6	7	11	23	30	-16
Nottm Forest	28	4	4	5	19	15	3	4	8	15	22	29	-3
Bradford	30	3	2	10	13	24	3	3	9	9	19	23	-21
Wimbledon	29	2	3	9	14	25	3	0	12	14	32	18	-29

January matches table

	P	W	D	L	F	A	Pts
Crystal Palace	4	3	1	0	10	3	10
Stoke	3	3	0	0	6	3	9
West Brom	3	2	1	0	6	2	7
Reading	3	2	1	0	5	2	7
Millwall	3	2	1	0	4	2	7
Cardiff	3	2	1	0	4	2	7
Derby	4	2	0	2	6	6	6
Ipswich	3	1	2	0	8	6	5
Coventry	3	1	2	0	7	2	5
Wigan	3	1	2	0	4	2	5
West Ham	3	1	1	1	6	4	4
Sheff Utd	4	1	1	2	6	6	4
Norwich	3	1	1	1	5	5	4
Crewe	3	1	0	2	6	8	3
Preston	2	1	0	1	4	5	3
Sunderland	2	1	0	1	2	2	3
Bradford	4	1	0	3	2	4	3
Gillingham	3	1	0	2	2	5	3
Burnley	3	0	3	0	1	1	3
Rotherham	3	0	1	2	7	9	1
Watford	3	0	1	2	2	8	1
Nottm Forest	3	0	1	2	0	2	1
Walsall	3	0	0	3	3	11	0
Wimbledon	3	0	0	3	1	5	0

January team stats details

Club Name	Ply	Shots On	Shots Off	Corners	Hit W'work	Caught Offside	Offside Trap	Fouls	Yellow Cards	Red Cards	Pens Awarded	Pens Con
Bradford	4	25	25	27	0	6	10	58	9	1	- (-)	-
Burnley	3	15	6	13	0	7	10	38	7	0	- (-)	-
Cardiff	3	14	23	11	0	13	4	29	4	1	1 (-)	1
Coventry	3	24	20	28	2	12	12	32	4	0	1 (-)	1
Crewe	3	19	18	7	1	19	10	21	1	0	- (-)	-
Crystal Palace	4	41	13	22	0	11	11	47	3	0	1 (1)	2
Derby	4	32	24	22	2	9	19	53	6	0	- (-)	-
Gillingham	3	22	14	18	1	14	5	44	6	2	- (-)	-
Ipswich	3	22	22	16	0	12	10	32	3	0	- (-)	-
Millwall	3	21	13	25	0	9	4	43	5	0	- (-)	-
Norwich	3	20	20	21	1	8	5	41	2	0	1 (1)	1
Nottm Forest	3	14	13	14	1	9	10	40	4	0	- (-)	-
Preston	2	13	7	17	2	11	2	23	6	0	1 (1)	-
Reading	3	15	13	12	0	6	8	30	1	0	- (-)	-
Rotherham	3	14	8	13	0	4	6	40	6	1	- (-)	-
Sheff Utd	4	17	23	22	1	10	13	45	2	0	1 (-)	-
Stoke	3	27	21	20	1	12	5	37	7	1	- (-)	-
Sunderland	2	10	8	10	0	4	9	22	3	0	- (-)	-
Walsall	3	16	14	11	1	3	5	36	4	1	- (-)	-
Watford	3	16	13	14	1	6	10	33	2	2	1 (1)	-
West Brom	3	16	15	16	1	14	1	42	3	1	- (-)	-
West Ham	3	19	16	17	1	9	11	34	2	0	- (-)	1
Wigan	3	20	22	22	1	4	15	36	4	0	- (-)	1
Wimbledon	3	22	22	14	0	5	22	39	5	0	- (-)	-

...January Player Stats..... Player Stats...... Player Stats......Pla

Monthly Top scorers

Paul Peschisolido (Derby)	4
Daniele Dichio (Millwall)	4
Geoff Horsfield (West Brom)	4
Andrew Johnson (Crystal Palace)	4
Martin Butler (Rotherham)	3
Shefki Kuqi (Ipswich)	2
Iwan Roberts (Norwich)	2
Carl Asaba (Stoke)	2
Nathan Ellington (Wigan)	2
Andrew Morrell (Coventry)	2

Penalties scored

1 Heidar Helguson (Watford), Graham Alexander (Preston), Darren Huckerby (Norwich), Andrew Johnson (Crystal P)

Assists

Matthew Etherington (West Ham)	3
Gary Teale (Wigan)	3
Peter Sweeney (Millwall)	2
Peter Thorne (Cardiff)	2
Gifton Noel-Williams (Stoke)	2
Michael Hughes (Crystal Palace)	2
Graham Alexander (Preston)	2

Quickest goals

0:40 mins - Jason Roberts (Preston vs Wigan)

0:59 mins - Lee Morris (Stoke vs Derby)

1:50 mins - Shaun Goater (Reading vs Derby)

2:36 mins - Stewart Talbot (Cardiff vs Rotherham)

2:51 mins - Tommy Miller (Ipswich vs Crewe)

Top Keeper

	Mins	Gls
Brian Jensen (Burnley)	286	1
Ed de Goey (Stoke)	194	1
Tony Warner (Millwall)	191	1
M Hahnemann (Reading)	292	2
Martyn Margetson (Cardiff)	289	2
Russell Hoult (West Brom)	287	2
Thomas Myhre (Crystal P)	286	2
Darren Ward (Nottm F)	286	2

Shots on target

Andrew Johnson (Crystal Palace)	11
Joel McAnuff (West Ham)	9
Daniele Dichio (Millwall)	8
Robert Blake (Burnley)	8
Andy Gray (Sheff Utd)	7
Geoff Horsfield (West Brom)	7
Gifton Noel-Williams (Stoke)	6
Julian Gray (Crystal Palace)	6
Manuel Manel (Derby)	6
Darel Russell (Stoke)	6

Shots off target

Peter Thorne (Cardiff)	9
Nathan Ellington (Wigan)	7
Wayne Allison (Sheff Utd)	7
Joel McAnuff (West Ham)	7
Robert Earnshaw (Cardiff)	6
Darren Wrack (Walsall)	6
Leon McKenzie (Norwich)	6
Nigel Reo-Coker (West Ham)	6
Shefki Kuqi (Ipswich)	6
Kris Commons (Stoke)	5

Caught offside

Patrick Agyemang (Gillingham)	9
Steve Jones (Crewe)	9
Robert Earnshaw (Cardiff)	8
David Connolly (West Ham)	8
Geoff Horsfield (West Brom)	7
Ade Akinbiyi (Stoke)	7
Andrew Johnson (Crystal Palace)	6
Julian Joachim (Coventry)	6
Dean Ashton (Crewe)	5

Free-kicks won

Wayne Allison (Sheff Utd)	15
Darren Huckerby (Norwich)	12
Geoff Horsfield (West Brom)	11
Andrew Johnson (Crystal Palace)	11
Gerry Taggart (Stoke)	10
Ricardo Fuller (Preston)	10
Paul Devlin (Watford)	10
Dennis Wise (Millwall)	10
Candido Costa (Derby)	10

Derby v Gillingham

Fouls conceded

Tony Grant (Burnley)	12
Geoff Horsfield (West Brom)	10
Gareth Taylor (Nottm Forest)	10
Michael Johnson (Derby)	9
Matthew Lawrence (Millwall)	8
Tom Huddlestone (Derby)	8
Ian Breckin (Wigan)	8
Gifton Noel-Williams (Stoke)	8
Malky Mackay (Norwich)	8

Fouls without a card

Gareth Taylor (Nottm Forest)	10
Tom Huddlestone (Derby)	8
Ian Breckin (Wigan)	8
Malky Mackay (Norwich)	8
Michael Tonge (Sheff Utd)	8
David Connolly (West Ham)	7
Christian Dailly (West Ham)	7
Wayne Routledge (Crystal Palace)	6
Danny Spiller (Gillingham)	6

Marco Reich made a great impression in this game. He brushed the post with a free-kick and later went off to a standing ovation.

Loan signing Leon Osman heads towards gaol. But it was Marcus Tudgay and substitute Izale McLeod who scored the vital winners in a great victory against promotion chasing Sheffield United.

Gillingham Defender Nyron Nosworthy shields the ball from Manel. Goals from Vincent and Edwards sealed a 2-1 victory for County.

Reading goalkeeper Marcus Hahnemann takes the ball away from Tom Huddlestone.
The 3-1 defeat saw Derby slump back into relegation trouble.

DERBY [0] 2 Cardiff [0] 2

In some eyes, the 2-2 draw against Cardiff City was viewed as a missed opportunity. But when Leon Osman ghosted in at the back post to bury a last-minute headed equaliser, the explosion of joy and relief suggested this was very much a point gained.

Skipper Ian Taylor celebrated his return from suspension by putting Derby ahead three minutes after the break. He moved to the near post to meet Candido Costa's corner and plant a firm header high into the net for his eighth goal of the season.

But the fear factor seemed to creep in. Derby became edgy and wasteful in possession and the team shape was often ragged in the second half. Cardiff took advantage with two goals around the hour mark.

First, Robert Earnshaw poked the ball high past Lee Grant from what looked an offside position. Two minutes later it was 2-1. Michael Johnson headed clear and then went to block Graham Kavanagh's shot from 20 yards but the ball deflected off him and looped into the top corner.

Earnshaw shot wide when well placed and just failed to turn in Peter Thorne's cross, then substitute Alan Lee was denied by Grant's fine stop as the visitors pushed for as third.

Grant kept out efforts from the lively Paul Parry and Earnshaw and Thorne saw his diving header blocked close to the line by Rob Edwards after Tom Huddlestone had given away a needless free kick.

The blustery conditions did not help, but the Rams looked comfortable when they got the ball down. Osman was again a key figure, looking dangerous operating from midfield where he can influence the game more with his bright, inventive thinking and late runs into the box.

And with 90 minutes on the clock, substitute Richard Jackson wandered into space on the right. His first cross was not so good, his second inch-perfect for Osman to give Martyn Margetson no chance.

Result.......Result.......Result.

DERBY ....(0) 2   **CARDIFF** ....(0) 2
Taylor 49   Earnshaw 60
Osman 90   Kavanagh 62

Att 20,958
Referee: M Pike

Stats......Stats.......Stats......Stats

DERBY						CARDIFF
1st	2nd	Total		Total	2nd	1st
3	3	6	Corners	7	4	3
3	3	6	Fouls	4	2	2
0	0	0	Yellow cards	2	1	1
0	0	0	Red cards	0	0	0
2	0	2	Caught Offside	7	5	2
3	5	8	Shots on target	8	4	4
5	3	8	Shots off target	8	5	3
0	0	0	Hit woodwork	0	0	0
50	50	50%	Possession	50%	50	50

 OUR defenders, for some reason, looked for offside against Rob Earnshaw which is not the way that we defend, and I thought that was poor.

George Burley

 THAT was a dagger to the heart. If we miss out on the play-offs by four or five points we'll look back on this day and rue what happened.

Lennie Lawrence

Other Div 1 Results

Bradford 1 West Ham 2, Burnley 1 Gillingham 0, Ipswich 1 Wigan 3, Millwall 1 Stoke 1, Nottm Forest 0 Coventry 1, Preston 3 West Brom 0, Rotherham 5 Reading 1, Sheff Utd 0 Crystal Palace 3, Walsall 1 Crewe 1, Watford 2 Sunderland 2, Wimbledon 0 Norwich 1

Goalkeeper Stats: Lee Grant
Saves: Catch 1, Parry 1,
Crosses: Catch 2, Parry 1

Derby Player Stats		Shots on target	Shots off target	Caught offside	Fouls conceded	Free-kicks won	Corners taken	Clearances	Defensive blocks
		L/R/H/Oth	L/R/H/Oth						
10 Michael Johnson	1st	-/-/-/-	-/-/-/-	-	-	-	-	1	-
	2nd	-/-/-/-	-/-/-/-	-	-	-	-	1	1
7 Ian Taylor	1st	-/-/1/-	-/-/1/-	-	-	-	-	-	-
	2nd	-/-/1/-	-/-/1/-	-	-	-	-	-	-
16 Youl Mawene	1st	-/-/-/-	-/-/-/-	-	-	-	-	1	2
	2nd	-/-/-/-	-/-/-/-	-	1	-	-	2	-
14 Richard Jackson	1st	-/-/-/-	-/-/-/-	-	-	-	-	-	-
▲ 86	2nd	-/-/-/-	-/-/-/-	-	-	-	-	-	-
18 Izale McLeod	1st	-/-/-/-	-/-/-/-	-	-	-	-	-	-
▲ 75	2nd	1/-/-/-	-/-/-/-	-	1	1	-	-	-
23 Marcus Tudgay	1st	-/-/-/-	-/-/-/-	-	-	-	-	-	-
▲ 83	2nd	-/-/-/-	-/-/-/-	-	-	-	-	-	-
8 Candido Costa	1st	-/-/-/-	-/-/-/-	1	1	-	2	-	-
▼ 75	2nd	-/-/-/-	-/-/-/-	-	-	-	2	-	-
32 Leon Osman	1st	-/-/-/-	-/1/-/-	-	-	-	-	-	-
	2nd	-/-/1/-	-/1/-/-	-	-	1	-	-	-
3 Jamie Vincent	1st	-/-/-/-	-/-/-/-	-	-	-	-	-	1
	2nd	-/-/-/-	-/-/-/-	-	-	-	-	-	1
22 Marco Reich	1st	-/1/-/-	-/1/-/-	-	-	1	1	-	-
	2nd	-/-/-/-	-/1/-/-	-	1	-	1	-	-
34 Noel Whelan	1st	-/-/-/-	-/1/-/-	1	1	-	-	-	-
▼ 83	2nd	-/1/-/-	-/-/-/-	-	-	-	-	-	-
2 Rob Edwards	1st	-/-/-/-	-/-/-/-	-	-	-	-	-	-
▼ 86	2nd	1/-/-/-	-/-/-/-	-	-	-	-	-	-
29 Tom Huddlestone	1st	-/1/-/-	-/1/-/-	-	1	1	-	2	-
	2nd	-/-/-/-	-/-/-/-	-	-	-	-	1	1

Subs not used: Camp, Bolder. - Formation: 4-4-2

Goalkeeper Stats: Martyn Margetson Saves: Catch 2

	Player Stats	Shots on target	Shots off target	Caught offside	Fouls conceded	Free-kicks won	Corners taken	Clearances	Defensive blocks
3	Chris Barker	-/-/-/-	-/-/-/-	-	1	1	-	2	-
19	Paul Parry	1/-/-/-	1/-/-/-	-	-	-	-	-	-
11	Peter Thorne ▼ 81 ■ 54	-/-/1/-	-/1/-/-	-	-	1	-	-	-
8	Graham Kavanagh ■ 1	-/1/-/-	-/1/-/-	-	1	-	7	1	-
24	Alan Lee ▲ 81	-/2/-/-	-/1/-/-	-	-	1	-	-	-
6	Daniel Gabbidon	-/-/-/-	-/-/1/-	-	-	-	-	6	1
2	Rhys Weston	-/-/-/-	-/-/-/-	-	-	1	-	2	1
12	Willie Boland	-/-/-/-	-/1/-/-	-	1	1	-	-	-
10	Robert Earnshaw ▼ 81	1/2/-/-	-/1/-/-	5	-	-	-	-	-
25	Richard Langley	-/-/-/-	-/1/-/-	-	1	1	-	-	-
9	Andy Campbell ▲ 81	-/-/-/-	-/-/-/-	2	-	-	-	-	-
21	Tony Vidmar	-/-/-/-	-/-/-/-	-	-	-	-	3	3

Subs not used: Alexander, Whalley, Prior. - Formation: 4-4-2

Wigan [1] 2 DERBY [0] 0

A meagre four points from 33 two in the last 11 League games on the road meant Derby's away fans had precious little hope for this game.

So there was nothing too surprising about the outcome of the club's first visit to Wigan Athletic's JJB Stadium. Goals from Nathan Ellington and substitute Lee McCulloch gave Wigan a 2-0 victory to keep their Premiership dreams alive.

Meanwhile, the threat of relegation still loomed large over the Rams. Reshaped and more resolute, they were never out of the game but neither were they convincing enough to emerge with a point or three.

It might have been so different had Noel Whelan and Izale McLeod accepted gilt-edged chances. Whelan's arrived on 14 minutes but his firmly-struck shot from 10 yards was brilliantly tipped over by John Filan. And McLeod had a clear sight of an equaliser after 67 minutes but his finish lacked conviction, allowing Filan to save again.

Burley's team deserved credit for running one of the division's top sides close but it was not enough. Grant did very well to keep out Ellington's effort before the home side went ahead on the stroke of half time.

Roberts went down over Grant and strong appeals for a penalty were still in the air when Mahon collected the ball on the left. He delivered a delicious cross and Ellington stole between the central defenders to plant a header past Grant.

Wigan wrapped up the points with a second 11 minutes from time.

Nicky Eaden crossed, Ellington headed up into the air and McCulloch hooked the dropping ball into the net. Burley insisted that there was a clear foul on his goalkeeper but McCulloch, sandwiched between Youl Mawene and Grant, did not appear to do much more than stand his ground.

Result.......Result.......Result.

WIGAN ....(1) 2   DERBY ....(0) 0
Ellington 45
McCulloch 78

Att 9,146
Referee: P Joslin

Stats......Stats.......Stats......Stats

WIGAN						DERBY
1st	2nd	Total		Total	2nd	1st
0	5	5	Corners	7	4	3
11	4	15	Fouls	11	6	5
0	0	0	Yellow cards	2	2	0
0	0	0	Red cards	0	0	0
1	1	2	Caught Offside	5	2	3
2	1	3	Shots on target	1	1	0
5	2	7	Shots off target	5	2	3
0	0	0	Hit woodwork	0	0	0
43	50	47%	Possession	53%	50	57

 AFTER last week's performance at Ipswich, a lot of people said a lot of nice things about us. But we had to make sure we carried on in that vein.

Paul Jewell

 I knew Wigan were an outstanding side - but we came here with a plan and we're very disappointed not to take something from the game.

George Burley

Other Div 1 Results

Coventry 0 Norwich 2, Crystal Palace 6 Stoke 3, Ipswich 3 Bradford 1, Millwall P Rotherham P, Nottm Forest 3 Walsall 3, Watford 2 Preston 0, West Brom 2 Cardiff 1

Wigan [1] 2 DERBY [0] 0

Goalkeeper Stats: Lee Grant Saves: Catch 1, Crosses: Catch 3

Derby Player Stats

Player		Shots on target L/R/H/Oth	Shots off target L/R/H/Oth	Caught offside	Fouls conceded	Free-kicks won	Corners taken	Clearances	Defensive blocks
10 Michael Johnson	1st	-/-/-/	-/-/-/	-	1	-	-	2	-
	2nd	-/-/-	-/-/-	-	-	-	-	1	-
7 Ian Taylor	1st	-/-/-	-/1/-/-	1	-	1	-	-	-
	2nd	-/-/-	-/-/-	-	1	-	-	-	-
14 Richard Jackson	1st	-/-/-	-/-/-	-	-	-	-	-	-
	2nd	-/-/-	-/-/-	-	-	-	1	-	-
16 Youl Mawene	1st	-/-/-	-/-/-	-	-	1	-	1	-
	2nd	-/-/-	-/-/-	-	-	-	-	-	-
18 Izale McLeod	1st	-/-/-	-/-/-	-	-	1	-	-	-
	2nd	-/1/-/-	-/-/-	2	-	1	-	-	-
32 Leon Osman	1st	-/-/-	-/-/-	1	-	5	1	-	-
	2nd	-/-/-	-/-/-	-	1	1	2	-	-
3 Jamie Vincent ▼ 77 ■ 62	1st	-/-/-	-/-/-	-	-	-	2	1	-
	2nd	-/-/-	-/-/-	-	1	1	-	-	-
34 Noel Whelan ▼ 63	1st	-/-/-	-/1/-/-	1	3	-	-	-	-
	2nd	-/-/-	-/-/-	-	1	-	-	-	-
22 Marco Reich ▲ 63	1st	-/-/-	-/-/-	-	-	-	-	-	-
	2nd	-/-/-	-/-/-	-	-	-	1	-	-
2 Rob Edwards	1st	-/-/-	-/-/-	-	-	1	-	1	-
	2nd	-/-/-	-/-/1/-	-	1	-	-	1	-
9 Manuel Manel ▲ 77	1st	-/-/-	-/-/-	-	-	-	-	-	-
	2nd	-/-/-	1/-/-/-	-	1	1	-	-	-
29 Tom Huddlestone ■ 89	1st	-/-/-	-/1/-/-	-	1	1	-	1	-
	2nd	-/-/-	-/-/-	-	-	-	-	1	-

Subs not used: Camp, Bolder, Tudgay. - Formation: 3-5-2

Goalkeeper Stats: John Filan Saves: Catch 2, Crosses: Catch 3

Player Stats

	Player	Shots on target	Shots off target	Caught offside	Fouls conceded	Free-kicks won	Corners taken	Clearances	Defensive blocks
10	Lee McCulloch ▲ 73	-/1/-/-	-/-/-	-	-	-	-	-	-
6	Ian Breckin	-/-/-	-/-/-	-	2	2	-	-	1
7	Andy Liddell ▲ 86	-/-/-	-/-/-	-	-	-	-	-	-
9	Nathan Ellington ▼ 86	1/-/1/-	-/2/-/-	2	4	-	-	-	-
18	Jason Jarrett ▼ 90	-/-/-	-/1/-/-	-	3	1	-	-	-
12	Michael Flynn ▲ 90	-/-/-	-/-/-	-	-	-	-	-	-
19	Nicky Eaden	-/-/-	-/-/-	-	1	-	-	-	-
26	Leighton Baines	-/-/-	-/-/-	-	-	-	-	1	-
30	Jason Roberts ▼ 73	-/-/-	-/-/-	-	1	1	-	-	-
5	Jason De Vos	-/-/-	-/-/-	-	1	2	-	1	-
21	Jimmy Bullard	-/-/-	-/-/-	-	2	2	4	-	-
20	Gary Teale	-/-/-	-/2/-/-	-	1	1	-	-	1
14	Alan Mahon	-/-/-	2/-/-/-	-	-	2	1	-	-

Subs not used: Walsh, Jackson. - Formation: 4-4-2

DERBY [0] 2 Crystal Palace [1] 1

A last throw of the dice by manager George Burley brought a victory and three precious points for Derby County when neither had looked likely.

Burley used his final substitution by calling for Manel and the Spanish striker answered the call by putting his struggles behind him to head an equaliser, his first senior goal for the Rams. Then Leon Osman, by far the most impressive of the many loan signings this season, completed the comeback by driving home the winner.

The 2-1 win over in-form Palace stretched the gap between Burley's team and the drop zone to three points. His decision to start with Izale McLeod as a lone striker raised just as many eyebrows.

Derby were poor for much of the first half, seemingly hoping that an individual like Reich or Osman would produce a decisive moment. And Palace went ahead after 16 minutes when a seemingly harmless punt downfield by Cedric Berthelin was flicked on by Neil Shipperley Michael Hughes. His run from midfield was not tracked and he expertly lobbed Lee Grant from the edge of the area.

But if Grant was partly at fault for Hughes' strike, he made amends with two saves to keep his side in the contest. He brilliantly tipped away an effort from Freedman and then plunged low to his right to push the ball out after Julian Gray's cross had taken a wicked deflection off Rob Edwards.

When Andy Johnson limped off after half an hour, much of Palace's sharpness and menace went with him.

Palace failed to deal with an Edwards long throw, Whelan flicked it on and Manel did well to stretch and steer his header wide of Berthelin from six yards. The tide had turned and the Rams went ahead a minute later.

Palace defender Tony Popovic passed across his own area and the ball fell to Osman and his low shot beat Berthelin.

Result.......Result.......Result.

DERBY ....(0) 2 **CRYSTAL PAL(1) 1**
Manel 70 — Hughes 16
Osman 76

Att 21,856
Referee: C Boyeson

Stats......Stats.......Stats......Stats

DERBY				CRYSTAL PALACE		
1st	2nd	Total		Total	2nd	1st
5	2	7	Corners	3	2	1
6	8	14	Fouls	14	6	8
1	1	2	Yellow cards	3	3	0
0	0	0	Red cards	0	0	0
0	2	2	Caught Offside	6	3	3
8	6	14	Shots on target	4	0	4
4	4	8	Shots off target	0	0	0
0	0	0	Hit woodwork	0	0	0
35	49	52%	Possession	48%	51	65

"I liked Leon the first time I saw him play for Everton reserves. He can play anywhere, he can create and he can score goals. He was outstanding."

George Burley

"**THIS** was probably the worst we've played in my nine games as manager. There's no point throwing the baby out with the bath water, though, this was a blip."

Iain Dowie

Other Div 1 Results

Bradford 2 Crewe 1, Burnley 4 Ipswich 2, Cardiff 4 Sunderland 0, Gillingham 0 Reading 1, Norwich 1 West Ham 1, Preston 1 Millwall 2, Rotherham 1 Nottm Forest 1, Sheff Utd 1 West Brom 2, Stoke 1 Wigan 1, Walsall 0 Watford 1, Wimbledon 0 Coventry 3

DERBY [0] 2 Crystal Palace [1] 1

Goalkeeper Stats: Lee Grant Saves: Catch 1, Parry 1

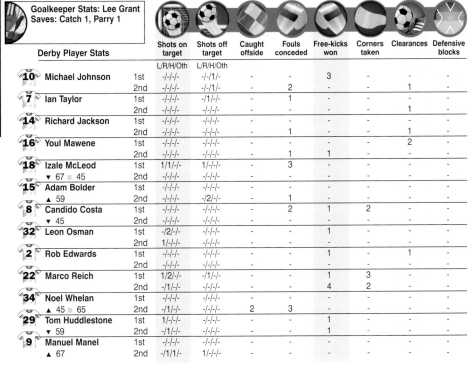

Derby Player Stats		Shots on target L/R/H/Oth	Shots off target L/R/H/Oth	Caught offside	Fouls conceded	Free-kicks won	Corners taken	Clearances	Defensive blocks
10 Michael Johnson	1st	-/-/-/-	-/-/1/-	-	-	3	-	-	-
	2nd	-/-/-/-	-/-/1/-	-	2	-	-	1	-
7 Ian Taylor	1st	-/-/-/-	-/1/-/-	-	1	-	-	-	-
	2nd	-/-/-/-	-/-/-/-	-	-	-	-	1	-
14 Richard Jackson	1st	-/-/-/-	-/-/-/-	-	-	-	-	-	-
	2nd	-/-/-/-	-/-/-/-	-	1	-	-	1	-
16 Youl Mawene	1st	-/-/-/-	-/-/-/-	-	-	-	-	2	-
	2nd	-/-/-/-	-/-/-/-	-	1	1	-	-	-
18 Izale McLeod ▼ 67 ■ 45	1st	1/1/-/-	1/-/-/-	-	3	-	-	-	-
	2nd	-/-/-/-	-/-/-/-	-	-	-	-	-	-
15 Adam Bolder ▲ 59	1st	-/-/-/-	-/-/-/-	-	-	-	-	-	-
	2nd	-/-/-/-	-/2/-/-	-	1	-	-	-	-
8 Candido Costa ▼ 45	1st	-/-/-/-	-/-/-/-	-	2	1	2	-	-
	2nd	-/-/-/-	-/-/-/-	-	-	-	-	-	-
32 Leon Osman	1st	-/2/-/-	-/-/-/-	-	-	1	-	-	-
	2nd	1/-/-/-	-/-/-/-	-	-	-	-	-	-
2 Rob Edwards	1st	-/-/-/-	-/-/-/-	-	-	1	-	1	-
	2nd	-/-/-/-	-/-/-/-	-	-	-	-	-	-
22 Marco Reich	1st	1/2/-/-	-/1/-/-	-	-	1	3	-	-
	2nd	-/1/-/-	-/-/-/-	-	-	4	2	-	-
34 Noel Whelan ▲ 45 ■ 65	1st	-/-/-/-	-/-/-/-	-	-	-	-	-	-
	2nd	-/1/-/-	-/-/-/-	2	3	-	-	-	-
29 Tom Huddlestone ▼ 59	1st	1/-/-/-	-/-/-/-	-	-	1	-	-	-
	2nd	-/1/-/-	-/-/-/-	-	-	1	-	-	-
9 Manuel Manel ▲ 67	1st	-/-/-/-	-/-/-/-	-	-	-	-	-	-
	2nd	-/1/1/-	1/-/-/-	-	-	-	-	-	-

Subs not used: Camp, Mills. - Formation: 4-4-2

Goalkeeper Stats: Cedric Berthelin Saves: Catch 5, Round Post 1, Crosses: Catch 1, Punch 2

	Player Stats	Shots on target	Shots off target	Caught offside	Fouls conceded	Free-kicks won	Corners taken	Clearances	Defensive blocks
8	Andrew Johnson ▼ 29	-/-/-/-	-/-/-/-	-	-	-	-	-	-
16	Tommy Black ▲ 80	-/-/-/-	-/-/-/-	-	-	-	1	-	-
4	Danny Butterfield	-/-/-/-	-/-/-/-	-	1	1	-	2	-
10	Shaun Derry ▲ 60	-/-/-/-	-/-/-/-	-	1	-	1	-	-
21	Julian Gray	-/-/-/-	-/-/-/-	1	2	2	-	-	1
17	Michael Hughes	1/-/-/-	-/-/-/-	1	1	1	1	-	-
6	Tony Popovic	-/-/-/-	-/-/-/-	2	-	-	-	6	-
20	Mark Hudson	-/-/-/-	-/-/-/-	-	1	1	-	2	2
15	Aki Riihilahti ▼ 60 ■ 59	-/-/-/-	-/-/-/-	-	2	2	-	-	-
11	Neil Shipperley ■ 71	-/-/1/-	-/-/-/-	1	5	3	-	-	-
3	Danny Granville ■ 79	-/-/-/-	-/-/-/-	-	1	2	-	1	-
9	Dougie Freedman ▲ 29	1/-/-/-	-/-/-/-	1	-	-	-	-	-
22	Wayne Routledge ▼ 80	-/1/-/-	-/-/-/-	-	-	2	-	-	-

Subs not used: Borrowdale, Leigertwood. - Formation: 4-4-2

Derby Played: 32 Won 8 Drawn 10 Lost 14 For 35 Against 52 Pos 21

Coventry [2] 2 DERBY [0] 0

Derby County manager George Burley had asked for back-to-back wins to help ease relegation fears but his calls clearly fell on deaf ears.

This was another disappointing result brought on by more woeful defending. That, coupled with Nottingham Forest's late winner against Bradford City, was enough to plunge Derby back into the unwelcoming waters of the Division One relegation zone. Five months and a dozen fixtures had now passed since they last won an away League match. Only four points from a possible 36 had been taken during that time.

Coventry's goals were both caused by set-pieces. Martin Grainger hoisted a harmless 20th-minute free-kick into the area, Calum Davenport faced little opposition in heading down and the unmarked Stephen Warnock saw his shot brilliantly parried by Lee Grant.

But the ball fell back to Warnock, who picked out Gary McSheffrey to sweep a shot home from a handful of yards. The second arrived 13 minutes later and was annoyingly similar.

This time, Warnock escaped his marker at Bjarni Gudjonsson's corner and headed down for the unattended Julian Joachim, who hooked the ball home from close range.

Problems seemed to exist in all departments of Derby's team. There was a lack of balance and goals up front, a midfield that possessed ability but found it difficult to stop the opposition playing and a defence with a tendency to look flimsy when put under pressure, particularly at set-pieces.

Derby actually enjoyed good spells in the game but failed to score. Scott Shearer made a fine save from Noel Whelan's shot after only four minutes and Leon Osman headed just over.

Even after Joachim put his side two up, Derby still finished the half strongly. Shearer moved sharply to save Osman's header and then Manel was close on three occasions.

Had Coventry possessed more quality, they would have added further goals on the break. It was their first home win in five League games and only the second time they had recorded back-to-back wins this season.

Result.......Result.......Result.

COVENTRY..........(2) 2   DERBY ....(0) 0
McSheffrey 20
Joachim 33

Att 16,042
Referee: I Williamson

Stats......Stats.......Stats......Stats

COVENTRY				DERBY		
1st	2nd	Total		Total	2nd	1st
2	3	5	Corners	6	2	4
13	6	19	Fouls	10	3	7
2	0	2	Yellow cards	2	0	2
0	0	0	Red cards	1	1	0
2	6	8	Caught Offside	5	3	2
9	2	11	Shots on target	10	2	8
0	5	5	Shots off target	0	0	0
0	0	0	Hit woodwork	0	0	0
29	44	46%	Possession	54%	56	71

I didn't see the incident for the sending off but I know Peter Clarke isn't the type of player who would go down for nothing.
Eric Black

MANEL says he didn't touch the boy so now I'm going to look at the video and if there's a case we will appeal.
George Burley

Other Div 1 Results

Crewe P Stoke P, Crystal Palace 1 Gillingham 0, Ipswich 2 Preston 0, Millwall 2 Burnley 0, Nottm Forest 2 Bradford 1, Reading 2 Sheff Utd 1, Sunderland P Norwich P, Watford 4 Wimbledon 0, West Brom 0 Rotherham 1, West Ham 1 Cardiff 0, Wigan 1 Walsall 0

Coventry [2] 2 DERBY [0] 0

Goalkeeper Stats: Lee Grant Saves: Catch 2, Parry 1, Crosses: Catch 2

Derby Player Stats		Shots on target	Shots off target	Caught offside	Fouls conceded	Free-kicks won	Corners taken	Clearances	Defensive blocks
		L/R/H/Oth	L/R/H/Oth						
10 Michael Johnson	1st	-/1/-/-	-/-/-/-	-	1	1	-	1	-
	2nd	-/-/-/-	-/-/-/-	-	-	-	-	3	-
7 Ian Taylor ■ 4	1st	-/1/-/-	-/-/-/-	-	1	-	-	-	-
	2nd	-/-/-/-	-/-/-/-	-	-	1	-	-	-
14 Richard Jackson	1st	-/-/-/-	-/-/-/-	-	1	-	-	-	-
	2nd	-/-/-/-	-/-/-/-	-	-	-	-	-	-
16 Youl Mawene	1st	-/-/-/-	-/-/-/-	-	2	1	-	2	-
	2nd	-/-/-/-	-/-/-/-	-	-	-	-	1	-
23 Marcus Tudgay ▲ 79	1st	-/-/-/-	-/-/-/-	-	-	-	-	-	-
	2nd	-/-/-/-	-/-/-/-	-	-	-	-	-	-
18 Izale McLeod ▲ 80	1st	-/-/-/-	-/-/-/-	-	-	-	-	-	-
	2nd	-/-/-/-	-/-/-/-	-	-	-	-	-	-
15 Adam Bolder	1st	-/-/-/-	-/-/-/-	-	-	2	-	-	-
	2nd	-/-/1/-	-/-/-/-	-	-	-	-	1	-
32 Leon Osman	1st	-/-/1/-	-/-/-/-	-	-	-	1	-	-
	2nd	-/-/-/-	-/-/-/-	-	1	3	1	-	-
22 Marco Reich ▼ 79 ■ 24	1st	-/1/-/-	-/-/-/-	-	1	1	3	-	-
	2nd	-/1/-/-	-/-/-/-	-	-	1	-	-	-
2 Rob Edwards ▼ 45	1st	-/-/-/-	-/-/-/-	-	1	1	-	-	-
	2nd	-/-/-/-	-/-/-/-	-	-	-	-	-	-
34 Noel Whelan ▼ 80	1st	-/2/-/-	-/-/-/-	2	-	4	-	-	-
	2nd	-/-/-/-	-/-/-/-	3	1	-	-	1	-
29 Tom Huddlestone ▲ 45	1st	-/-/-/-	-/-/-/-	-	-	-	-	-	-
	2nd	-/-/-/-	-/-/-/-	-	-	-	-	-	-
9 Manuel Manel ■ 60	1st	-/1/1/-	-/-/-/-	-	-	2	-	1	-
	2nd	-/-/-/-	-/-/-/-	-	1	-	-	-	-

Subs not used: Camp, Costa. - Formation: 4-4-2

Goalkeeper Stats: Scott Shearer Saves: Catch 1, Parry 1, Crosses: Catch 3

	Player Stats	Shots on target	Shots off target	Caught offside	Fouls conceded	Free-kicks won	Corners taken	Clearances	Defensive blocks
17	Michael Doyle	2/1/-/-	1/-/-/-	-	1	-	-	1	-
31	Bjarni Gudjonsson ▼ 80 ■ 22	-/-/1/-	-/-/-/-	-	1	3	3	1	-
37	Peter Clarke	-/-/-/-	-/1/-/-	-	4	1	-	-	-
9	Dele Adebola ▲ 80	-/-/-/-	-/1/-/-	2	-	-	-	-	-
6	Youssef Safri	-/-/-/-	1/-/-/-	-	5	1	-	-	-
20	Calum Davenport	-/-/1/-	-/-/-/-	-	2	-	-	5	-
35	Martin Grainger	-/-/-/-	-/-/-/-	-	-	2	-	1	-
22	Eric Deloumeaux ■ 9	-/-/-/-	-/-/-/-	-	1	1	-	1	1
26	Stephen Warnock ▼ 63	-/-/-/-	-/-/-/-	-	-	-	1	-	-
21	Julian Joachim	-/1/1/-	-/1/-/-	2	-	1	-	-	-
19	Gary McSheffrey	3/1/-/-	-/-/-/-	3	4	1	1	-	-
4	Muhamed Konjic ▲ 63	-/-/-/-	-/-/-/-	1	-	-	-	2	-

Subs not used: Ward, Shaw, Barrett. - Formation: 4-4-2

...February Team Stats.....Team Stats......Team Stats......Team S

League table at the end of February

	HOME						AWAY					Pts	Df
	P	W	D	L	F	A	W	D	L	F	A		
Norwich	32	12	2	2	27	12	6	7	3	23	15	63	23
West Brom	33	9	5	3	24	13	8	4	4	22	17	60	16
Wigan	33	9	6	2	21	10	6	6	4	25	22	57	14
Ipswich	33	10	2	5	39	26	5	6	5	23	26	53	10
Millwall	33	9	6	2	21	10	5	5	6	19	21	53	9
West Ham	32	7	5	4	25	17	6	8	2	20	14	52	14
Sheff Utd	33	8	4	4	28	18	7	3	7	20	22	52	8
Reading	33	9	4	4	25	21	6	3	7	16	22	52	-2
Crystal Palace	34	6	6	5	25	22	8	2	7	28	26	50	5
Sunderland	30	8	5	1	18	7	5	4	7	20	23	48	8
Cardiff	33	7	5	4	31	16	5	5	7	22	26	46	11
Coventry	33	5	8	4	18	17	6	5	5	25	19	46	7
Preston	32	9	3	4	32	19	4	4	8	15	22	46	6
Stoke	32	7	6	3	25	18	5	2	9	19	27	44	-1
Rotherham	33	6	6	4	22	18	4	5	8	17	27	41	-6
Crewe	32	9	2	5	24	16	2	5	9	16	28	40	-4
Watford	33	6	7	4	24	21	4	3	9	15	23	40	-5
Burnley	33	7	4	5	26	20	2	7	8	19	34	38	-9
Walsall	33	6	6	4	22	20	3	4	10	13	24	37	-9
Gillingham	32	7	1	8	17	21	3	6	7	16	24	37	-12
Nottm Forest	33	5	6	6	24	20	3	5	8	16	23	35	-3
Derby	33	6	4	6	24	27	2	6	9	11	27	34	-19
Bradford	34	4	2	11	16	27	3	3	11	11	24	26	-24
Wimbledon	32	2	3	11	14	29	3	0	13	14	36	18	-37

February matches table

	P	W	D	L	F	A	Pts
Watford	4	3	1	0	9	2	10
Wigan	4	3	1	0	7	2	10
Millwall	4	3	1	0	7	3	10
Crystal Palace	4	3	0	1	11	5	9
Coventry	4	3	0	1	6	2	9
Rotherham	4	2	1	1	8	4	7
Burnley	4	2	1	1	7	6	7
Reading	4	2	1	1	6	8	7
Norwich	3	2	1	0	4	1	7
West Ham	3	2	1	0	4	2	7
Ipswich	4	2	0	2	8	8	6
Nottm Forest	5	1	3	1	6	6	6
West Brom	4	2	0	2	4	6	6
Cardiff	4	1	1	2	7	5	4
Derby	4	1	1	2	4	7	4
Bradford	4	1	0	3	5	8	3
Preston	4	1	0	3	4	6	3
Sheff Utd	4	1	0	3	3	7	3
Stoke	3	0	2	1	5	8	2
Walsall	4	0	2	2	4	6	2
Crewe	3	0	1	2	2	4	1
Sunderland	2	0	1	1	2	6	1
Gillingham	4	0	1	3	0	3	1
Wimbledon	3	0	0	3	0	8	0

February team stats details

Club Name	Ply	Shots On	Shots Off	Corners	Hit W'work	Caught Offside	Offside Trap	Fouls	Yellow Cards	Red Cards	Pens Awarded	Pens Con
Bradford	4	31	17	25	0	12	18	59	11	1	- (-)	-
Burnley	4	22	13	23	0	8	14	50	7	0	- (-)	-
Cardiff	4	26	20	20	1	17	16	36	5	0	- (-)	-
Coventry	4	33	18	34	0	13	20	63	4	0	- (-)	-
Crewe	3	13	17	17	0	16	5	15	2	0	1 (-)	-
Crystal Palace	4	33	16	22	1	8	5	58	7	1	2 (2)	-
Derby	4	33	21	26	0	14	23	41	6	1	- (-)	-
Gillingham	4	20	14	18	1	6	6	56	4	0	2 (-)	1
Ipswich	4	35	31	29	2	15	21	39	5	0	- (-)	-
Millwall	4	35	17	26	0	10	6	75	8	0	- (-)	-
Norwich	3	20	15	12	2	20	2	40	2	0	- (-)	-
Nottm Forest	5	29	32	42	0	19	12	62	5	1	- (-)	-
Preston	4	26	20	22	0	13	10	45	2	0	1 (1)	-
Reading	4	21	5	16	1	14	12	46	7	0	2 (2)	3
Rotherham	4	23	18	21	0	10	11	54	5	0	2 (2)	1
Sheff Utd	4	28	20	36	1	10	13	55	11	1	- (-)	2
Stoke	3	23	5	15	1	4	3	46	5	0	1 (1)	3
Sunderland	2	9	9	9	1	5	8	19	1	1	- (-)	1
Walsall	4	19	19	25	0	10	14	47	2	0	- (-)	-
Watford	4	24	16	23	1	15	10	58	4	0	2 (2)	-
West Brom	4	33	17	26	0	12	13	54	3	0	- (-)	1
West Ham	3	28	16	26	3	11	14	38	3	1	- (-)	-
Wigan	4	33	29	34	1	10	12	56	2	2	- (-)	-
Wimbledon	3	13	12	14	1	6	10	33	4	3	- (-)	1

FEBRUARY STATS

Monthly Top scorers

Nathan Ellington (Wigan)	4
Dean Windass (Bradford)	3
Tim Cahill (Millwall)	2
Julian Joachim (Coventry)	2
Jorge Leitao (Walsall)	2
Lee Cook (Watford)	2
Bobby Zamora (West Ham)	2
Shefki Kuqi (Ipswich)	2
Marlon Harewood (West Ham)	2
Glen Little (Burnley)	2

Penalties scored

2 Michael Proctor (Rotherham), Shaun Goater (Reading), Neil Cox (Watford), Andrew Johnson (Crystal P)

Assists

Peter Sweeney (Millwall)	4
Darren Bent (Ipswich)	3
Stephen Warnock (Coventry)	2
Chris Sedgwick (Rotherham)	2
Danny Cadamarteri (Bradford)	2
Bobby Zamora (West Ham)	2
Jason Koumas (West Brom)	2

Quickest goals

2:14 mins - Andrew Impey (Nottm Forest vs Walsall)

3:14 mins - Patrick Suffo (Nottm Forest vs Coventry)

3:25 mins - Clive Clarke (Millwall vs Stoke)

4:05 mins - Andrew Johnson (Crystal Palace vs Stoke)

4:24 mins - Lee Cook (Watford vs Wimbledon)

Top Keeper

	Mins	Gls
Robert Green (Norwich)	287	1
Bertrand Bossu (Gillingham)	192	1
Andy Marshall (Millwall)	192	1
John Filan (Wigan)	381	2
Lenny Pidgeley (Watford)	381	2
Scott Shearer (Coventry)	376	2
S Bywater (West Ham)	286	2
Barry Roche (Nottm Forest)	126	1

Shots on target

Tim Cahill (Millwall)	11
Nathan Ellington (Wigan)	9
Bobby Zamora (West Ham)	9
Neil Shipperley (Crystal Palace)	8
Julian Joachim (Coventry)	8
Neil Clement (West Brom)	8
Andrew Johnson (Crystal Palace)	8
Robert Earnshaw (Cardiff)	7
Darren Huckerby (Norwich)	7
Marco Reich (Derby)	7

Shots off target

Chris Sedgwick (Rotherham)	8
Alan Mahon (Wigan)	8
Nathan Ellington (Wigan)	7
Marlon King (Nottm Forest)	6
Julian Gray (Crystal Palace)	6
Ricardo Fuller (Preston)	6
Darren Huckerby (Norwich)	6
Michael Doyle (Coventry)	5
Robert Earnshaw (Cardiff)	5
Danny Sonner (Nottm Forest)	5

Caught offside

Dean Ashton (Crewe)	10
Robert Earnshaw (Cardiff)	9
Darren Huckerby (Norwich)	9
Noel Whelan (Derby)	9
Lee Hughes (West Brom)	7
Lloyd Owusu (Reading)	7
Martin Butler (Rotherham)	6
Marlon King (Nottm Forest)	6
Gary Wales (Gillingham)	6

Free-kicks won

Martin Butler (Rotherham)	13
Geoff Horsfield (West Brom)	13
Ricardo Fuller (Preston)	12
Jason Roberts (Wigan)	12
Marlon King (Nottm Forest)	11
George McCartney (Sunderland)	11
Glen Little (Burnley)	11
Paul Devlin (Watford)	11
Leon Osman (Derby)	11

Derby v Cardiff

Fouls conceded

Robert Page (Sheff Utd)	11
Scott Fitzgerald (Watford)	11
Neil Shipperley (Crystal Palace)	11
Andy Hessenthaler (Gillingham)	10
Glen Little (Burnley)	10
Darren Ward (Millwall)	10
Jason Roberts (Wigan)	10
Adrian Williams (Reading)	10
Ricardo Fuller (Preston)	10

Fouls without a card

Scott Fitzgerald (Watford)	11
Darren Ward (Millwall)	10
Ricardo Fuller (Preston)	10
Thomas Gaardsoe (West Brom)	9
Nathan Ellington (Wigan)	9
James Harper (Reading)	9
Calum Davenport (Coventry)	8
Michael Jackson (Preston)	8
Danny Sonner (Nottm Forest)	8

Izale McLeod sees his shot blocked by a crowd of Wigan players. Derby's 3-0 loss meant that they had gained a meagre four points from a possible 33.

Proof of the victory over Crystal Palace that County fans had been praying for. The win meant that Derby stretched the gap between themselves and the relegation zone to 3 points.

Leon Osman with an attempt on goal. He later grabbed a last-minute equaliser when he ghosted in at the back post to head past Martyn Margetson.

Manel scored Derby's first goal in the long-awaited 2-1 win against Crystal Palace.

DERBY [0] 0 Crewe [0] 0

The character and commitment manager George Burley had asked for was there but sadly for Derby County the finish was not and they remained deep in relegation trouble.

They peppered the visitors' goal from start to finish, having around 26 attempts but had to be content with a goalless draw. Crewe 'keeper Ince stopped everything that was thrown at him, though much of it was from distance When Ince was beaten, the ball was twice hacked off the line and substitute Izale McLeod's late strike thudded against the bar.

The point left the Rams two behind fourth-bottom Gillingham.

Nottingham Forest's back-to-back wins meant that the pressure was on but you would not have guessed it from the Rams' confident start. Marco Reich pulled a shot wide and a Leon Osman drive was arrowing towards the net before a deflection took the ball over.

But what looked set to be Reich's night ended when the German limped off after 15 minutes. A hamstring injury appeared to be the problem and his disappointment was clear to see.

Candido Costa, the replacement, has been itching for a chance in recent weeks and was immediately in the action. His 20-yard drive was turned round the post by Ince, and Derby's urgency and desire was pleasing to see.

But Ince was proving a one-man barrier. He saved from Tudgay but also rode his luck when he failed to collect Huddlestone's ball in and Stephen Foster cleared.

One of Derby's shortcomings had been their failure to score during good spells. They had dominated the first half but had nothing to show for it. The pattern continued at the start of the second half as the Rams searched for a goal.

Belief started to blossom in the Crewe camp as the game became stretched but the Rams kept plugging away. The Rams gave everything they had but it was not quite enough to win.

Result.......Result.......Result.

DERBY ....(0) 0   CREWE ....(0) 0
Att 19,861
Referee: M Clattenburg

Stats......Stats.......Stats......Stats

DERBY				CREWE		
1st	2nd	Total		Total	2nd	1st
7	5	12	Corners	4	2	2
5	5	10	Fouls	12	8	4
0	0	0	Yellow cards	1	1	0
0	0	0	Red cards	0	0	0
3	0	3	Caught Offside	8	7	1
9	6	15	Shots on target	2	2	0
5	11	16	Shots off target	4	1	3
0	1	1	Hit woodwork	0	0	0
49	50	49%	Possession	51%	50	51

> I don't think there has been a more one-sided game at Pride Park for some time. You need a little bit of luck - but we didn't get it.
>
> **George Burley**

> OUR two outstanding players were the goalkeeper and defender Stephen Foster. They were at the heart of our resistance. We had to withstand tremendous pressure.
>
> **Dario Gradi**

Other Div 1 Results

Walsall 1 Sunderland 3

DERBY [0] 0 Crewe [0] 0

Goalkeeper Stats: Lee Grant
Saves: Catch 1, Crosses: Catch 3, Round Post 1

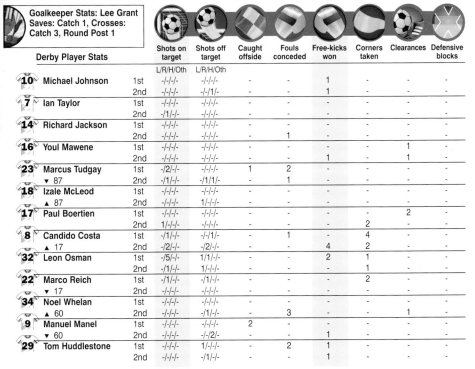

Derby Player Stats		Shots on target L/R/H/Oth	Shots off target L/R/H/Oth	Caught offside	Fouls conceded	Free-kicks won	Corners taken	Clearances	Defensive blocks
10 Michael Johnson	1st	-/-/-/-	-/-/-/-	-	-	1	-	-	-
	2nd	-/-/-/-	-/-/1/-	-	-	1	-	-	-
7 Ian Taylor	1st	-/-/-/-	-/-/-/-	-	-	-	-	-	-
	2nd	-/1/-/-	-/-/-/-	-	-	-	-	-	-
14 Richard Jackson	1st	-/-/-/-	-/-/-/-	-	-	-	-	-	-
	2nd	-/-/-/-	-/-/-/-	-	1	-	-	-	-
16 Youl Mawene	1st	-/-/-/-	-/-/-/-	-	-	-	-	1	-
	2nd	-/-/-/-	-/-/-/-	-	-	1	-	1	-
23 Marcus Tudgay ▼ 87	1st	-/2/-/-	-/-/-/-	1	2	-	-	-	-
	2nd	-/1/-/-	-/1/1/-	-	1	-	-	-	-
18 Izale McLeod ▲ 87	1st	-/-/-/-	-/-/-/-	-	-	-	-	-	-
	2nd	-/-/-/-	1/-/-/-	-	-	-	-	-	-
17 Paul Boertien	1st	-/-/-/-	-/-/-/-	-	-	-	-	2	-
	2nd	1/-/-/-	-/-/-/-	-	-	-	2	-	-
8 Candido Costa ▲ 17	1st	-/1/-/-	-/-/1/-	-	1	-	4	-	-
	2nd	-/2/-/-	-/2/-/-	-	-	4	2	-	-
32 Leon Osman	1st	-/5/-/-	1/1/-/-	-	-	2	1	-	-
	2nd	-/1/-/-	1/-/-/-	-	-	-	1	-	-
22 Marco Reich ▼ 17	1st	-/1/-/-	-/1/-/-	-	-	-	2	-	-
	2nd	-/-/-/-	-/-/-/-	-	-	-	-	-	-
34 Noel Whelan ▲ 60	1st	-/-/-/-	-/-/-/-	-	-	-	-	-	-
	2nd	-/-/-/-	-/1/-/-	-	3	-	-	1	-
9 Manuel Manel ▼ 60	1st	-/-/-/-	-/-/-/-	2	-	-	-	-	-
	2nd	-/-/-/-	-/-/2/-	-	-	1	-	-	-
29 Tom Huddlestone	1st	-/-/-/-	1/-/-/-	-	2	1	-	-	-
	2nd	-/-/-/-	-/1/-/-	-	-	1	-	-	-

Subs not used: Camp, Bolder. - Formation: 4-4-2

Goalkeeper Stats: Clayton Ince Saves: Catch 5, Round Post 1, Crosses: Catch 8, Parry 2, Punch 1

Player Stats		Shots on target	Shots off target	Caught offside	Fouls conceded	Free-kicks won	Corners taken	Clearances	Defensive blocks
4 Kenny Lunt		-/-/-/-	-/-/-/-	-	3	-	1	1	-
19 Justin Cochrane ▲ 67		-/-/-/-	-/-/-/-	-	-	-	-	-	-
14 Ben Rix ▼ 67		-/-/-/-	-/-/-/-	-	-	2	3	-	-
34 Craig Hignett ▼ 87		-/-/-/-	-/-/-/-	-	-	1	-	-	-
6 Stephen Foster		-/-/-/-	-/-/-/-	-	1	3	-	8	-
17 James Robinson ▲ 87		-/-/-/-	-/-/-/-	-	-	-	-	-	-
7 Neil Sorvel		-/-/-/-	-/-/-/-	-	1	-	-	1	-
3 Richard Walker		-/-/-/-	-/-/-/-	-	-	1	-	5	2
29 Billy Jones ■ 48		-/-/-/-	-/-/-/-	-	1	1	-	2	-
2 David Wright		-/-/-/-	-/-/-/-	-	3	2	-	3	1
10 Dean Ashton		-/1/1/-	1/2/-/-	5	2	-	-	1	-
9 Steve Jones		-/-/-/-	-/1/-/-	3	1	-	-	-	-

Subs not used: Tomlinson, Tonkin, Edwards. - Formation: 4-4-2

Derby Played: 34 Won 8 Drawn 11 Lost 15 For 35 Against 54 Pos 22

Paul Pechisolido became an instant Pride Park hero by firing Derby County to a vital victory over Rotherham United. Brought in to provide much-needed goals, he capped a typical livewire display with the winner around the hour mark.

And while Peschisolido was opening a door at one end, fellow debutant Jeff Kenna made sure the door at the back stayed tightly shut.

Rotherham put men behind the ball, closed down quickly and shackled Leon Osman. Peschisolido had a shot deflected wide and should have done better with an opportunity shortly before the break but Rotherham were the happier side at the interval.

Derby's midfield, unbalanced and unconvincing, needed attention and it was not surprising to see Candido Costa make way for Lee Holmes.

The 16-year-old brought natural width to left, Osman moved to the right, where he enjoyed more freedom, and skipper Ian Taylor returned to his preferred position in central midfield alongside Tom Huddlestone.

Suddenly there was better shape and balance and the tempo lifted. Taylor played in three different midfield positions during the game but looked most effective in the middle.

The decisive goal after 61 minutes came from a cross. Marcus Tudgay's clever pass released Richard Jackson down the right and his fine first-time cross reached Peschisolido at volleying height. Pollitt parried the effort but the striker was awake and quickly onto the rebound to bury the loose ball for the 99th League goal of his career.

Like Derby, Peschisolido improved as the game went on. He was a thorn in Rotherham's side, constantly looking to get in behind defenders. His link-up with Tudgay was highly promising and at times eye-catching.

If this is what competition for places did, Derby were hoping for more of it.

Result.......Result.......Result.

DERBY ....(0) 1   ROTHERHAM (0) 0
P Peschisolido 61

Att 21,741
Referee: A Leake

Stats......Stats.......Stats......Stats

DERBY				ROTHERHAM		
1st	2nd	Total		Total	2nd	1st
4	4	8	Corners	1	0	1
8	3	11	Fouls	17	10	7
0	0	0	Yellow cards	1	1	0
0	0	0	Red cards	0	0	0
1	0	1	Caught Offside	3	2	1
4	6	10	Shots on target	0	0	0
6	7	13	Shots off target	2	1	1
0	0	0	Hit woodwork	0	0	0
46	52	49%	Possession	51%	48	54

 WE'VE had a lot of games this season when we've been on top but haven't had a goalscorer to finish things off. That's why I brought Paul (Peschisolido) in.
George Burley

 I thought we probably just about shaded the first half but our use of the ball after the break was poor. We passed like a Third Division side.
Ronnie Moore

Other Div 1 Results

Bradford 0 Wigan 0, Cardiff 2 Norwich 1, Coventry 4 Burnley 0, Crewe 1 West Brom 2, Ipswich 1 Millwall 3, Nottm Forest 3 Crystal Palace 2, Preston 0 Gillingham 0, Reading 0 Stoke 0, Sunderland 2 West Ham 0, Walsall 1 Wimbledon 0, Watford 0 Sheff Utd 2

DERBY [0] 1 Rotherham [0] 0

Goalkeeper Stats: Lee Grant
Crosses: Catch 2, Punch 3

Derby Player Stats

Player		Shots on target L/R/H/Oth	Shots off target L/R/H/Oth	Caught offside	Fouls conceded	Free-kicks won	Corners taken	Clearances	Defensive blocks
10 Michael Johnson	1st	-/-/-/-	-/-/-/-	-	2	-	-	4	-
▼ 31	2nd	-/-/-/-	-/-/-/-	-	-	-	-	-	-
7 Ian Taylor	1st	-/-/-/-	-/-/-/-	-	2	1	-	-	-
	2nd	-/-/-/-	-/-/-/-	-	-	-	-	-	-
16 Youl Mawene	1st	-/-/-/-	-/-/-/-	-	1	-	-	2	-
	2nd	-/-/-/-	-/-/-/-	-	1	-	-	1	-
14 Richard Jackson	1st	-/-/-/-	-/1/-/-	-	-	-	-	-	-
	2nd	-/-/-/-	-/-/-/-	-	-	-	-	-	-
5 Jeff Kenna	1st	-/-/-/-	-/-/-/-	-	-	-	-	-	-
	2nd	-/-/-/-	-/-/-/-	-	1	2	-	-	-
11 Paul Peschisolido	1st	-/2/-/-	2/-/-/-	1	-	-	-	-	-
▼ 90	2nd	2/1/-/-	1/1/-/-	-	-	2	-	-	-
23 Marcus Tudgay	1st	-/-/-/-	-/-/1/-	-	3	1	-	-	-
	2nd	-/-/-/-	1/-/-/-	-	-	-	-	-	-
17 Paul Boertien	1st	-/-/-/-	-/-/-/-	-	-	-	-	-	-
▲ 31	2nd	-/-/-/-	-/-/-/-	-	-	1	-	2	-
8 Candido Costa	1st	-/-/-/-	-/1/-/-	-	-	3	3	-	-
▼ 45	2nd	-/-/-/-	-/-/-/-	-	-	-	-	-	-
32 Leon Osman	1st	-/-/-/-	-/1/-/-	-	-	1	1	-	-
	2nd	-/-/-/-	-/1/-/-	-	-	2	2	1	-
34 Noel Whelan	1st	-/-/-/-	-/-/-/-	-	-	-	-	-	-
▲ 90	2nd	-/-/-/-	-/-/-/-	-	-	1	-	-	-
30 Lee Holmes	1st	-/-/-/-	-/-/-/-	-	-	-	-	-	-
▲ 45	2nd	1/-/-/-	2/-/-/-	-	1	2	2	-	-
29 Tom Huddlestone	1st	-/2/-/-	-/-/-/-	-	-	1	-	-	-
	2nd	1/1/-/-	1/-/-/-	-	-	-	-	-	-

Subs not used: Oakes, Labarthe Tome. - Formation: 4-4-2

Goalkeeper Stats: Michael Pollitt Saves: Catch 2, Parry 2, Crosses: Catch 9, Punch 2

	Player Stats	Shots on target	Shots off target	Caught offside	Fouls conceded	Free-kicks won	Corners taken	Clearances	Defensive blocks
17	John Mullin ▲ 70	-/-/-/-	-/-/-/-	-	-	-	-	-	-
8	Chris Swailes	-/-/-/-	-/-/-/-	-	1	-	-	1	1
18	Scott Minto	-/-/-/-	-/-/-/-	-	3	2	-	-	-
29	Richard Barker ▼ 68	-/-/-/-	-/-/-/-	-	-	2	-	3	1
19	Phil Gilchrist	-/-/-/-	-/-/-/-	-	1	-	-	3	1
14	Will Hoskins ▲ 77	-/-/-/-	-/-/-/-	-	-	-	-	-	1
16	Paul Hurst	-/-/-/-	-/-/-/-	-	1	-	-	-	-
9	Martin Butler ■ 87	-/-/-/-	-/-/-/-	3	4	3	-	1	-
5	Darren Garner ▼ 77	-/-/-/-	-/-/1/-	-	1	-	1	-	1
7	Michael Proctor ▲ 68	-/-/-/-	-/-/-/-	-	1	1	-	1	-
6	Julien Baudet ▼ 70	-/-/-/-	-/-/-/-	-	2	1	-	2	-
2	Robbie Stockdale	-/-/-/-	-/-/-/-	-	2	1	-	2	-
10	Paul Warne	-/-/-/-	-/1/-/-	-	1	1	-	3	-

Subs not used: Montgomery, Daws. - Formation: 4-4-2

Derby Played: 35 Won 9 Drawn 11 Lost 15 For 36 Against 54 Pos 22

Watford [1] 2 DERBY [1] 1

Paul Pechisolido scored the 100th League goal of his career but there was little celebration for Derby County at Vicarage Road.

Peschisolido gave the Rams a dream start to their crucial Division One clash against Watford. He pounced to score after 10 minutes, his second goal in as many games since signing from Sheffield United.

But the home side hit back. Heidar Helguson equalised within nine minutes and Gavin Mahon struck early in the second half to secure a 2-1 victory. It was a massive win for Watford and a damaging defeat for the Rams in their relegation battle.

Stung by three recent defeats, Watford started in determined fashion and asked early questions of the Rams back line, but they were silenced when Peschisolido struck after only 10 minutes.

Costa's free kick delivery was perfect for Marcus Tudgay to head back across goal. Jerel Ifil dithered, rather than cleared, and Peschisolido capitalised. He nipped in and buried the ball low past Lenny Pidgley from inside the six-yard box.

Falling behind so early was a shattering blow but to their credit Watford bounced back. Grant brilliantly turned Helguson's downward header round the post but could do little to prevent Watford equalising in the 19th minute.

Devlin's persistence gave Lee Cook the chance to thump a shot high against the upright and Helguson was on hand to slot the rebound into the empty net.

And the Rams were behind eight minutes into the half. Helguson's headed flick from Neal Ardley's long ball forward caught out Kenna and Mahon's run from midfield was rewarded when he controlled the ball and fired under Grant.

Derby reverted to three at the back, but the momentum was with Watford. Strong claims for a penalty were waved away when Devlin went down over a challenge from Boertien and then Grant twice denied Helguson before diving full stretch to his right to palm away a volley from Fitzgerald.

Result.......Result.......Result.

WATFORD ....(1) 2   DERBY ....(1) 1
Helguson 19   Peschisolido 10
Mahon 53

Att 13,931
Referee: L Cable

Stats......Stats.......Stats......Stats

WATFORD				DERBY		
1st	2nd	Total		Total	2nd	1st
2	6	8	Corners	5	5	0
7	6	13	Fouls	14	4	10
0	1	1	Yellow cards	1	1	0
0	0	0	Red cards	0	0	0
3	1	4	Caught Offside	3	2	1
3	5	8	Shots on target	2	1	1
1	1	2	Shots off target	4	2	2
1	0	1	Hit woodwork	0	0	0
44	51	47%	Possession	53%	49	56

THAT was a massive must-win game and I thought the players and the crowd responded magnificently. It was particularly good after we gave away a sloppy goal.

Ray Lewington

THEY played the conditions better than us by playing the ball early and I thought we were out-muscled by their two big strikers.

George Burley

Other Div 1 Results

Cardiff 2 Reading 3, Norwich 3 Gillingham 0, Rotherham 1 Sheff Utd 1, Sunderland 1 Stoke 1, Walsall 1 Ipswich 3, West Brom 2 Wigan 1

Watford [1] 2 DERBY [1] 1

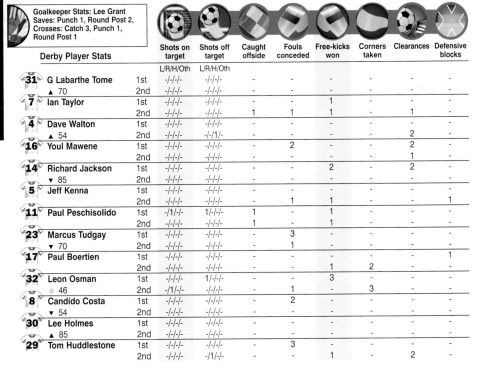

Goalkeeper Stats: Lee Grant
Saves: Punch 1, Round Post 2,
Crosses: Catch 3, Punch 1,
Round Post 1

Derby Player Stats		Shots on target L/R/H/Oth	Shots off target L/R/H/Oth	Caught offside	Fouls conceded	Free-kicks won	Corners taken	Clearances	Defensive blocks
31 G Labarthe Tome ▲ 70	1st	-/-/-	-/-/-	-	-	-	-	-	-
	2nd	-/-/-	-/-/-	-	-	-	-	-	-
7 Ian Taylor	1st	-/-/-	-/-/-	-	-	1	-	-	-
	2nd	-/-/-	-/-/-	1	1	1	-	1	-
4 Dave Walton ▲ 54	1st	-/-/-	-/-/-	-	-	-	-	-	-
	2nd	-/-/-	-/-/1/-	-	-	-	-	2	-
16 Youl Mawene	1st	-/-/-	-/-/-	-	2	-	-	2	-
	2nd	-/-/-	-/-/-	-	-	-	-	1	-
14 Richard Jackson ▼ 85	1st	-/-/-	-/-/-	-	-	2	-	2	-
	2nd	-/-/-	-/-/-	-	-	-	-	-	-
5 Jeff Kenna	1st	-/-/-	-/-/-	-	-	-	-	-	-
	2nd	-/-/-	-/-/-	-	1	1	-	-	1
11 Paul Peschisolido	1st	-/1/-/-	1/-/-/-	1	-	1	-	-	-
	2nd	-/-/-	-/-/-	1	-	1	-	-	-
23 Marcus Tudgay ▼ 70	1st	-/-/-	-/-/-	-	3	-	-	-	-
	2nd	-/-/-	-/-/-	-	1	-	-	-	-
17 Paul Boertien	1st	-/-/-	-/-/-	-	-	-	-	-	1
	2nd	-/-/-	-/-/-	-	-	1	2	-	-
32 Leon Osman ■ 46	1st	-/-/-	1/-/-/-	-	-	3	-	-	-
	2nd	-/1/-/-	-/-/-	-	1	-	3	-	-
8 Candido Costa ▼ 54	1st	-/-/-	-/-/-	-	2	-	-	-	-
	2nd	-/-/-	-/-/-	-	-	-	-	-	-
30 Lee Holmes ▲ 85	1st	-/-/-	-/-/-	-	-	-	-	-	-
	2nd	-/-/-	-/-/-	-	-	-	-	-	-
29 Tom Huddlestone	1st	-/-/-	-/-/-	-	3	-	-	-	-
	2nd	-/-/-	-/1/-/-	-	-	1	-	2	-

Subs not used: Oakes, Bolder. - Formation: 4-4-2

Goalkeeper Stats: Lenny Pidgeley Crosses: Catch 2, Round Post 1

	Player Stats	Shots on target	Shots off target	Caught offside	Fouls conceded	Free-kicks won	Corners taken	Clearances	Defensive blocks
3	Paul Mayo	-/-/-	-/-/-	-	1	1	-	-	-
12	Gavin Mahon	-/1/-/-	-/-/1/-	-	2	3	-	1	-
2	Neal Ardley	-/-/-	-/-/-	-	2	-	4	2	-
21	Scott Fitzgerald	-/1/-/-	-/-/-	1	2	-	-	-	-
22	Lee Cook ▼ 88	-/1/-/-	-/-/-	-	1	1	4	1	-
18	Heidar Helguson	2/-/1/-	-/1/-/-	3	2	3	-	-	-
6	Sean Dyche	-/-/-	-/-/-	-	-	3	-	2	-
8	Micah Hyde	-/-/1/-	-/-/-	-	1	2	-	-	-
4	Paolo Vernazza ▲ 88	-/-/-	-/-/-	-	-	-	-	-	-
25	Paul Devlin ■ 60	-/1/-/-	-/-/-	-	2	1	-	1	-
19	Jerel Ifil	-/-/-	-/-/-	-	-	-	-	-	-

Subs not used: Chamberlain, Dyer, Webber, Doyley. - Formation: 4-4-2

Derby Played: 36 Won 9 Drawn 11 Lost 16 For 37 Against 56 Pos 22

DERBY [3] 4 Nottm Forest [1] 2

Derby County sent fierce rivals Nottingham Forest back down the A52 as a beaten and worried outfit. Relegation fears added extra spice to an enthralling contest but the points and pride belonged to the Rams, thanks to a fully deserved 4-2 victory.

Much credit must go to the Derby players for an impressive, passionate display. The match was one they dare not lose and the players reacted to the gravity of the situation with sharpness and hunger.

A devastating start saw Derby go three up in 37 minutes, with striker Paul Peschisolido filling the role of maker and taker of chances. His clever pass dissected Forest's square backline and Ian Taylor strode forward, kept his cool and buried a low shot past Barry Roche in only the fourth minute.

The difficult conditions contributed to a bizarre second goal for the Rams. Roche was about to clear a back pass from Wes Morgan when the ball appeared to bobble off a stray plastic coffee cup. The ball came off the keeper's shin and dropped invitingly for Peschisolido to guide into an empty net.

Two minutes later, it was 3-0 when Marcus Tudgay's persistence and finely-weighted pass gave Peschisolido the chance to finish expertly with an angled shot across Roche. He now had four in three games following his move from Sheffield United and provided a much-needed cutting edge.

But Derby conceded a sloppy goal on the stroke of half-time to give the visitors a lifeline. Matthieu Louis-Jean's cross evaded a stretching Youl Mawene and Gareth Taylor muscled in behind a clearly injured Richard Jackson to head past Lee Grant from close range.

Forest then tested the home nerves with a second goal after 67 minutes. Andy Reid's cross was headed against the bar by Gareth Williams, who then smashed in the rebound.

But Derby wrapped up the points eight minutes from time. Peschisolido escaped down the left, picked out Tudgay on the edge of the area and his shot took a deflection before nestling in the net.

Result.......Result.......Result.

DERBY ....(3) 4   NOTTM FOR ..(1) 2
Taylor 4   Taylor 45
Peschisolido 28, 37   Williams 67
Tudgay 82

Att 32,390
Referee: D Pugh

Stats......Stats.......Stats......Stats

DERBY				NOTTM FOREST		
1st	2nd	Total		Total	2nd	1st
4	3	7	Corners	3	2	1
6	7	13	Fouls	16	6	10
0	0	0	Yellow cards	4	1	3
0	0	0	Red cards	0	0	0
1	2	0	Caught Offside	4	3	1
5	3	8	Shots on target	1	1	0
2	3	5	Shots off target	4	2	2
0	0	0	Hit woodwork	0	0	0
40	50	45%	Possession	55%	50	60

THIS is a massive result for us, we know we have to win games to stay in the First Division and derby matches are always special.
George Burley

PAUL PESCHISOLIDO was a thorn in our side, his movement caused us problems and he took his goals well but we gave them acres and acres of room.
Joe Kinnear

Other Div 1 Results

Burnley P Wimbledon P, Crewe 0 Cardiff 1, Crystal Palace 1 Norwich 0, Gillingham 2 Rotherham 0, Ipswich 4 Watford 1, Preston 1 Walsall 2, Reading 0 Sunderland 2, Sheff Utd 2 Bradford 0, Stoke P West Brom P, Wigan 2 Coventry 1

DERBY [3] 4 Nottm Forest [1] 2

Goalkeeper Stats: Lee Grant Crosses: Catch 2

Derby Player Stats

Player		Shots on target L/R/H/Oth	Shots off target L/R/H/Oth	Caught offside	Fouls conceded	Free-kicks won	Corners taken	Clearances	Defensive blocks
10 Michael Johnson	1st	-/-/1/-	-/-/-/-	-	1	1	-	1	-
	2nd	-/-/-/-	-/-/-/-	-	-	-	-	1	-
7 Ian Taylor	1st	-/1/-/-	-/-/-/-	-	-	1	-	-	-
	2nd	-/-/-/-	-/-/-/-	-	-	2	-	1	-
16 Youl Mawene	1st	-/-/-/-	-/-/-/-	-	1	-	-	-	-
	2nd	-/-/-/-	-/-/-/-	-	-	1	-	1	-
14 Richard Jackson ▼ 45	1st	-/-/-/-	-/-/-/-	-	-	-	-	1	-
	2nd	-/-/-/-	-/-/-/-	-	-	-	-	-	-
5 Jeff Kenna	1st	-/-/-/-	-/-/-/-	-	-	1	-	1	1
	2nd	-/-/-/-	-/-/-/-	-	-	1	-	1	-
11 Paul Peschisolido	1st	2/-/-/-	-/-/-/-	-	-	-	-	-	-
	2nd	-/-/-/-	-/1/-/-	2	2	1	-	-	-
23 Marcus Tudgay	1st	-/-/-/-	-/1/-/-	1	1	2	-	-	-
	2nd	-/3/-/-	-/-/-/-	-	1	-	-	-	-
17 Paul Boertien ▲ 45	1st	-/-/-/-	-/-/-/-	-	-	-	-	-	-
	2nd	-/-/-/-	-/-/-/-	-	-	-	-	1	-
32 Leon Osman	1st	-/-/-/-	-/1/-/-	-	-	-	-	-	-
	2nd	-/-/-/-	-/1/-/-	-	1	1	1	-	-
8 Candido Costa ▼ 72	1st	-/-/-/-	-/-/-/-	-	1	4	4	-	-
	2nd	-/-/-/-	-/-/-/-	-	-	-	2	-	-
30 Lee Holmes ▲ 72	1st	-/-/-/-	-/-/-/-	-	-	-	-	-	-
	2nd	-/-/-/-	-/-/-/-	-	-	-	-	-	-
29 Tom Huddlestone	1st	-/1/-/-	-/-/-/-	-	2	1	-	-	-
	2nd	-/-/-/-	1/-/-/-	-	3	-	-	-	-

Subs not used: Oakes, Labarthe Tome, Whelan. - Formation: 4-4-2

Goalkeeper Stats: Barry Roche Saves: Catch 2, Crosses: Catch 3

Player Stats

Player	Shots on target	Shots off target	Caught offside	Fouls conceded	Free-kicks won	Corners taken	Clearances	Defensive blocks
14 Eoin Jess	-/-/-/-	-/-/-/-	-	1	1	-	-	-
7 Andy Reid ▪ 34	-/-/-/-	1/-/-/-	-	1	2	3	-	-
36 Nick Barmby ▼ 35	-/-/-/-	-/-/-/-	-	-	-	-	-	-
23 Wes Morgan	-/-/-/-	-/-/-/-	-	1	-	-	-	1
35 Andrew Impey ▪ 33	-/-/-/-	1/-/-/-	-	-	2	-	-	-
10 Gareth Taylor ▪ 87	-/-/-/-	-/-/1/-	1	4	2	-	3	-
9 David Johnson ▲ 35	-/-/-/-	-/-/-/-	3	1	-	-	-	-
2 Matthieu Louis-Jean	-/-/-/-	-/-/-/-	-	2	1	-	-	-
8 Gareth Williams ▪ 42	-/1/-/-	-/1/-/-	-	4	2	-	-	-
21 Danny Sonner	-/-/-/-	-/-/-/-	-	1	2	-	-	-
5 Michael Dawson	-/-/-/-	-/-/-/-	-	1	1	-	5	-

Subs not used: Formann, Thompson, Doig, Westcarr. - Formation: 4-4-2

Derby Played: 37 Won 10 Drawn 11 Lost 16 For 41 Against 58 Pos 22

Sheff Utd [1] 1 DERBY [1] 1

Skipper Ian Taylor converted a controversial penalty to lift Derby County out of the Division One relegation zone. His 10th goal of the season gave the Rams a fully-deserved 1-1 draw against promotion hopefuls Sheffield United at Bramall Lane.

Andy Gray had put United ahead on 21 minutes, helped by dithering defending, but Taylor levelled four minutes later. There were chances for both sides to win it and each had efforts cleared off the line.

The draw ended a run of five consecutive defeats away from home for the Rams and dumped Burnley into the bottom three. This was a big point and coupled with the marvellous victory over Nottingham Forest, it had been a good few days.

But it was sloppy defending that handed United the lead after 21 minutes. Edwards dithered when he should have cleared and was robbed by Peter Ndlovu. The ball fell for Gray who squeezed a low shot past Grant.

Derby were level four minutes in controversial circumstances. Leon Osman went down over a challenge from Nick Montgomery and the referee pointed to the penalty spot. He looked to be wrong on two counts as Montgomery appeared to play the ball and the incident also seemed to take place outside the area.

The official was still having his ear bent by Warnock as Taylor coolly stroked his penalty past Paddy Kenny. Both sides also went close to taking an interval lead. Marcus Tudgay had a header cleared off the line while at the other end, a scrambling Grant was relieved to see Gray's deflected shot drop just wide.

United finished the half with Montgomery's low shot going inches wide and they pressed the Rams back at the start of the second. Kenny held efforts from Tudgay and Huddlestone and Ndlovu volleyed wide before Warnock made a double change.

It rather summed up United's night but Derby were delighted with the point.

Result.......Result.......Result.

SHEFF UTD ....(1) 1   DERBY ....(1) 1
Gray 21   Taylor 25(p)

Att 21,351
Referee: L Mason

Stats......Stats.......Stats......Stats

SHEFF UTD				DERBY		
1st	2nd	Total		Total	2nd	1st
3	6	9	Corners	4	1	3
6	7	13	Fouls	13	4	9
3	1	4	Yellow cards	3	0	3
0	0	0	Red cards	0	0	0
2	1	3	Caught Offside	4	2	2
3	2	5	Shots on target	12	5	7
2	5	7	Shots off target	2	0	2
0	0	0	Hit woodwork	0	0	0
29	41	35%	Possession	65%	59	71

THE penalty was the major decision of the whole evening. We were on top at the time and really it knocked the stuffing out of us.
Neil Warnock

OUR home form has been excellent. We haven't lost at home in the new year, but we've struggled away. Here we showed the character that's needed.
George Burley

Other Div 1 Results

Crewe 2 Stoke 0, Sunderland 2 Gillingham 1

Goalkeeper Stats: Lee Grant
Saves: Parry 1, Crosses: Tip Over 1, Catch 1

Derby Player Stats

			Shots on target	Shots off target	Caught offside	Fouls conceded	Free-kicks won	Corners taken	Clearances	Defensive blocks
			L/R/H/Oth	L/R/H/Oth						
10	Michael Johnson	1st	-/-/-/-	-/-/-/-	-	-	-	-	-	-
▼ 8		2nd	-/-/-/-	-/-/-/-	-	-	-	-	-	-
7	Ian Taylor	1st	-/-/-/-	-/-/-/-	-	1	-	-	-	-
		2nd	-/-/-/-	-/-/-/-	-	1	1	-	2	-
4	Dave Walton	1st	-/-/2/-	-/-/-/-	-	2	1	-	1	-
▲ 8		2nd	-/-/-/-	-/-/-/-	-	-	-	-	-	-
16	Youl Mawene	1st	-/-/-/-	-/-/-/-	-	-	-	-	3	1
		2nd	-/-/-/-	-/-/-/-	-	-	-	-	-	-
23	Marcus Tudgay	1st	-/-/-/-	-/-/-/-	-	1	2	-	-	-
▼ 90		2nd	1/1/-/-	-/-/-/-	1	1	2	-	-	-
17	Paul Boertien	1st	-/-/-/-	-/-/-/-	-	-	-	-	-	-
		2nd	-/-/-/-	-/-/-/-	-	-	1	-	2	-
15	Adam Bolder	1st	-/1/-/-	-/1/-/-	-	2	1	1	-	-
■ 40		2nd	-/-/-/-	-/-/-/-	-	1	1	1	1	-
32	Leon Osman	1st	-/1/-/-	-/-/-/-	-	2	1	2	-	-
■ 34		2nd	-/2/-/-	-/-/-/-	-	-	2	-	-	-
8	Candido Costa	1st	-/-/-/-	-/-/-/-	-	-	-	-	-	-
▲ 78		2nd	-/-/-/-	-/-/-/-	-	-	-	-	-	-
2	Rob Edwards	1st	-/-/-/-	-/-/-/-	-	-	-	-	3	-
		2nd	-/-/-/-	-/-/-/-	-	-	-	-	-	-
34	Noel Whelan	1st	-/-/-/-	-/-/-/-	-	-	-	-	-	-
▲ 90		2nd	-/-/-/-	-/-/-/-	-	-	-	-	-	-
29	Tom Huddlestone	1st	-/-/-/-	-/-/-/-	-	1	-	-	-	-
		2nd	1/-/-/-	-/-/-/-	-	-	-	-	1	-
9	Manuel Manel	1st	-/1/1/-	-/-/1/-	2	-	1	-	-	-
▼ 78 ■ 37		2nd	-/-/-/-	-/-/-/-	1	1	-	-	-	-

Subs not used: Oakes, Labarthe Tome. - Formation: 4-4-2

Goalkeeper Stats: Patrick Kenny Saves: Catch 4, Block 1, Crosses: Catch 2

	Player Stats	Shots on target	Shots off target	Caught offside	Fouls conceded	Free-kicks won	Corners taken	Clearances	Defensive blocks
18	Michael Tonge	-/-/-/-	-/2/-/-	-	1	1	8	2	-
32	Jonathan Forte ▲ 67	-/-/-/-	-/-/-/-	-	-	-	-	-	-
17	Phil Jagielka	-/-/-/-	-/-/-/-	-	1	1	-	-	-
4	Nick Montgomery	-/-/-/-	1/1/-/-	-	1	1	-	-	-
14	Wayne Allison ▲ 81	-/-/-/-	-/-/-/-	-	-	-	-	-	-
11	Jack Lester	-/1/1/-	-/-/1/-	1	1	1	-	-	-
16	Peter Ndlovu ▼ 67 ■ 32	-/-/-/-	1/1/-/-	-	1	1	-	-	-
6	Robert Page ■ 24	-/-/-/-	-/-/-/-	1	1	1	-	2	3
5	Chris Morgan ■ 64	-/-/-/-	-/-/-/-	-	6	2	-	-	-
30	Dries Boussatta ▼ 81 ▲ 67	-/-/-/-	-/-/-/-	-	-	-	1	-	-
2	Robert Kozluk	-/-/-/-	-/-/-/-	-	-	2	-	1	-
19	Andy Gray	-/2/1/-	-/-/-/-	1	1	2	-	-	-
8	Stuart McCall ▼ 67 ■ 25	-/-/-/-	-/-/-/-	-	-	1	-	-	-

Subs not used: Shaw, Francis. - Formation: 4-4-2

Sunderland [1] 2 DERBY [0] 1

Derby County returned empty-handed but not despondent from their trip to the Stadium of Light. However, with Burnley picking up points at Bradford City, Derby slipped back into the drop zone.

The game was another of those away-days when Derby could have returned with something to show for their efforts. There was spirit and commitment but much of this only appeared once they trailed to goals from John Oster and Tommy Smith.

Skipper Ian Taylor took advantage of another soft penalty decision to give Derby a lifeline and Manel and substitute Adam Bolder could have made things very interesting had they accepted rather than squandered excellent chances just before and after the interval.

Sunderland boasted confident and clever width in Julio Arca and Oster and Derby never got to grips with the pair. Arca had a hand in both Sunderland's goals and received a standing ovation when he was substituted near the end.

Gary Breen headed just over, Darren Byfield hit a shot into the side netting and Lee Grant had made a double save from Arca and Byfield before he was beaten after 31 minutes. He parried Arca's shot and the ball fell to Oster, who did well to steer home the rebound.

And Grant was picking the ball out of the net again five minutes after the break. Making the most of a numerical advantage on the left, Arca stepped inside and flighted a ball in for the unmarked Smith to send a header looping over Grant.

The odds were stacked against a Derby comeback. Sunderland had not lost at home in the League since August, a run of 18 games, but this did not deter George Burley's men from giving it a good go.

The drive and urgency lacking in the first half suddenly emerged. Bolder should have reduced the deficit two minutes after Smith had struck but somehow headed wide from eight yards.

And Derby were given an unexpected lifeline when referee Graham Salisbury awarded a penalty against Sunderland captain, George McCartney, for handball. It looked another strange decision but this mattered little to Taylor, who sent Mart Poom the wrong way from the spot.

Result.......Result.......Result.

SUNDERLAND ....(1) 2   DERBY ....(0) 1
Oster 31   Taylor 64(p)
Smith 50

Att 30,838
Referee: G Salisbury

Stats......Stats.......Stats......Stats

SUNDERLAND   DERBY

1st	2nd	Total		Total	2nd	1st
4	1	5	Corners	3	3	0
6	3	9	Fouls	8	3	5
0	0	0	Yellow cards	0	0	0
0	0	0	Red cards	0	0	0
2	8	10	Caught Offside	4	2	2
3	2	5	Shots on target	6	5	1
5	2	7	Shots off target	7	3	4
0	0	0	Hit woodwork	0	0	0
51	55	53%	Possession	47%	45	49

IT was a scrap. They had a go at us as you would expect but I can't praise the lads enough for their efforts.
Mick McCarthy

WE could have folded at 2-0 but we didn't. In fact we had three or four good chances which we should have at least hit the target with.
George Burley

Other Div 1 Results

Bradford 1 Burnley 2, Cardiff 2 Sheff Utd 1, Coventry 1 Reading 2, Norwich 1 Stoke 0, Nottm Forest 2 Crewe 0, Rotherham 1 Preston 0, Walsall 1 Millwall 1, Watford 1 Wigan 1, West Brom 2 Crystal Palace 0, West Ham 2 Gillingham 1, Wimbledon 1 Ipswich 2

Sunderland [1] 2 DERBY [0] 1

Goalkeeper Stats: Lee Grant
Saves: Punch 1, Crosses: Catch 2, Punch 1

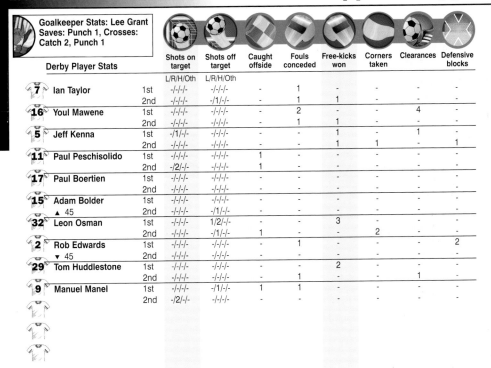

Derby Player Stats		Shots on target L/R/H/Oth	Shots off target L/R/H/Oth	Caught offside	Fouls conceded	Free-kicks won	Corners taken	Clearances	Defensive blocks
7 Ian Taylor	1st	-/-/-/-	-/-/-/-	-	1	-	-	-	-
	2nd	-/-/-/-	-/1/-/-	-	1	1	-	-	-
16 Youl Mawene	1st	-/-/-/-	-/-/-/-	-	2	-	-	4	-
	2nd	-/-/-/-	-/-/-/-	-	1	1	-	-	-
5 Jeff Kenna	1st	-/1/-/-	-/-/-/-	-	-	1	-	1	-
	2nd	-/-/-/-	-/-/-/-	-	-	1	1	-	1
11 Paul Peschisolido	1st	-/-/-/-	-/-/-/-	1	-	-	-	-	-
	2nd	-/2/-/-	-/-/-/-	1	-	-	-	-	-
17 Paul Boertien	1st	-/-/-/-	-/-/-/-	-	-	-	-	-	-
	2nd	-/-/-/-	-/-/-/-	-	-	-	-	-	-
15 Adam Bolder ▲ 45	1st	-/-/-/-	-/-/-/-	-	-	-	-	-	-
	2nd	-/-/-/-	-/1/-/-	-	-	-	-	-	-
32 Leon Osman	1st	-/-/-/-	1/2/-/-	-	-	3	-	-	-
	2nd	-/-/-/-	-/1/-/-	1	-	-	2	-	-
2 Rob Edwards ▼ 45	1st	-/-/-/-	-/-/-/-	-	1	-	-	-	2
	2nd	-/-/-/-	-/-/-/-	-	-	-	-	-	-
29 Tom Huddlestone	1st	-/-/-/-	-/-/-/-	-	-	2	-	-	-
	2nd	-/-/-/-	-/-/-/-	-	1	-	-	1	-
9 Manuel Manel	1st	-/-/-/-	-/1/-/-	1	1	-	-	-	-
	2nd	-/2/-/-	-/-/-/-	-	-	-	-	-	-

Subs not used: Oakes, Costa, Walton, Labarthe Tome. Formation: 4-3-1-2

Goalkeeper Stats: Mart Poom Saves: Catch 1, Punch 1, Crosses: Catch 3

	Player Stats	Shots on target	Shots off target	Caught offside	Fouls conceded	Free-kicks won	Corners taken	Clearances	Defensive blocks
18	Phil Babb	-/-/-/-	-/-/-/-	-	-	-	-	1	2
10	Marcus Stewart ▲ 75	-/-/-/-	-/-/-/-	1	1	-	-	-	-
21	Paul Thirlwell	-/-/-/-	-/1/-/-	-	1	-	-	-	-
33	Julio Arca ▼ 76	1/-/-/-	-/-/1/-	-	2	1	4	-	-
7	Matthew Piper ▲ 81	-/-/-/-	-/-/-/-	2	-	-	-	-	-
11	Tommy Smith ▼ 81	-/2/1/-	-/-/1/-	2	-	-	-	-	-
17	Darren Byfield ▼ 75	-/-/-/-	-/1/-/-	3	1	3	-	-	-
4	Jason McAteer	-/-/-/-	-/-/-/-	-	-	3	-	-	-
12	John Oster	1/-/-/-	-/1/-/-	1	1	-	1	-	-
14	Colin Cooper ▲ 76	-/-/-/-	-/-/-/-	-	1	-	-	1	1
16	Darren Williams	-/-/-/-	-/-/-/-	-	2	-	-	-	-
3	George McCartney	-/-/-/-	1/-/-/-	1	-	1	-	-	-
5	Gary Breen	-/-/-/-	-/-/1/-	-	-	-	-	2	-

Subs not used: Thornton, Myhre. - Formation: 4-4-2

Derby Played: 39 Won 10 Drawn 12 Lost 17 For 43 Against 61 Pos 22

...March Team Stats.....Team Stats......Team Stats......Team S

League table at the end of March

		HOME					AWAY						
	P	W	D	L	F	A	W	D	L	F	A	Pts	Df
Norwich	38	15	3	2	34	13	6	7	5	24	18	73	27
West Brom	38	12	5	3	31	14	9	5	4	24	18	73	23
Sunderland	37	11	7	1	28	13	7	4	7	25	24	65	16
West Ham	39	10	6	4	36	20	6	9	4	22	21	63	17
Millwall	38	10	6	2	25	11	7	6	7	25	25	63	14
Sheff Utd	39	10	5	4	33	20	8	4	8	24	25	63	12
Wigan	38	10	6	3	25	14	6	8	5	27	25	62	13
Ipswich	39	11	2	6	44	30	7	6	7	29	33	62	10
Reading	39	9	5	5	25	23	8	4	8	24	29	60	-3
Cardiff	38	9	5	6	37	22	6	5	7	23	26	55	12
Coventry	39	7	8	5	27	20	7	5	7	27	24	55	10
Crystal Palace	38	7	7	5	28	24	8	2	9	30	31	54	3
Preston	39	10	4	5	35	22	4	6	10	20	31	52	2
Stoke	38	9	6	3	30	19	5	4	11	20	31	52	0
Crewe	39	10	2	7	27	19	3	6	11	21	36	47	-7
Nottm Forest	39	7	6	6	30	23	4	5	10	20	29	45	-2
Rotherham	38	7	7	5	25	21	4	5	10	17	30	45	-9
Walsall	39	7	7	6	26	27	4	5	10	15	25	45	-11
Burnley	38	7	6	5	28	22	3	8	9	22	40	44	-12
Watford	39	7	8	5	27	25	4	3	12	17	32	44	-13
Gillingham	38	9	1	8	21	22	3	7	10	18	31	44	-14
Derby	39	8	5	6	29	29	2	7	11	14	32	42	-18
Bradford	39	5	3	12	19	29	4	3	12	13	27	33	-24
Wimbledon	37	2	3	14	15	33	3	0	15	14	42	18	-46

March matches table

	P	W	D	L	F	A	Pts
Sunderland	7	5	2	0	15	7	17
West Brom	5	4	1	0	9	2	13
West Ham	7	3	2	2	13	10	11
Sheff Utd	6	3	2	1	9	5	11
Millwall	5	3	1	1	10	5	10
Nottm Forest	6	3	1	2	10	9	10
Norwich	6	3	1	2	8	4	10
Coventry	6	3	0	3	11	8	9
Ipswich	6	3	0	3	11	11	9
Cardiff	5	3	0	2	7	6	9
Derby	6	2	2	2	8	7	8
Reading	6	2	2	2	8	9	8
Stoke	6	2	2	2	6	5	8
Walsall	6	2	2	2	6	8	8
Crewe	7	2	1	4	8	11	7
Gillingham	6	2	1	3	6	8	7
Bradford	5	2	1	2	5	5	7
Preston	7	1	3	3	8	12	6
Burnley	5	1	3	1	5	8	6
Wigan	5	1	2	2	6	7	5
Crystal Palace	4	1	1	2	5	7	4
Watford	6	1	1	4	5	13	4
Rotherham	5	1	1	3	3	6	4
Wimbledon	5	0	0	5	1	10	0

March team stats details

Club Name	Ply	Shots On	Shots Off	Corners	Hit W'work	Caught Offside	Offside Trap	Fouls	Yellow Cards	Red Cards	Pens Awarded	Pens Con
Bradford	5	28	24	34	1	19	27	74	7	0	- (-)	-
Burnley	5	15	13	32	0	23	15	57	10	0	- (-)	1
Cardiff	5	42	31	28	2	24	3	51	3	1	1 (-)	-
Coventry	6	40	35	36	1	13	34	68	6	1	3 (2)	2
Crewe	7	32	28	31	0	26	24	58	3	0	2 (2)	2
Crystal Palace	4	19	20	32	2	6	17	39	7	0	- (-)	-
Derby	6	53	47	39	1	18	40	69	4	0	2 (2)	2
Gillingham	6	23	26	24	0	18	13	72	10	1	- (-)	-
Ipswich	6	49	30	39	3	24	16	62	6	1	1 (1)	2
Millwall	5	22	24	31	0	16	8	81	12	0	2 (-)	-
Norwich	6	38	28	36	0	27	5	97	8	0	1 (1)	-
Nottm Forest	6	33	31	42	2	21	10	80	12	1	- (-)	-
Preston	7	53	59	51	5	26	11	102	7	2	2 (2)	3
Reading	6	23	26	18	0	17	24	69	5	2	- (-)	-
Rotherham	5	13	23	21	0	9	14	73	9	0	- (-)	-
Sheff Utd	6	30	23	42	0	18	18	68	11	0	1 (1)	1
Stoke	6	28	22	19	2	21	14	86	13	0	1 (1)	1
Sunderland	7	45	31	42	2	32	28	95	12	2	1 (1)	-
Walsall	6	22	21	33	2	11	33	74	3	0	- (-)	-
Watford	6	34	15	40	2	20	21	80	7	0	- (-)	-
West Brom	5	37	33	27	0	23	9	59	5	0	1 (1)	-
West Ham	7	56	33	47	1	29	33	59	10	1	2 (2)	4
Wigan	5	23	30	23	0	13	20	83	9	2	1 (1)	2
Wimbledon	5	9	11	22	1	9	26	59	4	0	- (-)	-

MARCH STATS

Monthly Top scorers

Darren Bent (Ipswich)	5
Matthew Etherington (West Ham)	4
Paul Peschisolido (Derby)	4
Jason Roberts (Wigan)	3
Darren Byfield (Sunderland)	3
Tim Cahill (Millwall)	3
Andy Gray (Sheff Utd)	3
Gareth Taylor (Nottm Forest)	3
Heidar Helguson (Watford)	3
Gary McSheffrey (Coventry)	3

Penalties scored

2 Dean Ashton (Crewe), Gary McSheffrey (Coventry), Ian Taylor (Derby), Graham Alexander (Preston)

Assists

Bjarni Gudjonsson (Coventry)	4
Glen Little (Burnley)	3
Andy Reid (Nottm Forest)	3
Dean Bowditch (Ipswich)	3
David Connolly (West Ham)	2
Paul Merson (Walsall)	2
Danny Granville (Crystal Palace)	2

Quickest goals

1:12 mins - Matt Fryatt (Preston vs Walsall)

1:26 mins - Bjarni Gudjonsson (Coventry vs Preston)

2:59 mins - Bobby Zamora (West Ham vs Gillingham)

3:03 mins - Gareth Taylor (Wimbledon vs Nottm Forest)

3:28 mins - Gareth Williams (Nottm Forest vs Crystal Palace)

Top Keeper

	Mins	Gls
Russell Hoult (West Brom)	480	2
Robert Green (Norwich)	575	4
Patrick Kenny (Sheff Utd)	579	5
Ed de Goey (Stoke)	563	5
Lars Hirschfeld (Gillingham)	98	1
Andy Marshall (Millwall)	486	5
Mart Poom (Sunderland)	670	7
Jonathan Gould (Preston)	95	1

Shots on target

Bobby Zamora (West Ham)	17
David Healy (Preston)	14
Heidar Helguson (Watford)	12
Darren Bent (Ipswich)	11
Gary McSheffrey (Coventry)	11
Dean Ashton (Crewe)	10
Leon Osman (Derby)	10
Tommy Miller (Ipswich)	10
Paul Peschisolido (Derby)	10
Kevin Kyle (Sunderland)	9

Shots off target

David Healy (Preston)	14
Leon Osman (Derby)	12
Nathan Ellington (Wigan)	12
Ricardo Fuller (Preston)	11
Robert Earnshaw (Cardiff)	10
Andy Reid (Nottm Forest)	9
Kevin James (Nottm Forest)	8
Gareth Taylor (Nottm Forest)	8
Steve Jones (Crewe)	8
Richard Cresswell (Preston)	7

Caught offside

Ade Akinbiyi (Stoke)	15
Darren Bent (Ipswich)	13
Robert Earnshaw (Cardiff)	13
Bobby Zamora (West Ham)	13
Dean Ashton (Crewe)	12
Steve Jones (Crewe)	11
Heidar Helguson (Watford)	10
Julian Joachim (Coventry)	9
Richard Cresswell (Preston)	9

Free-kicks won

Darren Huckerby (Norwich)	22
Martin Butler (Rotherham)	22
Gerry Taggart (Stoke)	18
Heidar Helguson (Watford)	17
Alan Lee (Cardiff)	17
Mamady Sidibe (Gillingham)	16
Leon Osman (Derby)	15
Dean Windass (Bradford)	15
Glen Little (Burnley)	15

Derby v Forrest

Fouls conceded

Gareth Taylor (Nottm Forest)	22
Heidar Helguson (Watford)	20
Daniele Dichio (Millwall)	19
Gary McSheffrey (Coventry)	18
Dean Windass (Bradford)	17
Ade Akinbiyi (Stoke)	16
Jason Jarrett (Wigan)	16
Kevin Kyle (Sunderland)	15
Alan Lee (Cardiff)	15

Fouls without a card

Dean Windass (Bradford)	17
Marcus Tudgay (Derby)	14
Dean Ashton (Crewe)	14
Michael Jackson (Preston)	13
Tom Huddlestone (Derby)	12
Malky Mackay (Norwich)	11
Neil Emblen (Walsall)	11
Dave Kitson (Reading)	11
Robert Edwards (Preston)	10

Marcus Tudgay looks dejected after missing one of many chances that Derby created. The 0-0 draw was little reward for football they played.

Although Lee Grant conceded two goals Derby still secured a great 4-2 win against Forest. score was 4-2. is Derby's keeper Lee Grant.

Paul Peschisolido scores his second goal and Derby's third. In the fantastic 4-2 win against Forest. A devastating opening 37 minutes saw Derby go 3-0 ahead.

Leon Osman attempts to hold off a defender during the 2-1 defeat by Sunderland. The loss meant that Derby slipped back into the relegation zone at a crucial point of the season.

Derby's players surround Marcus Tudgay after he secured the win against Forest with an 82nd minute goal.

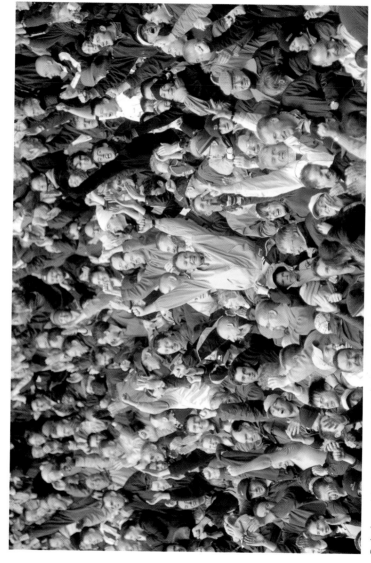

Derby fans celebrating their team's third goal in the win against Forest.

DERBY [0] 0 Walsall [0] 1

When you are walking a relegation tightrope, bad luck or controversial refereeing can send you toppling. That is why the 1-0 home defeat by Walsall was such a massive blow.

The nature of the defeat was hard to swallow as major decisions went against the Rams, none more so than the match-winning penalty four minutes from time. A towering headed clearance from Ian Roper dropped between Rams defenders Youl Mawene and Michael Johnson.

Lee Bradbury used his hand to pull back Johnson to gain the advantage and then Johnson hauled down Bradbury in the area. Bradbury, who never looked like scoring during two loan spells with the Rams earlier this season put away an unconvincing spot-kick. It was his first senior goal for almost a year. But as well as looking at the referee with bewilderment, the Rams also had to look at their own shortcomings.

They had enough of the ball to win several games and did play well, up to a point, but their inability to turn all that possession into a much-needed goal was worrying. Though when crosses were made from less predictable angles, they troubled Walsall. When Leon Osman picked out Manel, he headed past James Walker, only for the effort to be ruled out for offside.

Derby pressed and there were some close calls for Walsall. A stretching Roper deflected a shot narrowly wide of his own post, Peschisolido drove a shot into the side-netting and then Manel's strike hit Bazeley but dropped inches the wrong side of the post with half the stadium cheering a goal.

Bradbury did not impress, but it was his disputed penalty that gave him a winning return to Pride Park and pushed a grateful Walsall closer to Division One safety.

A first home defeat of the year left Derby in the relegation zone, two points adrift with six games to play.

Result.......Result.......Result.

DERBY ....(0) 0   WALSALL ......(0) 1
                                    Bradbury 86(p)

Att 23,574
Referee: M Jones

Stats......Stats.......Stats......Stats

DERBY				WALSALL		
1st	2nd	Total		Total	2nd	1st
6	5	11	Corners	1	0	1
6	4	10	Fouls	16	7	9
0	0	0	Yellow cards	3	3	0
0	1	1	Red cards	0	0	0
2	2	4	Caught Offside	8	7	1
4	7	11	Shots on target	4	1	3
4	5	9	Shots off target	4	2	2
0	0	0	Hit woodwork	1	1	0
37	51	44%	Possession	56%	49	63

IT was shocking. There's no doubt about it, the referee has won the game for Walsall today and that could be very costly for us.

George Burley

THE decision was controversial because the linesman, I believe, saw it differently to the referee. I would be disappointed if I was in their camp.

Colin Lee

Other Div 1 Results

Burnley 3 Norwich 5, Crewe 0 Rotherham 0, Gillingham 1 Cardiff 2, Preston 1 Bradford 0, Reading 2 West Ham 0, Sheff Utd 1 Nottm Forest 2, Stoke 1 Coventry 0, Wigan 0 Wimbledon 1

DERBY [0] 0 Walsall [0] 1

Goalkeeper Stats: Lee Grant
Saves: Catch 1, Parry 1

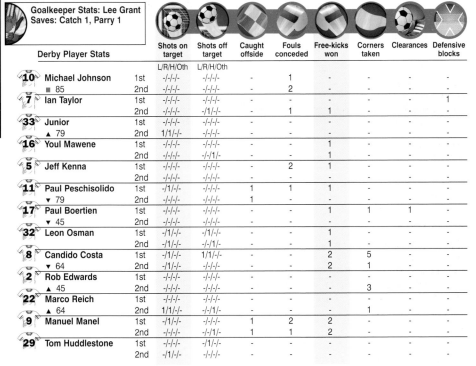

Derby Player Stats		Shots on target L/R/H/Oth	Shots off target L/R/H/Oth	Caught offside	Fouls conceded	Free-kicks won	Corners taken	Clearances	Defensive blocks
10 Michael Johnson	1st	-/-/-/-	-/-/-/-	-	1	-	-	-	-
▪ 85	2nd	-/-/-/-	-/-/-/-	-	2	-	-	-	-
7 Ian Taylor	1st	-/-/-/-	-/-/-/-	-	-	-	-	-	1
	2nd	-/-/-/-	-/1/-/-	-	1	1	-	-	-
33 Junior	1st	-/-/-/-	-/-/-/-	-	-	-	-	-	-
▲ 79	2nd	1/1/-/-	-/-/-/-	-	-	-	-	-	-
16 Youl Mawene	1st	-/-/-/-	-/-/-/-	-	-	1	-	-	-
	2nd	-/-/-/-	-/-/1/-	-	-	1	-	-	-
5 Jeff Kenna	1st	-/-/-/-	-/-/-/-	-	2	1	-	-	-
	2nd	-/-/-/-	-/-/-/-	-	-	-	-	-	-
11 Paul Peschisolido	1st	-/1/-/-	-/-/-/-	1	1	1	-	-	-
▼ 79	2nd	-/-/-/-	-/-/-/-	1	-	-	-	-	-
17 Paul Boertien	1st	-/-/-/-	-/-/-/-	-	-	1	1	1	-
▼ 45	2nd	-/-/-/-	-/-/-/-	-	-	-	-	-	-
32 Leon Osman	1st	-/1/-/-	-/1/-/-	-	-	1	-	-	-
	2nd	-/1/-/-	-/-/1/-	-	-	1	-	-	-
8 Candido Costa	1st	-/1/-/-	1/1/-/-	-	-	2	5	-	-
▼ 64	2nd	-/1/-/-	-/-/-/-	-	-	2	1	-	-
2 Rob Edwards	1st	-/-/-/-	-/-/-/-	-	-	-	-	-	-
▲ 45	2nd	-/-/-/-	-/-/-/-	-	-	-	3	-	-
22 Marco Reich	1st	-/-/-/-	-/-/-/-	-	-	-	-	-	-
▲ 64	2nd	1/1/-/-	-/-/1/-	-	-	-	1	-	-
9 Manuel Manel	1st	-/1/-/-	-/-/-/-	1	2	2	-	-	-
	2nd	-/-/-/-	-/-/1/-	1	1	2	-	-	-
29 Tom Huddlestone	1st	-/-/-/-	-/1/-/-	-	-	-	-	-	-
	2nd	-/1/-/-	-/-/-/-	-	-	-	-	-	-

Subs not used: Oakes, Bolder. - Formation: 4-4-2

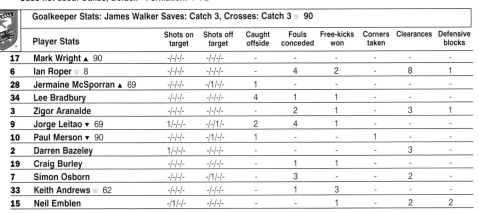

Goalkeeper Stats: James Walker Saves: Catch 3, Crosses: Catch 3 ▪ 90

Player Stats	Shots on target	Shots off target	Caught offside	Fouls conceded	Free-kicks won	Corners taken	Clearances	Defensive blocks
17 Mark Wright ▲ 90	-/-/-/-	-/-/-/-	-	-	-	-	-	-
6 Ian Roper ▪ 8	-/-/-/-	-/-/-/-	-	4	2	-	8	1
28 Jermaine McSporran ▲ 69	-/-/-/-	-/1/-/-	1	-	-	-	-	-
34 Lee Bradbury	-/-/-/-	-/-/-/-	4	1	1	-	-	-
3 Zigor Aranalde	-/-/-/-	-/-/-/-	-	2	1	-	3	1
9 Jorge Leitao ▼ 69	1/-/-/-	-/-/1/-	2	4	1	-	-	-
10 Paul Merson ▼ 90	-/-/-/-	-/1/-/-	1	-	-	1	-	-
2 Darren Bazeley	1/-/-/-	-/-/-/-	-	-	-	-	3	-
19 Craig Burley	-/-/-/-	-/-/-/-	-	1	1	-	-	-
7 Simon Osborn	-/-/-/-	-/1/-/-	-	3	-	-	2	-
33 Keith Andrews ▪ 62	-/-/-/-	-/-/-/-	-	1	3	-	-	-
15 Neil Emblen	-/1/-/-	-/-/-/-	-	-	1	-	2	2

Subs not used: Petterson, Carbon, Taylor. - Formation: 4-4-2

West Ham [0] 0 DERBY [0] 0

Derby County showed the character needed to survive the Division One relegation battle by taking a valuable point with a gutsy performance at West Ham United. And by the time the final whistle had blown on Saturday's goalless draw at Upton Park, manager George Burley was convinced his team should have had three points.

With stoppage time being played, substitute Manel was released by Leon Osman's cute pass and beat Pavel Srnicek. The flag was straight up for offside but television replays showed that the Spanish striker was onside and that the assistant referee had got it wrong.

Victory would have lifted Derby out of the bottom three and for a second game they had suffered at the hands of the officials. The early kick-off appeared to suit West Ham and they were on top in the first half.

Front men Bobby Zamora and David Connolly were a handful and Marlon Harewood had his moments, despite playing on the right of midfield. But Derby's stubborn resistance kept West Ham out. It was Derby's first clean sheet in six games and full marks to them because West Ham had not been short of goals on their own patch.

Realising that West Ham's confidence was draining away, Derby grew in stature and belief. Their first shot on target had come only three minutes before the break but they were much more of a threat in the second half.

Tom Huddlestone stretched Srnicek with a quickly-taken free kick, Marcus Tudgay fired over from a good position after Osman's menacing run and Vincent should have done a lot better with a couple of free kicks.

Paul Peschisolido had another quiet game up front. After a scorching start to his Rams career with four goals in three games, he had not been such a threat in his last three appearances, despite his commendable work-rate.

Result.......Result.......Result.

WEST HAM..........(0) 0   DERBY ....(0) 0

Att 28,207
Referee: J P Robinson

Stats......Stats.......Stats......Stats

WEST HAM						DERBY
1st	2nd	Total		Total	2nd	1st
4	3	7	Corners	3	2	1
3	11	14	Fouls	9	3	6
0	0	0	Yellow cards	0	0	0
0	0	0	Red cards	0	0	0
5	1	6	Caught Offside	7	3	4
3	0	3	Shots on target	3	2	1
3	1	4	Shots off target	5	4	1
0	0	0	Hit woodwork	0	0	0
53	53	53%	Possession	47%	47	47

 YOU could tell this was a team who desperately needed a goal to lift them. The task in front of us is difficult but we're up to it.
Alan Pardew

YOU know it's going to be tough with West Ham going for promotion but we've improved in the last few months and came here thinking we had a chance.
George Burley

Other Div 1 Results

Bradford 2 Reading 1, Cardiff 0 Crystal Palace 2, Coventry 4 Millwall 0, Nottm Forest 0 Stoke 0, Rotherham 1 Ipswich 3, Walsall 0 Burnley 1, Watford 2 Crewe 1, West Brom 1 Gillingham 0, Wimbledon 3 Preston 3

Goalkeeper Stats: Lee Grant
Saves: Round Post 1,
Crosses: Catch 1

Derby Player Stats

Player		Shots on target L/R/H/Oth	Shots off target L/R/H/Oth	Caught offside	Fouls conceded	Free-kicks won	Corners taken	Clearances	Defensive blocks
7 Ian Taylor	1st	-/-/-/-	-/-/-/-	1	-	1	-	-	-
	2nd	-/-/-/-	-/-/1/-	-	-	3	-	-	-
16 Youl Mawene	1st	-/-/-/-	-/-/-/-	-	2	-	-	-	-
	2nd	-/-/-/-	-/-/-/-	-	-	1	-	1	-
11 Paul Peschisolido ▼ 82	1st	-/-/-/-	-/-/-/-	2	1	-	-	-	-
	2nd	-/-/-/-	-/-/-/-	1	1	2	-	-	-
23 Marcus Tudgay	1st	-/-/-/-	-/-/-/-	1	-	-	-	-	-
	2nd	-/-/-/-	-/1/-/-	1	1	2	-	1	-
15 Adam Bolder ▲ 54	1st	-/-/-/-	-/-/-/-	-	-	-	-	-	-
	2nd	-/-/-/-	-/-/-/-	-	-	1	-	-	-
32 Leon Osman	1st	1/-/-/-	-/-/-/-	-	-	-	-	-	-
	2nd	-/-/-/-	-/1/-/-	-	-	1	1	-	-
3 Jamie Vincent	1st	-/-/-/-	-/-/-/-	-	-	1	1	-	-
	2nd	1/-/-/-	1/-/-/-	-	-	-	1	1	-
30 Lee Holmes ▼ 54	1st	-/-/-/-	-/-/-/-	-	-	1	-	-	-
	2nd	-/-/-/-	-/-/-/-	-	-	-	-	-	-
9 Manuel Manel ▲ 82	1st	-/-/-/-	-/-/-/-	-	-	-	-	-	-
	2nd	-/-/-/-	-/-/-/-	1	1	-	-	-	-
29 Tom Huddlestone	1st	-/-/-/-	1/-/-/-	-	3	-	-	-	-
	2nd	-/1/-/-	-/-/-/-	-	-	1	-	-	-

Subs not used: Oakes, Edwards, Costa. - Formation: 4-3-3

Goalkeeper Stats: Pavel Srnicek Saves: Catch 2, Parry 1, Crosses: Punch 1

	Player Stats	Shots on target	Shots off target	Caught offside	Fouls conceded	Free-kicks won	Corners taken	Clearances	Defensive blocks
6	Michael Carrick	-/-/-	-/-/-	-	2	-	4	-	-
10	Marlon Harewood ▼ 80	-/-/-	-/-/-	1	-	-	-	-	-
11	Steve Lomas	-/-/-	-/-/-	-	1	1	-	1	-
7	Christian Dailly	-/-/-	1/1/-/-	-	1	2	-	-	-
8	David Connolly	-/1/-/-	-/-/-	2	-	2	-	-	-
20	Nigel Reo-Coker ▲ 66	-/-/-	-/-/-	-	1	-	-	-	-
35	Chris Cohen ▼ 66	-/-/-	1/-/-/-	-	1	-	-	1	-
2	Tomas Repka	-/-/-	-/-/-	-	2	-	-	-	-
25	Bobby Zamora ▼ 66	1/1/-/-	-/-/-	3	1	2	-	-	-
29	Brian Deane ▲ 66	-/-/-	-/-/1/-	-	1	-	-	-	-
26	Joel McAnuff ▲ 80	-/-/-	-/-/-	-	1	-	-	-	-
5	Jon Harley	-/-/-	-/-/-	-	3	-	3	-	-
17	Hayden Mullins	-/-/-	-/-/-	-	-	1	-	1	-

Subs not used: Forde, Melville. - Formation: 4-4-2

DERBY [1] 3 Bradford [0] 2

George Burley had asked for a change of luck. And he certainly got it after a bizarrre own goal handed his relegation-threatened Derby County team a late and crucial winner in the 3-2 home victory over Bradford City.

Derby had suffered some bad luck leaving them pleading for a break in the battle to beat the drop. With six minutes remaining and the scores level at 2-2, they got it when Bradford's Robert Wolleaston looked set to hack Leon Osman's goal-bound shot away from his own line.

Instead, he thumped his clearance against the back of his grounded goalkeeper Alan Combe and the ball rebounded into the net. Relief swept round Pride Park Stadium because the Rams had made ridiculously hard work of beating a poor Bradford team who were already virtually condemned to Division Two football.

Goals from Osman and skipper Ian Taylor, his 12th of the season, had seemingly put them in a comfortable position before panic set in. Battling Bradford hit back with two goals in 12 minutes from Peter Atherton and Wolleaston.

From the start, a number of Derby's players looked edgy, trying to force the issue rather than taking an extra touch or pass to compose themselves. But they still took the lead after 20 minutes. A lay off from Marcus Tudgay found Osman who, displaying quick feet in a tight situation, cleverly twisted and shot across the face of goal.

After the break, the Rams were pinned back by Bradford's bold start.Grant made some good saves that took on added importance when Derby went two-up after 64 minutes.

Osman curled in a free kick and Taylor capitalised on some dreadful marking to head home at the back post. A two-goal cushion should have been enough to see Derby to a comfortable win but they allowed Bradford to hit back with two goals in 12 mad minutes.

Summerbee's cross picked out Windass who headed down for Atherton to poke the ball past Grant then Richard Jackson's weak clearance gave Wolleaston the chance to shoot, Jeff Kenna made the block but the ball fell for Wolleaston again and he found the net with a low shot.

Result.......Result.......Result.

DERBY ....(1) 3 BRADFORD ..(0) 2
Osman 36   Atherton 67
Taylor 64   Wolleaston 79
Combe 84 (og)

Att 21,593
Referee: H Webb

Stats......Stats.......Stats......Stats

DERBY				BRADFORD		
1st	2nd	Total		Total	2nd	1st
2	3	5	Corners	6	4	2
2	6	8	Fouls	16	8	8
0	1	1	Yellow cards	2	1	1
0	0	0	Red cards	0	0	0
1	2	3	Caught Offside	4	0	4
3	2	5	Shots on target	4	4	0
3	2	5	Shots off target	5	4	1
1	0	1	Hit woodwork	0	0	0
42	53	47%	Possession	53%	47	58

 YOU just hope at some stage that you'll get the rub of the green and the winner was fortunate but, thankfully, we got it to get three points.
George Burley

 THE writing is on the wall, we were relegated today, even though it's mathematically possible to get out of it. The lads gave 100%.
Bryan Robson

Other Div 1 Results

Burnley 2 Watford 3, Crewe 3 Coventry 1, Crystal Palace 1 West Ham 0, Gillingham 3 Walsall 0, Ipswich 1 Sunderland 0, Millwall 1 West Brom 1, Preston 2 Nottm Forest 2, Reading 0 Norwich 1, Sheff Utd 2 Wimbledon 1, Stoke 0 Rotherham 2

DERBY [1] 3 Bradford [0] 2

Goalkeeper Stats: Lee Grant
Saves: Round Post 1,
Crosses: Catch 2, Punch 2

Derby Player Stats

			Shots on target L/R/H/Oth	Shots off target L/R/H/Oth	Caught offside	Fouls conceded	Free-kicks won	Corners taken	Clearances	Defensive blocks
7	Ian Taylor	1st	-/-/-/-	-/-/-/-	-	-	-	-	-	-
		2nd	-/-/1/-	-/-/-/-	-	-	-	-	-	-
14	Richard Jackson	1st	-/-/-/-	-/-/-/-	-	-	1	-	1	-
		2nd	-/-/-/-	-/-/-/-	-	1	-	-	-	-
16	Youl Mawene	1st	-/-/-/-	-/-/-/-	-	1	1	-	3	-
		2nd	-/-/-/-	-/-/-/-	-	-	1	-	2	-
5	Jeff Kenna	1st	-/-/-/-	-/-/-/-	-	-	-	-	-	-
	■ 65	2nd	-/-/-/-	-/-/-/-	-	1	-	-	-	-
11	Paul Peschisolido	1st	-/1/-/-	1/-/-/-	-	-	-	-	-	-
		2nd	1/-/-/-	-/-/-/-	2	-	1	-	-	-
23	Marcus Tudgay	1st	-/-/1/-	-/1/-/-	1	1	1	-	-	-
		2nd	-/-/-/-	-/-/1/-	-	-	3	-	-	-
15	Adam Bolder	1st	-/-/-/-	-/-/-/-	-	-	-	-	-	-
	▲ 35	2nd	-/-/-/-	-/1/-/-	-	1	-	-	-	2
8	Candido Costa	1st	-/-/-/-	-/-/-/-	-	-	3	1	-	-
	▼ 35	2nd	-/-/-/-	-/-/-/-	-	-	-	-	-	-
32	Leon Osman	1st	1/-/-/-	-/1/-/-	-	-	1	-	-	-
		2nd	-/-/-/-	-/-/-/-	-	1	2	3	-	-
3	Jamie Vincent	1st	-/-/-/-	-/-/-/-	-	-	1	1	1	1
	▼ 49	2nd	-/-/-/-	-/-/-/-	-	-	-	-	-	-
29	Tom Huddlestone	1st	-/-/-/-	-/-/-/-	-	-	-	-	-	-
		2nd	-/-/-/-	-/-/-/-	-	-	-	-	1	1
6	Pablo Mills	1st	-/-/-/-	-/-/-/-	-	-	-	-	-	-
	▲ 49	2nd	-/-/-/-	-/-/-/-	-	2	1	-	1	-

Subs not used: Oakes, Manel, Junior. - Formation: 4-4-2

Goalkeeper Stats: Alan Combe Saves: Parry 1, Crosses: Catch 3

Player Stats

		Shots on target	Shots off target	Caught offside	Fouls conceded	Free-kicks won	Corners taken	Clearances	Defensive blocks
5	David Wetherall	-/-/-/-	-/-/1/-	-	-	-	-	5	-
17	Jason Gavin ▼ 86	-/-/-/-	-/-/-/-	-	1	-	-	1	-
3	Paul Heckingbottom ■ 82	-/-/-/-	-/-/-/-	-	6	1	-	1	1
10	Dean Windass	-/-/-/-	-/-/2/-	1	1	1	-	1	-
8	Michael Branch	-/1/-/-	-/1/-/-	3	-	-	-	-	-
9	Nicky Summerbee ■ 3	-/-/-/-	-/-/-/-	-	1	-	6	-	-
18	Ben Muirhead ▲ 75	-/-/-/-	-/-/-/-	-	-	2	-	-	-
2	Peter Atherton	-/1/-/-	-/-/-/-	-	-	-	-	-	-
20	Robert Wolleaston	-/2/-/-	1/-/-/-	-	1	1	-	-	-
12	Danny Cadamarteri ▲ 61	-/-/-/-	-/-/-/-	-	2	2	-	-	-
6	Mark Bower ▲ 86	-/-/-/-	-/-/-/-	-	-	1	-	-	-
16	Lewis Emanuel ▼ 61	-/-/-/-	-/-/-/-	-	2	-	-	-	-
19	Gareth Edds ▼ 75	-/-/-/-	-/-/-/-	-	2	-	-	3	-

Subs not used: Paston, Kearney. - Formation: 4-4-2

Derby Played: 42 Won 11 Drawn 13 Lost 18 For 46 Against 64 Pos 22

Derby County's hopes of surviving their torrid season received a significant boost when their biggest win for more than six years lifted them out of the Division One relegation zone.

A four-goal first-half blitz set up a thumping 5-1 victory over Preston North End at Pride Park Stadium on a day when everything fell for the Rams. They dismantled Preston in the opening 45 minutes, racing into a 4-0 lead thanks to doubles from Spanish striker Manel and the excellent Marcus Tudgay.

Only two minutes had gone when Leon Osman's volley was blocked and the ball rebounded off Manel's knee and into the net. Preston appeared to be settling without really threatening when Derby hit them with three more goals.

The first came when Richard Jackson and Paul Peschisolido were involved in the move before Manel's inviting lay-off saw Tudgay take a good first touch before expertly clipping the ball past Jonathan Gould from an angle.

Derby were being helped by Preston's apparent lack of interest in closing down and they capitalised with a third goal on 32 minutes. Manel was given time and space to curl a 30-yarder against the underside of the bar, Peschisolido was quickly to the loose ball and unselfishly picked out Tudgay, who finished from close range for his sixth goal of the season.

And Derby fans were also on their feet again five minutes later but to celebrate another goal. Tom Huddlestone's free-kick took a slight deflection off the wall and Gould could only parry when he perhaps should have done better, leaving Manel to steer the ball high into an empty net.

But Derby appear unsure of how to handle leads. Despite being four-up, they found themselves on the back foot for a 20-minute spell as Preston suddenly woke up. Chris Lucketti pulled one back after 55 minutes, heading in after a hesitant Derby watched rather than dealt with Paul McKenna's cross.

Fit-again Marco Reich and Junior were introduced and they figured in the fifth goal to put the result beyond doubt. Preston defender Michael Jackson could do little as Reich's shot struck his arm and referee Paul Taylor, who made some strange decisions throughout, gave Derby another fortunate penalty to follow the ones at Sheffield United and Sunderland.

Result.......Result.......Result.

DERBY ....(4) 5   **PRESTON** ......(0) 1
Manel 2, 37   Mawene 55 (og)
Tudgay 27, 32
Junior 76(p)

Att 24,162
Referee: P Taylor

Stats......Stats.......Stats......Stats

DERBY				PRESTON		
1st	2nd	Total		Total	2nd	1st
4	4	8	Corners	6	5	1
8	9	17	Fouls	13	4	9
0	0	0	Yellow cards	4	1	3
0	0	0	Red cards	0	0	0
0	0	0	Caught Offside	2	0	2
11	4	15	Shots on target	6	2	4
1	2	3	Shots off target	8	6	2
0	0	0	Hit woodwork	0	0	0
50	58	54%	Possession	46%	42	50

WE'VE reached 49 points but I've said that we need 52 or more so we need to win at least one more, if not two, games.
George Burley

WE had chances to get back in it and make it 4-3 but all credit to Derby, they were up for it. I feel embarrassed by our first-half display.
Craig Brown

Other Div 1 Results

Bradford 2 Wimbledon 3, Cardiff 2 Burnley 0, Crystal Palace 1 Wigan 1, Gillingham 1 Ipswich 2, Norwich 5 Walsall 0, Nottm Forest 2 Millwall 2, Reading 1 Crewe 1, Rotherham 1 Watford 1, Sheff Utd 0 Stoke 1, West Ham 2 Coventry 0

DERBY [4] 5 Preston [0] 1

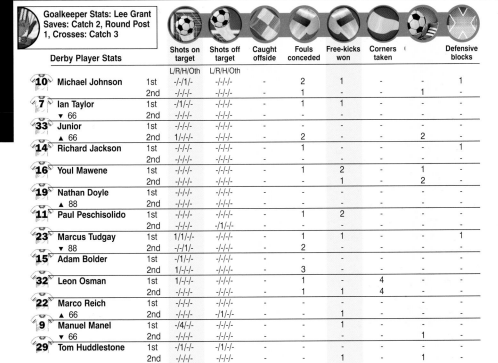

Goalkeeper Stats: Lee Grant Saves: Catch 2, Round Post 1, Crosses: Catch 3

Derby Player Stats		Shots on target L/R/H/Oth	Shots off target L/R/H/Oth	Caught offside	Fouls conceded	Free-kicks won	Corners taken	Defensive blocks
10 Michael Johnson	1st	-/-/1/-	-/-/-	-	2	1	-	1
	2nd	-/-/-	-/-/-	-	1	-	-	-
7 Ian Taylor ▼ 66	1st	-/1/-/-	-/-/-	-	1	1	-	-
	2nd	-/-/-	-/-/-	-	-	-	-	-
33 Junior ▲ 66	1st	-/-/-	-/-/-	-	-	-	-	-
	2nd	1/-/-/-	-/-/-	-	2	-	-	-
14 Richard Jackson	1st	-/-/-	-/-/-	-	1	-	-	1
	2nd	-/-/-	-/-/-	-	-	-	-	-
16 Youl Mawene	1st	-/-/-	-/-/-	-	1	2	-	-
	2nd	-/-/-	-/-/-	-	-	1	-	-
19 Nathan Doyle ▲ 88	1st	-/-/-	-/-/-	-	-	-	-	-
	2nd	-/-/-	-/-/-	-	-	-	-	-
11 Paul Peschisolido	1st	-/-/-	-/-/-	-	1	2	-	-
	2nd	-/-/-	-/1/-/-	-	-	-	-	1
23 Marcus Tudgay ▼ 88	1st	1/1/-/-	-/-/-	-	1	1	-	1
	2nd	-/-/1/-	-/-/-	-	2	-	-	-
15 Adam Bolder	1st	-/1/-/-	-/-/-	-	-	-	-	-
	2nd	1/-/-/-	-/-/-	-	3	-	-	-
32 Leon Osman	1st	1/-/-/-	-/-/-	-	1	-	4	-
	2nd	-/-/-	-/-/-	-	1	1	4	-
22 Marco Reich ▲ 66	1st	-/-/-	-/-/-	-	-	-	-	-
	2nd	-/-/-	-/1/-/-	-	-	1	-	-
9 Manuel Manel ▼ 66	1st	-/4/-/-	-/-/-	-	-	1	-	-
	2nd	-/-/-	-/-/-	-	-	-	-	-
29 Tom Huddlestone	1st	-/1/-/-	-/1/-/-	-	-	-	-	-
	2nd	-/-/-	-/-/-	-	1	-	-	-

Subs not used: Oakes, Mills. - Formation: 4-4-2

PRESTON NORTH END FC

Goalkeeper Stats: Jonathan Gould Saves: Catch 2, Parry 1, Crosses: Catch 4, Punch 1

	Player Stats	Shots on target	Shots off target	Caught offside	Fouls conceded	Free-kicks won	Corners taken	Clearances	Defensive blocks
6	Marlon Broomes ■ 14	-/-/-	-/-/-	-	2	1	-	2	1
25	Richard Cresswell ■ 36	1/-/-/-	-/-/1/-	-	-	2	-	3	-
2	Graham Alexander	-/1/-/-	-/-/-	-	-	1	3	2	-
34	Simon Lynch ▲ 86	-/-/-	-/-/-	-	-	-	-	-	-
33	Mark Jackson ▲ 86	-/-/-	-/-/-	-	-	-	-	-	-
4	Dickson Etuhu ▼ 86	-/-/-	1/-/-/-	-	-	-	-	1	1
11	David Healy	-/2/-/-	-/2/1/-	1	-	2	-	-	-
27	Alan McCormack ▼ 86 ■ 24	-/2/-/-	-/1/-/-	-	2	3	1	-	-
5	Michael Jackson ■ 79	-/-/-	-/-/-	-	3	1	-	2	2
20	Chris Lucketti	-/-/-	-/-/-	-	-	1	-	-	-
9	Ricardo Fuller	-/-/-	-/1/1/-	1	5	5	-	1	-
16	Paul McKenna	-/-/-	-/-/-	-	-	1	2	-	-

Subs not used: Lucas, Armstrong, Elebert. - Formation: 4-4-2

Burnley [1] 1 DERBY [0] 0

Another annoying and preventable away-day failure meant that the threat of relegation still loomed large over Derby County with only two games remaining. Playing an equally edgy Burnley at Turf Moor presented an opportunity for the Rams to virtually secure their status in Division One.

But they failed to seize the moment.

Instead, Burnley's 1-0 victory sees them relieved and planning ahead, while another week or more of worry lay in front of George Burley and his players. As the scoreline suggests, the home side just about shaded a tense, closely-fought, often exciting encounter in which some of the football belied the lowly positions of both teams.

The Rams saw plenty of the ball and, at times, their movement and passing was good but they were wasteful at key moments and that is why they returned empty-handed. Spanish striker Manel, a two-goal hero against Preston in the previous game, was the main culprit.

His miss after 24 minutes, when he side-footed over from little more than six yards was inexplicable. Such openings cannot be squandered when you are scrapping for survival and had Manel accepted that gilt-edged chance, along with others at Sheffield United and Sunderland, the Rams may well have been safe.

There were four presentable opportunities to dent Burnley's confidence before Graham Branch grabbed the winning goal four minutes before the break.

Youl Mawene looked favourite to deal with Mark McGregor's long punt forward but the French defender was uncertain rather than decisive in his challenge. This allowed Branch to steal the ball and curl a low shot past Lee Grant, who should also have done better.

Result.......Result.......Result.

BURNLEY ....(1) 1   **DERBY** ....(0) 0
Branch 42

Att 16,189
Referee: E Evans

Stats......Stats.......Stats......Stats

BURNLEY				DERBY		
1st	2nd	Total		Total	2nd	1st
4	3	7	Corners	8	5	3
5	5	10	Fouls	9	6	3
0	3	3	Yellow cards	0	0	0
0	0	0	Red cards	0	0	0
4	3	7	Caught Offside	2	2	0
4	1	5	Shots on target	2	1	1
1	0	1	Shots off target	4	1	3
0	0	0	Hit woodwork	0	0	0
39	46	42%	Possession	58%	54	61

IT feels good to celebrate back-to-back wins and a couple of clean sheets. I thought Derby were excellent and contributed in full to a great game.

Stan Ternent

IT was disappointing to lose but the commitment was first class and now we've got to do the same again in the final two games.

George Burley

Other Div 1 Results

Coventry 1 Rotherham 1, Crewe 2 Crystal Palace 3, Ipswich 1 Nottm Forest 2, Millwall 0 Reading 1, Preston 2 Cardiff 2, Stoke 0 West Ham 2, Walsall 0 Sheff Utd 1, Watford 1 Norwich 2, West Brom 2 Bradford 0, Wigan 0 Sunderland 0, Wimbledon 1 Gillingham 2

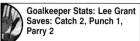

Goalkeeper Stats: Lee Grant Saves: Catch 2, Punch 1, Parry 2

Derby Player Stats		Shots on target	Shots off target	Caught offside	Fouls conceded	Free-kicks won	Corners taken	Clearances	Defensive blocks
		L/R/H/Oth	L/R/H/Oth						
10 Michael Johnson	1st	-/-/-/-	-/-/-/-	-	-	1	-	1	-
	2nd	-/-/-/-	-/-/-/-	-	1	-	-	2	-
7 Ian Taylor	1st	-/-/-/-	-/-/1/-	-	-	-	-	-	-
	2nd	-/-/1/-	-/-/-/-	-	1	-	-	-	-
33 Junior ▲ 80	1st	-/-/-/-	-/-/-/-	-	-	-	-	-	-
	2nd	-/-/-/-	-/-/-/-	-	-	-	-	-	-
14 Richard Jackson	1st	-/-/-/-	-/-/-/-	-	-	1	-	1	-
	2nd	-/-/-/-	-/-/-/-	-	-	-	-	-	1
16 Youl Mawene	1st	-/-/-/-	-/-/-/-	-	-	-	-	-	-
	2nd	-/-/-/-	-/-/-/-	-	-	2	-	-	-
11 Paul Peschisolido ▼ 80	1st	-/-/-/-	-/-/-/-	-	-	-	-	-	-
	2nd	-/-/-/-	-/1/-/-	-	-	-	-	-	-
23 Marcus Tudgay	1st	-/-/-/-	-/-/-/-	-	1	-	-	-	1
	2nd	-/-/-/-	-/-/-/-	-	-	-	-	-	-
15 Adam Bolder ▼ 70	1st	-/-/-/-	-/-/-/-	-	-	-	2	-	-
	2nd	-/-/-/-	-/-/-/-	-	-	-	1	-	-
32 Leon Osman	1st	-/1/-/-	-/-/-/-	-	-	-	1	-	-
	2nd	-/-/-/-	-/-/-/-	-	-	-	2	-	-
22 Marco Reich ▲ 70	1st	-/-/-/-	-/-/-/-	-	-	-	-	-	-
	2nd	-/-/-/-	-/-/-/-	-	-	-	1	-	-
29 Tom Huddlestone	1st	-/-/-/-	-/-/-/-	-	2	-	-	-	-
	2nd	-/-/-/-	-/-/-/-	-	4	1	1	1	-
9 Manuel Manel	1st	-/-/-/-	-/1/1/-	-	-	2	-	-	-
	2nd	-/-/-/-	-/-/-/-	2	-	2	-	-	-

Subs not used: Oakes, Mills, Doyle. - Formation: 4-4-2

Goalkeeper Stats: Brian Jensen Saves: Catch 1, Crosses: Catch 6

	Player Stats	Shots on target	Shots off target	Caught offside	Fouls conceded	Free-kicks won	Corners taken	Clearances	Defensive blocks
14	Mark McGregor	-/-/-/-	-/-/-/-	-	-	-	-	-	-
25	Neil Wood ▲ 70	-/-/-/-	-/-/-/-	-	1	-	-	-	-
7	Glen Little ▼ 70	-/-/-/-	-/-/-/-	3	1	1	-	-	-
4	Paul Weller	-/-/-/-	-/-/-/-	-	1	2	-	1	-
8	Robert Blake ▼ 77	-/1/-/-	-/1/-/-	1	1	2	6	-	-
3	Mohammed Camara ■ 77	-/-/-/-	-/-/-/-	-	-	-	-	-	-
16	Lenny Johnrose	-/-/-/-	-/-/-/-	-	2	1	-	-	-
6	Graham Branch ■ 90	1/1/-/-	-/-/-/-	3	2	-	-	-	-
2	Lee Roche	-/-/-/-	-/-/-/-	-	-	-	-	-	1
5	David May	-/1/1/-	-/-/-/-	-	2	-	1	1	1
18	Luke Chadwick ▲ 77 ■ 85	-/-/-/-	-/-/-/-	-	-	2	-	-	-

Subs not used: Adebola, Moore, Abbey. - Formation: 4-4-2

Derby Played: 44 Won 12 Drawn 13 Lost 19 For 51 Against 66 Pos 21

...April Team Stats.....Team Stats......Team Stats......Team S

League table at the end of April

		HOME					AWAY						
	P	W	D	L	F	A	W	D	L	F	A	Pts	Df
Norwich	43	17	3	2	41	13	9	7	5	32	22	88	38
West Brom	43	14	5	3	34	14	11	6	4	29	21	86	28
Sunderland	43	12	7	2	31	14	8	5	9	27	29	72	15
Ipswich	45	12	2	8	48	35	9	7	7	35	36	72	12
West Ham	44	11	7	4	38	20	7	9	6	24	24	70	18
Wigan	44	11	7	4	28	15	7	9	6	31	28	70	16
Crystal Palace	44	9	8	5	33	25	11	2	9	37	34	70	11
Sheff Utd	45	11	6	6	37	25	9	4	9	25	28	70	9
Reading	44	10	6	6	28	25	9	4	9	26	31	67	-2
Millwall	44	10	8	4	27	15	7	7	8	27	31	66	8
Cardiff	44	10	5	7	39	24	7	7	8	27	32	63	10
Coventry	44	8	9	5	32	21	7	5	10	28	30	59	9
Stoke	43	10	6	5	31	23	6	5	11	21	31	59	-2
Preston	44	11	6	5	40	26	4	7	11	24	39	58	-1
Nottm Forest	44	7	9	6	32	25	6	6	10	26	33	54	0
Watford	44	8	8	6	30	28	6	4	12	23	36	54	-11
Burnley	44	9	6	7	36	30	4	8	10	23	42	53	-13
Crewe	44	11	3	8	32	23	3	7	12	23	39	52	-7
Rotherham	44	7	8	7	28	27	5	7	10	20	31	51	-10
Gillingham	44	10	1	11	26	29	4	7	11	20	33	50	-16
Derby	**44**	**10**	**5**	**7**	**37**	**33**	**2**	**8**	**12**	**14**	**33**	**49**	**-15**
Walsall	44	7	7	8	26	29	5	5	12	16	33	48	-20
Bradford	44	6	3	13	23	33	4	3	15	15	33	36	-28
Wimbledon	44	2	4	16	20	40	5	0	17	19	48	25	-49

April matches table

	P	W	D	L	F	A	Pts
Crystal Palace	6	5	1	0	12	4	16
Norwich	5	5	0	0	15	4	15
West Brom	5	4	1	0	8	3	13
Ipswich	6	3	1	2	10	8	10
Watford	5	3	1	1	9	7	10
Burnley	6	3	0	3	9	10	9
Nottm Forest	5	2	3	0	8	6	9
Wigan	6	2	2	2	7	4	8
Cardiff	6	2	2	2	6	8	8
Wimbledon	7	2	1	4	10	13	7
Derby	**5**	**2**	**1**	**2**	**8**	**5**	**7**
Reading	5	2	1	2	5	4	7
Sunderland	6	2	1	3	5	6	7
Sheff Utd	6	2	1	3	5	8	7
West Ham	5	2	1	2	4	3	7
Stoke	5	2	1	2	2	4	7
Preston	5	1	3	1	9	12	6
Gillingham	6	2	0	4	7	9	6
Rotherham	6	1	3	2	6	7	6
Crewe	5	1	2	2	7	7	5
Coventry	5	1	1	3	6	7	4
Bradford	5	1	0	4	6	10	3
Millwall	6	0	3	3	4	10	3
Walsall	5	1	0	4	1	10	3

April team stats details

Club Name	Ply	Shots On	Shots Off	Corners	Hit W'work	Caught Offside	Offside Trap	Fouls	Yellow Cards	Red Cards	Pens Awarded	Pens Con
Bradford	5	33	27	35	1	14	20	75	11	1	- (-)	-
Burnley	6	20	18	33	0	23	15	59	11	0	1 (1)	2
Cardiff	6	28	31	31	0	20	16	65	13	1	2 (1)	2
Coventry	5	35	39	38	1	8	26	77	4	0	2 (1)	2
Crewe	5	22	18	13	1	16	17	54	7	0	2 (2)	1
Crystal Palace	6	34	35	27	1	18	15	97	10	0	2 (2)	1
Derby	**5**	**36**	**26**	**35**	**1**	**16**	**19**	**53**	**1**	**1**	**1 (1)**	**-**
Gillingham	6	40	27	30	0	29	18	70	6	0	2 (1)	-
Ipswich	6	42	42	39	3	12	17	72	8	0	1 (1)	2
Millwall	6	17	25	22	3	18	11	86	10	2	- (-)	1
Norwich	5	43	27	29	1	23	10	71	6	0	- (-)	-
Nottm Forest	5	26	19	17	2	15	9	71	6	1	- (-)	-
Preston	5	38	35	37	2	12	3	68	7	0	- (-)	1
Reading	5	25	17	30	0	12	14	40	3	1	- (-)	-
Rotherham	6	36	31	32	4	16	17	68	7	0	- (-)	1
Sheff Utd	6	30	32	39	2	19	25	84	10	0	3 (2)	1
Stoke	5	15	20	25	0	12	2	57	8	0	- (-)	-
Sunderland	6	36	30	35	1	22	32	66	11	1	- (-)	2
Walsall	5	19	21	19	1	25	22	67	6	0	1 (1)	1
Watford	5	28	22	21	3	24	24	73	4	0	1 (1)	1
West Brom	5	26	21	24	2	25	11	60	7	2	- (-)	-
West Ham	5	24	19	27	0	18	23	70	8	1	1 (1)	-
Wigan	6	37	41	30	1	20	37	85	9	2	- (-)	-
Wimbledon	7	34	31	38	3	20	34	64	5	0	1 (1)	2

...April Player Stats..... Player Stats...... Player Stats......Pla

Monthly Top scorers

Mathias Svensson (Norwich)	5
Darren Huckerby (Norwich)	4
Dave Kitson (Reading)	4
Wayne Gray (Wimbledon)	3
Patrick Agyemang (Gillingham)	3
Martin Butler (Rotherham)	3
Jason Roberts (Wigan)	3
Paul McKenna (Preston)	3
Nathan Ellington (Wigan)	3
David Johnson (Nottm Forest)	3

Penalties scored

2 Dean Ashton (Crewe), Andrew Johnson (Crystal Palace)

Assists

Andrew Johnson (Crystal Palace)	4
Lloyd Dyer (West Brom)	3
Darren Huckerby (Norwich)	3
Nicky Summerbee (Bradford)	3
Nicky Southall (Gillingham)	3
Julian Gray (Crystal Palace)	2
Matthew Richards (Ipswich)	2

Quickest goals

1:35 mins - Damien Francis (Norwich vs Walsall)
1:42 mins - Manuel Manel (Derby vs Preston)
3:19 mins - Marlon King (Preston vs Nottm Forest)
3:56 mins - Martin Butler (Rotherham vs Watford)
4:12 mins - Malvin Kamara (Bradford vs Wimbledon)

Top Keeper

	Mins	Gls
Thomas Myhre (Sunderland)	265	1
Pavel Srnicek (West Ham)	192	1
John Filan (Wigan)	475	3
Russell Hoult (West Brom)	435	3
Nico Vaesen (Crystal P)	580	4
S Bywater (West Ham)	278	2
Jamie Ashdown (Reading)	478	4
Robert Green (Norwich)	473	4

Shots on target

Nathan Ellington (Wigan)	14
Darren Huckerby (Norwich)	12
Darren Bent (Ipswich)	11
Andrew Johnson (Crystal Palace)	9
Leon McKenzie (Norwich)	9
Mathias Svensson (Norwich)	9
Danny Cadamarteri (Bradford)	8
Michael Proctor (Rotherham)	8
Jason Roberts (Wigan)	8
Mamady Sidibe (Gillingham)	7

Shots off target

Nathan Ellington (Wigan)	11
Kevin Kyle (Sunderland)	11
Jimmy Bullard (Wigan)	9
Gary McSheffrey (Coventry)	9
Robert Earnshaw (Cardiff)	9
Dean Windass (Bradford)	8
Wayne Gray (Wimbledon)	8
Darren Bent (Ipswich)	7
Ricardo Fuller (Preston)	7
Michael Doyle (Coventry)	7

Caught offside

Mamady Sidibe (Gillingham)	12
Lee Bradbury (Walsall)	11
Kevin Kyle (Sunderland)	10
Jason Roberts (Wigan)	10
Hameur Bouazza (Watford)	10
Darren Bent (Ipswich)	9
Robert Earnshaw (Cardiff)	9
Bobby Zamora (West Ham)	9
Geoff Horsfield (West Brom)	9

Free-kicks won

Alan Lee (Cardiff)	20
Dave Kitson (Reading)	18
Danny Spiller (Gillingham)	18
Kevin Kyle (Sunderland)	17
Gary Smith (Wimbledon)	17
Richard Langley (Cardiff)	16
Jack Lester (Sheff Utd)	16
Shaun Barker (Rotherham)	15
Kris Commons (Stoke)	15

Derby v Preston

Fouls conceded

Chris Morgan (Sheff Utd)	18
Jason Roberts (Wigan)	18
Jason Jarrett (Wigan)	18
Daniele Dichio (Millwall)	17
Alan Lee (Cardiff)	16
Aki Riihilahti (Crystal Palace)	14
Paul Evans (Nottm Forest)	14
Calum Davenport (Coventry)	13
Wes Morgan (Nottm Forest)	13

Fouls without a card

Calum Davenport (Coventry)	13
Neil Shipperley (Crystal Palace)	13
Gareth Taylor (Nottm Forest)	13
Dave Kitson (Reading)	12
Mamady Sidibe (Gillingham)	12
Andy Gray (Sheff Utd)	12
Bruce Dyer (Watford)	11
Julian Gray (Crystal Palace)	11
Sean Dyche (Watford)	10

Derby's players form a huddle before the match. A 0-0 draw against promotion hopefuls West Ham at Upton Park was a strong result.

Manel celebrates Derby's first goal with Ian Taylor and Marcus Tudgay. County's survival hopes received a significant boost as they lifted themselves out of the relegation zone with their biggest win for six years.

Leon Osman clashes with Steve Lomas in the hard-faught 0-0 with West Ham at Upton Park.

Junior celebrates after scoring a penalty against Preston. This was his first game back after injury and successfully confirmed his return to form.

151

DERBY [1] 2 Millwall [0] 0

Relief swept around Pride Park Stadium after Adam Bolder and Marco Reich fired Derby County to Division One safety with two wonderful strikes.

The ball ripped into Millwall's net twice and the 2-0 victory coupled with Walsall's predicted failure at Crystal Palace earlier in the day was enough to book another season in the second tier of English football.

Joy at surviving such a dismal campaign was an understandable reaction among the club's loyal supporters as they stood and applauded. Derby had been haunted by the prospect of relegation for much of the season. Shocking and inexplicable away form meant they had to save themselves at home and they have done so by displaying promotion form.

Twenty five points from eight wins and two draws in 11 home games since the turn of the year is excellent. A poor Millwall side never looked capable of standing in the way.

Derby were clearly more hungry, more competitive than their opponents but they squandered opportunities early in the game to ease the tension. Then another penalty gave skipper Ian Taylor the chance to stretch his 100 per cent record from the spot to seven.

Marco Reich delivered a teasing cross and Millwall defender Robbie Ryan appeared to do little more than stand his ground and Marcus Tudgay went down. Referee Mark Cowburn pointed to the spot, booked the unfortunate Ryan but Andy Marshall clawed away Taylor's penalty.

Derby needed a goal to soothe the nerves, and it arrived five minutes before the break. Bolder had only replaced the injured Michael Johnson eight minutes earlier when he spotted his moment. Charlie Hearn dithered on the ball and Bolder snapped in, won possession and sent a fine volley from 20 yards past the scrambling Marshall and into the bottom corner.

One-goal leads are never enough and Derby went in search of another. Marshall saved Manel's volley with his legs and Reich and Peschisolido had shots blocked.

But there was no hiding from the fact that the last two seasons had been awful. Next time there is a celebration at Pride Park, let it be for the right reasons and not merely survival.

Result.......Result.......Result.

DERBY ....(1) 2   **MILLWALL** ....(0) 0
Bolder 40
Reich 72

Att 26,056
Referee: M Cowburn

Stats......Stats.......Stats......Stats

DERBY				MILLWALL		
1st	2nd	Total		Total	2nd	1st
4	1	5	Corners	4	1	3
12	9	21	Fouls	15	7	8
0	1	1	Yellow cards	2	1	1
0	0	0	Red cards	0	0	0
1	1	2	Caught Offside	9	5	4
1	6	7	Shots on target	2	1	1
6	1	7	Shots off target	6	2	4
0	0	0	Hit woodwork	0	0	0
36	49	52%	Possession	48%	51	64

IT'S been a long and hard season and I'm pleased we're staying up because more than anything, it's reward for the fans who've stayed loyal to the club.

George Burley

MAYBE the FA Cup final is on people's minds but to be honest, I don't really know what they're thinking at the moment.

Dennis Wise

Other Div 1 Results

Bradford 0 Stoke 2, Cardiff 1 Wimbledon 1, Crystal Palace 1 Walsall 0, Gillingham 2 Coventry 5, Norwich 3 Preston 2, Nottm Forest 1 Wigan 0, Reading 1 West Brom 0, Rotherham 3 Burnley 0, Sunderland 1 Crewe 1, West Ham 4 Watford 0

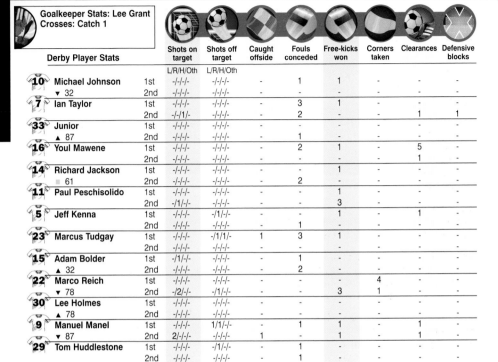

Goalkeeper Stats: Lee Grant
Crosses: Catch 1

Derby Player Stats		Shots on target L/R/H/Oth	Shots off target L/R/H/Oth	Caught offside	Fouls conceded	Free-kicks won	Corners taken	Clearances	Defensive blocks
10 Michael Johnson ▼ 32	1st	-/-/-/-	-/-/-/-	-	1	1	-	-	-
	2nd	-/-/-/-	-/-/-/-	-	-	-	-	-	-
7 Ian Taylor	1st	-/-/-/-	-/-/-/-	-	3	1	-	-	-
	2nd	-/-/1/-	-/-/-/-	-	2	-	-	1	1
33 Junior ▲ 87	1st	-/-/-/-	-/-/-/-	-	-	-	-	-	-
	2nd	-/-/-/-	-/-/-/-	-	1	-	-	-	-
16 Youl Mawene	1st	-/-/-/-	-/-/-/-	-	2	1	-	5	-
	2nd	-/-/-/-	-/-/-/-	-	-	-	-	1	-
14 Richard Jackson ■ 61	1st	-/-/-/-	-/-/-/-	-	-	1	-	-	-
	2nd	-/-/-/-	-/-/-/-	-	2	-	-	-	-
11 Paul Peschisolido	1st	-/-/-/-	-/-/-/-	-	-	1	-	-	-
	2nd	-/1/-/-	-/-/-/-	-	-	3	-	-	-
5 Jeff Kenna	1st	-/-/-/-	-/1/-/-	-	-	1	-	1	-
	2nd	-/-/-/-	-/-/-/-	-	1	-	-	-	-
23 Marcus Tudgay	1st	-/-/-/-	-/1/1/-	1	3	1	-	-	-
	2nd	-/-/-/-	-/-/-/-	-	-	-	-	-	-
15 Adam Bolder ▲ 32	1st	-/1/-/-	-/-/-/-	-	1	-	-	-	-
	2nd	-/-/-/-	-/-/-/-	-	2	-	-	-	-
22 Marco Reich ▼ 78	1st	-/-/-/-	-/-/-/-	-	-	-	4	-	-
	2nd	-/2/-/-	-/1/-/-	-	-	3	1	-	-
30 Lee Holmes ▲ 78	1st	-/-/-/-	-/-/-/-	-	-	-	-	-	-
	2nd	-/-/-/-	-/-/-/-	-	-	-	-	-	-
9 Manuel Manel ▼ 87	1st	-/-/-/-	1/1/-/-	-	1	1	-	1	-
	2nd	2/-/-/-	-/-/-/-	1	-	1	-	1	-
29 Tom Huddlestone	1st	-/-/-/-	-/1/-/-	-	1	-	-	-	-
	2nd	-/-/-/-	-/-/-/-	-	1	-	-	-	-

Subs not used: Oakes, Mills. - Formation: 4-4-2

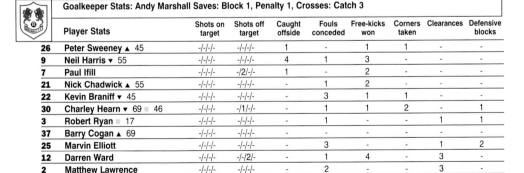

Goalkeeper Stats: Andy Marshall Saves: Block 1, Penalty 1, Crosses: Catch 3

	Player Stats	Shots on target	Shots off target	Caught offside	Fouls conceded	Free-kicks won	Corners taken	Clearances	Defensive blocks
26	Peter Sweeney ▲ 45	-/-/-/-	-/-/-/-	1	-	1	1	-	-
9	Neil Harris ▼ 55	-/-/-/-	-/-/-/-	4	1	3	-	-	-
7	Paul Ifill	-/-/-/-	-/2/-/-	1	-	2	-	-	-
21	Nick Chadwick ▲ 55	-/-/-/-	-/-/-/-	-	1	2	-	-	-
22	Kevin Braniff ▼ 45	-/-/-/-	-/-/-/-	-	3	1	1	-	-
30	Charley Hearn ▼ 69 ■ 46	-/-/-/-	-/1/-/-	-	1	1	2	-	1
3	Robert Ryan ■ 17	-/-/-/-	-/-/-/-	-	1	-	-	1	1
37	Barry Cogan ▲ 69	-/-/-/-	-/-/-/-	-	-	-	-	-	-
25	Marvin Elliott	-/-/-/-	-/-/-/-	-	3	-	-	1	2
12	Darren Ward	-/-/-/-	-/-/2/-	-	1	4	-	3	-
2	Matthew Lawrence	-/-/-/-	-/-/-/-	-	2	-	-	3	-
18	John Sutton	-/-/1/-	-/-/-/-	3	2	4	-	-	-
8	David Livermore	-/-/-/-	-/1/-/-	-	-	3	-	-	-

Subs not used: Gueret, McCammon. - Formation: 4-4-2

Derby Played: 45 Won 13 Drawn 13 Lost 19 For 53 Against 66 Pos 20

Derby County may have gone into the final match already safe in Division One but they will take their woeful away record into next season with them.

Jermaine Darlington hit the winner after 26 minutes and the Rams could not find a reply to a team without an away win for more than seven months and had taken just six points from the last 54 on the road.

Wimbledon had not won at home in their previous 14 League games and were one defeat short of the worst-ever League season. A chance then for the Rams to go out on a high. But apart from a 25-minute spell after half-time when Dons goalkeeper Scott Bevan made a handful of saves, their performance was awful.

While the Rams started at a pedestrian pace, the home side threatened a goal on three occasions in the opening 20 minutes. Dean Lewington headed over when he should at least have hit the target, Lee Grant went full stretch to turn Malvin Kamara's low shot round a post before Adam Bolder, stationed by an upright, cleared Wade Small's header.

Wimbledon met little defensive opposition down Derby's left when they went ahead. Small got away from Marco Reich too easily and his low cross was flicked past Grant from four yards.

But there was more purpose to Derby's play after the break. Taylor thumped a shot straight at Bevan, who then saved one-handed after Junior's shot took a deflection off Peschisolido. Bolder pulled a shot wide after good link-up play between Junior and Peschisolido and Reich was twice denied by Bevan.

But Wimbledon have been praised for the character they have shown during a difficult season and found a second wind.

So a disappointing season had at last come to an end. Suffering Derby fans will be hoping and praying for a much better campaign next season.

Result......Result.......Result.

WIMBLEDON ......(1) 1	DERBY ....(0) 0	

Darlington 25

Att 6,509
Referee: P Crossley

Stats......Stats.......Stats......Stats

	WIMBLEDON				DERBY	
1st	2nd	Total		Total	2nd	1st
5	3	8	Corners	7	4	3
4	9	13	Fouls	12	5	7
0	0	0	Yellow cards	3	2	1
0	0	0	Red cards	0	0	0
2	6	8	Caught Offside	4	1	3
5	2	7	Shots on target	8	7	1
2	2	4	Shots off target	4	2	2
0	0	0	Hit woodwork	0	0	0
43	44	44%	Possession	56%	56	57

 IT shows today how far we've come in the last two months and that we're not dead and buried. The old Wimbledon spirit is still there.

Stuart Murdoch

 WE have the nucleus of a decent squad, though not strong enough yet to challenge for the play-offs, and I'll be trying to add to it this summer.

George Burley

Other Div 1 Results

Burnley 1 Sunderland 2, Coventry 2 Crystal Palace 1, Crewe 1 Norwich 3, Ipswich 1 Cardiff 1, Millwall 1 Bradford 0, Preston 3 Sheff Utd 3, Stoke 0 Gillingham 0, Walsall 3 Rotherham 2, Watford 1 Reading 0, West Brom 0 Nottm Forest 2, Wigan 1 West Ham 1

Wimbledon [1] 1 DERBY [0] 0

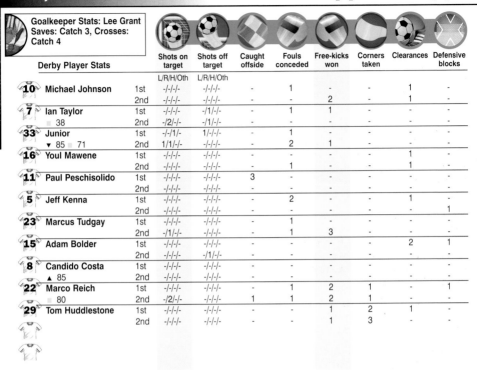

Goalkeeper Stats: Lee Grant Saves: Catch 3, Crosses: Catch 4

Derby Player Stats		Shots on target L/R/H/Oth	Shots off target L/R/H/Oth	Caught offside	Fouls conceded	Free-kicks won	Corners taken	Clearances	Defensive blocks
10 Michael Johnson	1st	-/-/-/-	-/-/-/-	-	1	-	-	1	-
	2nd	-/-/-/-	-/-/-/-	-	-	2	-	1	-
7 Ian Taylor — 38	1st	-/-/-/-	-/1/-/-	-	1	1	-	-	-
	2nd	-/2/-/-	-/1/-/-	-	-	-	-	-	-
33 Junior ▼85 71	1st	-/-/1/-	1/-/-/-	-	1	-	-	-	-
	2nd	1/1/-/-	-/-/-/-	-	2	1	-	-	-
16 Youl Mawene	1st	-/-/-/-	-/-/-/-	-	-	-	-	1	-
	2nd	-/-/-/-	-/-/-/-	-	1	-	-	1	-
11 Paul Peschisolido	1st	-/-/-/-	-/-/-/-	3	-	-	-	-	-
	2nd	-/-/-/-	-/-/-/-	-	-	-	-	-	-
5 Jeff Kenna	1st	-/-/-/-	-/-/-/-	-	2	-	-	1	-
	2nd	-/-/-/-	-/-/-/-	-	-	-	-	-	1
23 Marcus Tudgay	1st	-/-/-/-	-/-/-/-	-	1	-	-	-	-
	2nd	-/1/-/-	-/-/-/-	-	1	3	-	-	-
15 Adam Bolder	1st	-/-/-/-	-/-/-/-	-	-	-	-	2	1
	2nd	-/-/-/-	-/1/-/-	-	-	-	-	-	-
8 Candido Costa ▲85	1st	-/-/-/-	-/-/-/-	-	-	-	-	-	-
	2nd	-/-/-/-	-/-/-/-	-	-	-	-	-	-
22 Marco Reich — 80	1st	-/-/-/-	-/-/-/-	-	1	2	1	-	1
	2nd	-/2/-/-	-/-/-/-	1	1	2	1	-	-
29 Tom Huddlestone	1st	-/-/-/-	-/-/-/-	-	-	1	2	1	-
	2nd	-/-/-/-	-/-/-/-	-	-	1	3	-	-

Subs not used: Oakes, Mills, Manel, Holmes. - Formation: 4-4-2

Goalkeeper Stats: Scott Bevan Saves: Tip Over 1, Catch 4, Punch 1, Crosses: Catch 5, Punch 1

	Player Stats	Shots on target	Shots off target	Caught offside	Fouls conceded	Free-kicks won	Corners taken	Clearances	Defensive blocks
29	Ben Harding ▲ 45	-/-/-/-	-/-/-/-	-	-	2	3	1	-
7	Harry Ntimban-Zeh	-/-/-/-	-/1/-/-	-	1	3	-	3	-
28	Malvin Kamara ▼ 87	-/2/-/-	1/-/-/-	-	4	2	-	-	-
10	Dean Holdsworth ▲ 87	-/-/-/-	-/-/-/-	-	-	-	-	-	-
18	Wayne Gray	-/-/1/-	-/1/-/-	4	2	1	-	-	-
20	Gary Smith ▼ 45	-/-/-/-	-/-/-/-	-	-	-	5	-	-
8	Wade Small	-/2/-/-	-/-/-/-	2	1	3	-	-	-
19	Ben Chorley	-/-/-/-	-/-/-/-	-	1	-	-	2	-
5	Mark Williams	-/2/-/-	-/-/-/-	-	1	-	-	3	1
24	Jermaine Darlington	-/-/-/-	-/-/-/-	2	-	-	-	1	-
17	Shola Oyedele	-/-/-/-	-/-/-/-	-	1	-	-	2	-
25	Dean Lewington	-/-/-/-	-/-/1/-	-	2	1	-	2	-

Subs not used: Hawkins, Martin, Puncheon. - Formation: 4-4-2

Derby Played: 46 Won 13 Drawn 13 Lost 20 For 53 Against 67 Pos 20

...May Team Stats.....Team Stats......Team Stats......Team S

League table at the end of May

		HOME					AWAY					Pts	Df
	P	W	D	L	F	A	W	D	L	F	A		
Norwich	46	18	3	2	44	15	10	7	6	35	24	94	40
West Brom	46	14	5	4	34	16	11	6	6	30	26	86	22
Sunderland	46	13	8	2	33	15	9	5	9	29	30	79	17
West Ham	46	12	7	4	42	20	7	10	6	25	25	74	22
Ipswich	46	12	3	8	49	36	9	7	7	35	36	73	12
Crystal Palace	46	10	8	5	34	25	11	2	10	38	36	73	11
Wigan	46	11	8	4	29	16	7	9	7	31	29	71	15
Sheff Utd	46	11	6	6	37	25	9	5	9	28	31	71	9
Reading	46	11	6	6	29	25	9	4	10	26	32	70	-2
Millwall	46	11	8	4	28	15	7	4	9	27	33	69	7
Stoke	46	11	7	5	35	24	7	5	11	23	31	66	3
Coventry	46	9	9	5	34	22	8	5	10	33	32	65	13
Cardiff	46	10	6	7	40	25	7	8	8	28	33	65	10
Nottm Forest	46	8	9	6	33	25	7	6	10	28	33	60	3
Preston	46	11	7	5	43	29	4	7	12	26	42	59	-2
Watford	46	9	8	6	31	28	6	4	13	23	40	57	-14
Rotherham	46	8	8	7	31	27	5	7	11	22	34	54	-8
Crewe	46	11	3	9	33	26	3	8	12	24	40	53	-9
Burnley	46	9	6	8	37	32	4	8	11	23	45	53	-17
Derby	46	11	5	7	39	33	2	8	13	14	34	52	-14
Gillingham	46	10	1	12	28	34	4	8	11	20	34	51	-19
Walsall	46	8	7	8	29	31	5	5	13	16	34	51	-20
Bradford	46	6	3	14	23	35	4	3	16	15	34	36	-31
Wimbledon	46	3	4	16	21	40	5	1	17	20	49	29	-48

May matches table

	P	W	D	L	F	A	Pts
Stoke	3	2	1	0	6	1	7
Sunderland	3	2	1	0	4	2	7
Coventry	2	2	0	0	7	3	6
Norwich	3	2	0	1	6	4	6
Nottm Forest	2	2	0	0	3	0	6
West Ham	2	1	1	0	5	1	4
Wimbledon	2	1	1	0	2	1	4
Rotherham	2	1	0	1	5	3	3
Walsall	2	1	0	1	3	3	3
Derby	**2**	**1**	**0**	**1**	**2**	**1**	**3**
Crystal Palace	2	1	0	1	2	2	3
Reading	2	1	0	1	1	1	3
Millwall	2	1	0	1	2	3	3
Watford	2	1	0	1	1	4	3
Cardiff	2	0	2	0	2	2	2
Preston	2	0	1	1	5	6	1
Sheff Utd	1	0	1	0	3	3	1
Crewe	2	0	1	1	2	4	1
Gillingham	2	0	1	1	2	5	1
Ipswich	1	0	1	0	1	1	1
Wigan	2	0	1	1	2	1	1
Burnley	2	0	0	2	1	5	0
West Brom	3	0	0	3	1	7	0
Bradford	2	0	0	2	0	3	0

May team stats details

Club Name	Ply	Shots On	Shots Off	Corners	Hit W'work	Caught Offside	Offside Trap	Fouls	Yellow Cards	Red Cards	Pens Awarded	Pens Con
Bradford	2	5	8	9	0	5	7	30	1	0	- (-)	1
Burnley	2	5	10	7	0	5	18	16	3	0	- (-)	1
Cardiff	2	10	12	13	0	7	2	31	3	0	- (-)	-
Coventry	2	16	7	11	0	7	4	30	3	0	- (-)	-
Crewe	2	13	9	11	1	11	6	16	2	0	- (-)	-
Crystal Palace	2	11	10	17	0	3	8	16	3	0	1 (-)	-
Derby	**2**	**15**	**11**	**12**	**0**	**6**	**17**	**33**	**4**	**0**	**1 (-)**	**-**
Gillingham	2	17	8	20	0	3	1	27	5	1	- (-)	-
Ipswich	1	8	6	10	0	0	1	13	0	0	- (-)	-
Millwall	2	6	7	12	0	13	3	29	3	0	1 (1)	1
Norwich	3	24	21	20	2	5	8	37	5	0	1 (1)	1
Nottm Forest	2	7	9	8	1	13	4	16	0	0	- (-)	-
Preston	2	21	14	14	1	10	6	40	5	1	- (-)	-
Reading	2	6	13	8	0	7	7	29	2	0	- (-)	-
Rotherham	2	13	4	11	0	17	12	35	2	0	3 (3)	2
Sheff Utd	1	9	5	7	2	4	7	19	3	0	- (-)	-
Stoke	3	13	10	10	0	3	5	31	3	0	- (-)	-
Sunderland	3	27	11	26	0	17	14	39	3	0	- (-)	-
Walsall	2	12	13	10	0	4	2	34	6	1	- (-)	1
Watford	2	14	5	8	0	7	7	30	3	0	- (-)	1
West Brom	3	16	17	23	0	8	5	34	4	1	- (-)	-
West Ham	2	18	5	10	0	4	11	22	1	0	1 (1)	-
Wigan	2	10	14	20	1	8	12	20	1	0	- (-)	-
Wimbledon	2	16	4	10	1	10	10	26	3	0	- (-)	-

MAY STATS

Monthly Top scorers

Gifton Noel-Williams (Stoke)	3
Gary McSheffrey (Coventry)	2
Andy Gray (Sheff Utd)	2
Dean Ashton (Crewe)	2
David Johnson (Nottm Forest)	2
Kris Commons (Stoke)	2
Michael Doyle (Coventry)	2
David Healy (Preston)	2
Kevin Kyle (Sunderland)	1
Robbie Stockdale (Rotherham)	1

Penalties scored

2 Michael Proctor (Rotherham)

Assists

Kris Commons (Stoke)	2
Marcus Stewart (Sunderland)	2
Gary McSheffrey (Coventry)	2
Michael Proctor (Rotherham)	2
Patrick Agyemang (Gillingham)	2
Sean Thornton (Sunderland)	2
Graham Alexander (Preston)	2

Quickest goals

1:17 mins - Gifton Noel-Williams
(Bradford vs Stoke)
1:58 mins - Leon McKenzie
(Norwich vs Preston)
3:22 mins - Gareth Williams (West
Brom vs Nottm Forest)
3:37 mins - Muhamed Konjic
(Coventry vs Crystal Palace)
4:21 mins - Paul McKenna
(Norwich vs Preston)

Top Keeper

	Mins	Gls
S Bywater (West Ham)	192	1
Scott Bevan (Wimbledon)	191	1
Mart Poom (Sunderland)	191	1
Lee Grant (Derby)	191	1
Jamie Ashdown (Reading)	190	1
John Filan (Wigan)	192	2
Nico Vaesen (Crystal P)	191	2
Martyn Margetson (Cardiff)	191	2

Shots on target

Kevin Kyle (Sunderland)	10
Dean Ashton (Crewe)	8
Gary McSheffrey (Coventry)	6
Michael Proctor (Rotherham)	5
Bruce Dyer (Watford)	5
Gifton Noel-Williams (Stoke)	5
Ricardo Fuller (Preston)	5
Nathan Ellington (Wigan)	4
Darren Huckerby (Norwich)	4
Marlon Harewood (West Ham)	4

Shots off target

Lee Hughes (West Brom)	8
Nathan Ellington (Wigan)	6
Darren Huckerby (Norwich)	6
Eddie Lewis (Preston)	5
Jorge Leitao (Walsall)	4
Kevin Kyle (Sunderland)	4
Robert Blake (Burnley)	4
Darel Russell (Stoke)	4
Gary McSheffrey (Coventry)	4
Jermaine Wright (Ipswich)	3

Caught offside

Kevin Kyle (Sunderland)	7
Michael Proctor (Rotherham)	6
Martin Butler (Rotherham)	6
Marlon King (Nottm Forest)	6
Dean Ashton (Crewe)	6
Ricardo Fuller (Preston)	6
David Johnson (Nottm Forest)	5
Lee Hughes (West Brom)	5
Steve Jones (Crewe)	5

Free-kicks won

Wayne Routledge (Crystal P)	12
Ricardo Fuller (Preston)	9
Robert Blake (Burnley)	8
Kris Commons (Stoke)	7
Danny Cadamarteri (Bradford)	7
Marco Reich (Derby)	7
Darren Huckerby (Norwich)	7
Leon McKenzie (Norwich)	6
Richard Langley (Cardiff)	6

Wimbledon v Derby

Fouls conceded

Phil Babb (Sunderland)	9
Dave Kitson (Reading)	9
Bruce Dyer (Watford)	8
Clive Clarke (Stoke)	8
Gary McSheffrey (Coventry)	8
Chris Lucketti (Preston)	7
Eric Deloumeaux (Coventry)	7
Sean Gregan (West Brom)	7
Paul Ritchie (Walsall)	7

Fouls without a card

Phil Babb (Sunderland)	9
Bruce Dyer (Watford)	8
Chris Lucketti (Preston)	7
Eric Deloumeaux (Coventry)	7
Sean Gregan (West Brom)	7
Danny Cadamarteri (Bradford)	6
Graham Alexander (Preston)	6
Michael Branch (Bradford)	6
Marcus Tudgay (Derby)	5

© Raymond's Press Agency

Junior battles with two Wimbledon defenders. Derby had their chances during the game, but failed to make an impression on already relegated Wimbledon.

The 2-0 win against Millwall, coupled with Walsall's predicted failure at Crystal Palace earlier that same day was enough to book another season in the second tier of English football.

The Coca-Cola Championship Fixtures 2004-2005

21
23
19
9
11
15

13

August		result
7 Leeds (0-0)	(A)	0,1
11 Leicester	(H)	1,2
14 Ipswich (1-2)	(H)	3,2
21 QPR (2-0)	(A)	2,0
28 Crewe (1-2)	(H)	2,4
30 Stoke (0-0)	(A)	0,1

September		result
11 Reading (0-0)	(H)	2,1
14 Millwall	(A)	1,3
18 Cardiff	(A)	2,0
25 Wigan (1-1)	(H)	1,1
29 West Ham (1-1)	(H)	1,1

October		result
2 Sunderland (0-0)	(A)	0,0
16 Watford (1-2)	(H)	2,2
19 Wolverhampton	(A)	0,2
23 Burnley	(A)	2,0
30 Rotherham (1-2)	(H)	3,2

November		result
3 Brighton	(H)	3,0
6 Watford	(A)	2,2
13 Gillingham (1-0)	(A)	2,0
20 Sheff Utd (0-0)	(H)	0,1
27 Preston	(A)	0,3

December		result
4 Coventry	(H)	2,2
11 Nottm Forest (1-0)	(H)	3,0
18 Plymouth (2-0)	(A)	2,0

December (continued)		result
26 Wigan	(A)	2,1
28 Millwall	(H)	0,3

January		result
1 Cardiff (0-1)	(H)	0,1
3 Reading (1-0)	(A)	1,0
15 Sunderland (0-0)	(H)	0,2
22 West Ham (1-1)	(A)	2,1

February		result
5 Brighton (2-1)	(A)	3,2
12 Wolverhampton	(H)	
19 Rotherham	(A)	
23 Burnley	(H)	
26 Nottm Forest	(A)	

March		result
5 Plymouth	(H)	
12 Leicester	(A)	
16 QPR	(H)	
19 Leeds (0-0)	(H)	2,0

April		result
2 Ipswich	(A)	
5 Crewe	(A)	
9 Stoke	(H)	
16 Sheff Utd	(A)	
23 Gillingham	(H)	
30 Coventry	(A)	

May		result
8 Preston	(H)	
EMBARGOED		